THE CRAFT OF CREATIVITY

THE CRAFT

OF

Creativity

MATTHEW A. CRONIN

and JEFFREY LOEWENSTEIN

Stanford Business Books

AN IMPRINT OF STANFORD UNIVERSITY PRESS • STANFORD, CALIFORNIA

Stanford University Press
Stanford, California

Special discounts for bulk quantities of Stanford Business Books are available to corporations, professional associations, and other organizations. For details and discount information, contact the special sales department of Stanford University Press. Tel: (650) 725-0820, Fax: (650) 725-3457

Printed in the United States of America on acid-free, archival-quality paper

Library of Congress Cataloging-in-Publication Data

Names: Cronin, Matthew A. (Professor of management), author. | Loewenstein, Jeffrey, author.
Title: The craft of creativity / Matthew A. Cronin and Jeffrey Loewenstein.
Description: Stanford, California : Stanford Business Books, an imprint of Stanford University Press, 2018. | Includes bibliographical references and index.
Identifiers: LCCN 2017031231 | ISBN 9780804787376 (cloth : alk. paper) | ISBN 9781503605077 (pbk. : alk. paper)
Subjects: LCSH: Creative ability. | Creative thinking. | Creative ability in business.
Classification: LCC BF408 .C7578 2018 | DDC 153.3/5—dc23
LC record available at https://lccn.loc.gov/2017031231
ISBN 9781503605510 (electronic)

Cover design: Matt Tanner
Typeset by Bruce Lundquist in 10/14 Minion

For Hayes, who made it possible for me to start this work,
and for Jason, who made it possible for me to complete it
—Matt

For my craftiest creators, Jacki, Emma, and Alina
—Jeff

CONTENTS

PREFACE AND ACKNOWLEDGMENTS

Faced with the choice between changing one's mind and proving that there is
no need to do so, almost everyone gets busy on the proof.
—John Kenneth Galbraith

Creativity is touted by educators, scientists, and business leaders as important,[1]
but bemoaned as all too scarce.[2] The lack of creativity is not for lack of trying.
There are many calls to promote creativity and earnest attempts to support it
in our schools and workplaces.[3] It is why so much is written on how to help
people to be more creative. Searching "how to be creative" will produce 812
books on Amazon and one million sites on Google. Yet for all this effort and
knowledge, the results have not been encouraging. Most people still struggle to
be creative or assume that they are not and cannot be creative. Creativity may
even be on the decline.[4]

Creativity is personal for us. One of us played music professionally before
becoming an academic. The other studied visual arts. Both of us realized we
were even more interested in studying the creative process than in employing
it in these areas. Both of us married people far more artistically talented than
ourselves and whose creativity is a continuing source of joy. Creativity saved
one of our spouse's lives.

Heather has a lung disease, called interstitial pulmonary fibrosis, which is
poorly understood despite killing as many people per year as breast cancer. The
only known treatment is a lung transplant. Heather had been on a slow decline
for about a year. She was in the hospital, about to be put on a ventilator, and
she probably had about a month left to live.

When the call arrived that they had a matching lung, there was a catch. On
paper, the lung had some uncertainties (the donor was a smoker, for instance),

and so it had been rejected by twenty other hospitals. But the surgeons, Drs. Sanchez and Kon, didn't just accept the results of the formula. Sanchez flew to Chicago to look at the lung, and he saw it differently; he said it was viable. Then there was another issue: the lung was not a classic match. There was a problem with mismatching antigens. Dr. Iacono, Heather's pulmonologist, planned to use a new technique called the Toronto Protocol, whereby both Heather and the donated lung would have their antigens "reset" to zero before the operation. The protocol worked, the lung worked, and Heather has a new lease on life. The invention of the protocol and the willingness of the doctors to consider new possibilities, even ones others had rejected, ended up saving Heather's life. Creativity matters.

That all of us already know something about creativity is both helpful and a challenge. If the concept of creativity was something esoteric that people did not know about already, like *interstitial pulmonary fibrosis*, then our challenge as authors would be to explain what it is using concepts already understood. But creativity does not seem esoteric. Even though creativity is every bit as complex as interstitial pulmonary fibrosis, most people already think they know a fair amount about creativity. The challenge is that there is a great deal more to know about creativity, and we are going to have to give up some of our current ways of thinking about creativity to learn to be more creative.

We wrote this book in the hope that we could help people change their perspective on creativity and become more creative. And as you will see, changing perspectives is not "out with the old, in with the new" or "forget everything you *think* you know about creativity . . ." People have some excellent ideas about creativity already. But they also have some misconceptions, and there are a few notions that simply might be overlooked.

To provide a new perspective on creativity required understanding existing perspectives. A good deal of discussion and listening helped too. We thank Denise Rousseau for encouraging us from the beginning. We thank Roni Reiter-Palmon and Jing Zhou for their very thoughtful reviews. We thank Colin Fisher, Jonathan Cromwell, and Sarah Harvey for providing insights on framing the argument, and Laura Thomas for help with our initial draft. We thank an array of colleagues for discussions on these topics, most notably Jack Goncalo, Jill Perry-Smith, Chris Shalley, Bernard Nijstadt, Teresa Amabile, and Keith Sawyer. We are extraordinarily grateful to Jennifer Mueller for her perspective on our work as it developed and for thinking about the kind of bread we were trying to make. We thank Margo Beth Fleming, whose sage advice has kept us on track since she first told Matt, "You know, somewhere in all that rambling are some pretty good ideas." Finally, we thank our families for their continued tolerance/support/nonviolence as we disappeared into the void of writing during these past few years.

THE CRAFT OF CREATIVITY

1

PERSPECTIVES ON CREATIVITY

You keep using that word. . . . I do not think it means what you think it means.
—Inigo Montoya in *The Princess Bride*, by William Goldman

We do not think creativity means what you think it means. For many people, creativity is a rare gift bestowed on exceptional people. This is why, when we approached a magician named Turley to interview him about creativity, his reply was, "I am not creative."

Early in his adult life, Turley was teaching developmentally disabled adults and realized that they were unlikely to find appropriate work, but that they would be greatly helped by such work. He figured out that landscaping offered a useful variety of tasks. So he started a landscaping business and ran it for ten years, employing developmentally disabled adults. Later, Turley gained national publicity for his magic act with a $35 want ad in the *Washington Post*: "Lost at birthday party: Magician's tuxedo jacket, 96 hidden pockets, snake in right sleeve, and dove in one of the pockets. If found, contact Turley the magician. . . ." When the newspaper came out, Turley sent copies of the want ad to local radio stations with an anonymous note: "I read this and maybe you could help this guy out." The item was picked up and covered across the country. Turley was also creative in the ways we expected, having generated original magic tricks. His is a sufficient talent that he has performed for several U.S. presidents. And Turley told us, "I am not creative."

We heard this from many people. Grammy-winning producer Bob Dawson hesitated about being interviewed because he didn't think of himself as creative. Dancer, choreographer, and veteran of stage and screen Dan Joyce didn't really see himself as creative either. And who were the people we spoke to who were most likely to see themselves as creative? It was the novices who had not yet achieved anything.

It feels backward for the novices to see themselves as more creative than accomplished professionals. But with a shift in thinking it becomes perfectly conceivable. All that is necessary is to move away from thinking about creative people and about creative products such as magic tricks or songs and instead think about the creative process. Novices told us they were having new ideas all the time. But when we asked what the ideas were, we found that nearly all of them were ideas that had long since become ordinary for people like Bob, Dan, and Turley. Experts feel less creative than novices because experts have already thought about their topics so much they encounter fewer new ideas.

A shift in focus from creative people and creative products to the creative process is helpful both in understanding novice and expert experience with creativity and in learning to be more creative. We should all want to be more creative. In our view, being creative means developing different ways of thinking so that what was inconceivable becomes thinkable. As a result, in our view creativity is no more about rare geniuses writing operas or equations than it is about neighborhood plumbers installing water heaters. If you can think about it, no matter what "it" is, then you can think creatively about it. Creativity is not "out there" in the world, it is "in here" in all of our heads.

People have some control over their heads. This is why they can have some control over their creativity. But we realize that some intuitions about creativity suggest otherwise. Many people tell us that creative ideas seem to come from nowhere, as gifts from the muses. These are the stories we often hear about the creative geniuses behind wondrous works of art, scientific breakthroughs, and technological marvels. These stories of inspirations support the belief that creativity is important. Yet these stories can also sow doubt about whether the many earnest attempts to support creativity in schools and workplaces can possibly do any good. The same doubt results from people saying such things as, "Some people just seem to have it" and "We were probably just lucky." These statements suggest that creativity is beyond people's control. These intuitions are misleading. It is possible to learn to go through the creative process more efficiently and effectively than has been done in the past. We think there is a skill, a craft, to creativity.

We interviewed many people about creativity. In these interviews, people often told us, "You can't learn to be creative." Yet when we asked our interviewees if they themselves had gotten more creative over time, almost everyone said—usually with some expression of surprise—that they had. For example, composer Jesse Guessford realized that while he had fewer ideas than he used to have, the ideas he generated were much more likely to be good ones. Many people we interviewed realized that their efficiency in generating creative products was far better than it had been initially and so they needed fewer creative ideas. Over their careers, they had learned how to navigate the creative process.

Creativity must be a learnable skill, because many research studies have found predictable interventions that can foster creativity. For example, moderate background noise, relative to quiet or loud noise, can help people be creative.[1] And people who have lived abroad, relative to those who have only lived in the country in which they were born, appear to be more likely to solve creativity problems.[2] That researchers can find that certain conditions can reliably increase people's chances of generating creative ideas means that there is something we can do to help ourselves be creative. We could try implementing those interventions ourselves.

Before you turn the TV on for background noise or consider looking for an overseas job assignment, you might consider a few more findings. Scholars report that creativity increases with mindfulness[3] and mindlessness,[4] positive moods[5] and negative moods,[6] and hard work[7] and play.[8] While individual research findings on creativity are intriguing, when looked at collectively they are confusing. Worse, despite all the research indicating ways to help people be creative, a wide range of scholars, educators, and business leaders bemoan the lack of creativity in the world and tell us that we seem to be generating less creativity than ever.[9] The problem with looking only at individual research findings is that each study only provides a sentence or two of the full story of creativity. We need to know how the sentences fit together to tell that story.

To understand the larger story of creativity, we need to examine the creative process. This means we need to expand beyond the most common definition of creativity: "*the production of novel and useful ideas.*"[10] This definition tells us something about what to expect when the story ends. We should find ourselves with something "novel and useful." But this definition does not reveal anything about the story itself. It is as if we are reading the last page of a book, where it describes how marvelous the view is from the summit of a mountain. It sounds nice, but what happened in the three hundred pages leading up to that moment? How did they make the climb? Worse, we seem to have some funny notions about what is involved in the production of ideas. We mostly hear about sudden "Aha!" moments of illumination. Producing ideas is not described as a story unfolding over time but as a magic moment when all of a sudden we blink and find ourselves on top of a mountain, gazing out at a wonderful view. There has to be more to the story.

For example, one story of creativity is about "the train that runs between Tokyo and Hakata [that] is, like the TGV in France, one of the fastest trains in the world. This train is the 500-Series Shinkansen, operated by JR West and known for its futuristic design and characteristic long 'nose' on the front of the train. The Shinkansen enables us to move comfortably and quietly at 300 km/h."[11] The long nose of the 500-Series Shinkansen train is quite different from the short, boxy front end previously found on most trains (Figure 1.1). How the train got its long nose is a story of creativity.

The people who generated that story were Eiji Nakatsu, head engineer for development of the 500-Series Shinkansen, and his staff. Nakatsu said, "You might assume that the challenge for the Shinkansen is how to make it run faster, but thanks to current technology it is now not so hard to make it run faster. In fact, the greater challenge for us is how to make it run quietly. Half of the entire Sanyo Shinkansen Line (from Osaka to Hakata) is made up of tunnel sections. When a train rushes into a narrow tunnel at high speed, this generates atmospheric pressure waves that gradually grow into waves like tidal waves. These reach the tunnel exit at the speed of sound, generating low-frequency waves that produce a large boom and aerodynamic vibration so intense that residents 400

FIGURE 1.1. The 500-Series Shinkansen Train. Source: By Rsa—Rsa が新大阪駅で撮影, CC BY-SA 3.0, https://commons.wikimedia.org/w/index.php?curid=9777034.

meters away from the tunnel exit have registered complaints. . . . Then, one of our young engineers told me that when the train rushes into a tunnel, he felt as if the train had shrunk. This must be due to a sudden change in air resistance, I thought. The question that occurred to me—is there some living thing that manages sudden changes in resistance as a part of daily life? Yes, there is, the kingfisher. To catch its prey, a kingfisher dives from the air, which has low resistance, into high-resistance water, and moreover does this without splashing. I wondered if this is possible because of the keen edge and streamlined shape of its beak. We conducted tests to measure pressure waves arising from shooting bullets of various shapes into a pipe and through a series of simulation tests of running the trains in tunnels . . . these tests and experiments were performed at the RTRI (Railway Technical Research Institute) with JR West staff. Data analysis showed the ideal shape for this Shinkansen is almost identical to a kingfisher's beak. . . . This [nose] shape has . . . reduced air resistance by 30% and electricity use by 15% compared with the 300-Series Shinkansen, while speeds have increased by 10% over the former series."

This is a very short version of the story of rethinking a part of the design of the Shinkansen train. While we can tell the story in a paragraph that takes two minutes to read, it took Nakatsu years to navigate and resolve this story. The story started when engineers working on the train recognized an objective. They needed to make the train travel more quietly. This might have meant changing the tracks, the wheels, the car bodies, the tunnels, or any number of other things. That it would come to be the front end of the train that would be redesigned was not initially conceivable. At the outset of a story, we might not even know we will be climbing a mountain. We might just be jolting ourselves out of our normal routines and deciding that we need to leave town. The creative process often includes some realization that the normal way of going about things is not enough, that creativity might be necessary.

If we are not going to do the normal thing and walk out the door and go to work, we have to go somewhere else. But where? The creative process is centrally concerned with taking new directions, or less metaphorically, with shifts in thinking. The junior engineer sharing a simple feeling about riding the train led the senior engineer to think about an aspect of the train's travel that was not previously in focus: the change in air resistance as the train entered the tunnel. The tunnel boom was happening as the train exited the tunnel, and a junior engineer's simple feeling about entering the tunnel could easily have been ignored. The junior engineer's feeling was not obviously relevant for making the train travel more quietly, and in itself it did not directly suggest changing the shape of the front of the train. Nakatsu's transformation of the junior engineer's observation into a question about managing a change in resistance—not just air resistance, but any resistance—was a new interpretation of the problem they were solving. It was not directly about being quieter; it was about managing a transition in resistance as a means to being quieter. Nakatsu's story was changing and developing in unexpected ways.

As the story continued, Nakatsu asked himself a question about living things and considered an analogy to kingfishers diving into water. The question and analogy might seem to be the most original aspect of this creative process. For this reason though, it is important to note how firmly the creative process rests on ordinary thinking. The question and the answer relied on the engineer's history. Nakatsu described it like this: "One day, I happened to see a notice for a lecture in a newspaper; attending the lecture, I had the honor of meeting Mr. Seiichi Yajima, then an aircraft design engineer and also a member of the Wild Bird Society of Japan. From him I learned how much of current aircraft technology has been based on studies of the functions and structures of birds. . . . [he] had recommended that I read a book, *Aircraft Designing Theory* by Dr. Masao Yamana and Dr. Hiroshi Nakaguchi. This book says, 'A tree, a blade of grass, a bird or a fish, all can be brilliant and everlasting teachers.'" Given this history, thinking about whether the train's problem of needing to make the transition from low to high resistance was already solved in nature, and by a bird, is a little more understandable. This does not mean it was easy or routine. Nakatsu had to have actually studied birds and had to ask himself the question about living things managing changes in resistance to have made the analogy between the kingfisher diving into water and the Shinkansen train entering a tunnel. And of course, the analogy might not have been helpful. Stories can have dead ends, backtracking, and restarts. But Nakatsu's question and identification of the kingfisher were not random events. Instead, the process of shifting thinking rests on ordinary learning and skill while also requiring a change in how learning and skill are applied. Nakatsu had never made this analogy before, and had not thought about the front of the train in this way before.

Even after identifying the kingfisher analogy, there were numerous further questions to address. That the shape of the train's front end actually did matter and that the kingfisher's beak shape ended up being a useful model for the train were results of further testing. Whether shooting bullets through a pipe was a routine act or the result of further creativity, we do not know. We do not know how many other questions Nakatsu asked himself, how many other conversations he had with other engineers, how many other possibilities they tried apart from the shape of the front of the train. Recollections about innovations are usually incomplete. Recollections tend to give the impression of more direct and obvious journeys than actually occurred. Even so, Nakatsu's story with the front end of the 500-Series Shinkansen shows that his thinking changed multiple times over several years.

It can be tempting to emphasize one key moment in a story, a key turning point in the creative process, but this is a mischaracterization. The analogy with kingfisher birds is a classic, sudden moment of insight. But that insight followed from identifying the tunnel boom problem, listening to the young engineer's description of his experience riding trains, Nakatsu's turning of that description into a new problem to solve, Nakatsu's transformation of that description into a new question he could ask, and Nakatsu's drawing on a pool of knowledge he had developed. Further, the insight about the kingfisher analogy did not directly provide a solution, but rather indicated a new direction in which to look. The front end of the train ended up looking like a kingfisher's beak, but they did not simply make a large copy of a kingfisher's beak. Instead, they took the idea that the beak shape might matter and tested whether different shapes for the train's nose might matter. The testing of bullets and other simulations might well have involved other shifts in thinking. How the Shinkansen got its long nose is a tale of many steps and many shifts in thinking that combined to form a substantially different perspective on the train that made thinkable what had once been inconceivable. The creative process is not a moment but a journey.

One journey is related to other journeys. The creative process around one problem might relate to other creative processes we undertake. This also helps to reveal why going through the creative process is a learnable skill. Changing the front of the Shinkansen train was not Nakatsu's first or last creative effort. He had learned lessons for himself, such as drawing analogies from birds, that he could consider when faced with a need to change his thinking to solve a new problem. For example, Nakatsu also redesigned the train's pantographs—the devices that extend up from the train to transfer electricity from power lines to the train. At high speeds, the pantographs produced a very loud whistle. The analogy Nakatsu made this time was based on thinking about the pantographs as *flying* noisily through the air, when he needed them to fly silently. To a bird watcher, it is not hard then to think of an owl, a bird well known for flying silently. One reason that people can become more skilled at going through the creative process is that one time they go through the process can relate to and build upon previous times they have gone through the process.

This other journey through the creative process that Nakatsu experienced, comparing the train's pantograph to an owl, highlights the scale of the creative process. We can examine particular moments of insight when we shift our thinking, but the creative process is more than those moments or even a string of such moments. Shifts in thinking may not reveal any answers but begin a process of building new understandings. When Nakatsu made the analogy between the pantograph and an owl, he had no idea how it is that owls accomplish their silent flying and so had no idea how thinking about owls might lead to a quieter pantograph. Nakatsu had learned how owls fly silently from a story by Mr. Yajima, who gave a lecture called "Flight of Birds and Airplanes" at the meeting of the Osaka branch of the World Bird Society of Japan. Owls fly quietly because of their feather serrations. But this was only the beginning. The creative process is not about jumping directly to the end of the story or even just envisioning the end of the story. Instead, the creative process is about changing how we are thinking. Sometimes we can identify new pathways for our stories to take that were previously inconceivable. Sometimes we have to build those new pathways and it is hard to conceive how. In either case, it can change the entire story, what we thought it was about, and where we thought we were headed with it.

In the case of Nakatsu exploring the owl analogy, it led to some surprising developments. First, they had to build knowledge of how serration feathers worked, which was aided by a further clever development. "We conducted wind tunnel tests to analyze the noise level coming from a flying owl, using a stuffed owl courtesy of the Osaka Municipal Tennoji Zoo." They learned that owls' serration feathers generate small vortexes in the airflow that break up the larger vortexes which produce noise. This lesson drawn from studying owl wing plumage was applied to the support structure of the pantograph. "It took 4 years of strenuous effort by our younger engineers to practically apply this principle. Finally, 'serrations' were inscribed on the main part of the pantograph, and this succeeded in reducing noise enough to meet the world's strictest standards. This technology is called a 'vortex generator.'"

In their lengthy pursuit of a quieter pantograph for their train, Nakatsu and his colleagues had an insight that owls might be helpful, they built new knowledge about owl flight, they generated an innovative solution for the train over four years of work, and they forged a new technology, vortex generators, that would be applied to many other products including airplanes, ships, windmills, skis, and ice skates. Their long creative process was very fruitful, and it ended at a substantially different place than they could initially, or even as they were in the midst of it, have conceived.

The most exciting aspect of Nakatsu's creative stories to us, when we first learned about them, was that they were strikingly familiar. We have studied how students solve engineering problems. These kinds of challenges are common activities in engineering classrooms. In our studies, as in Nakatsu's stories, we observed a drawn-out process of turning the inconceivable into the thinkable, and then onward to the actual.

One engineering challenge we conducted asked student teams to make products that would transport an egg from a launching point up and over a seven-foot wall and down to a target fifteen feet away, safe and sound. The teams had to make products using a given set of household materials. We gave every team a few cardboard boxes and tubes, some sheets of newspaper, string, tape, scissors, and the like—fourteen items in total. The teams created an enormous variety of solutions. But as with the long nose and the pantographs of the Shinkansen train, to understand how they arrived at their inventions, it was critical to follow the process they went through as they grappled with and reinterpreted the challenge.

Teams facing the engineering challenge were not always creative. Plenty of teams tried straightforward approaches. For example, one team saw the cardboard tubes and started taping them together. They were going to roll the egg down the tube from the top of the wall to the target. They noticed that they did not have enough tubes to get all the way there. So they took cardboard boxes and opened them up on both ends so they could extend the tunnel until they had fashioned a long enough tunnel to get the egg to the target. Sometimes that worked and sometimes it did not work if the eggs rolled into the side walls.

Another group started the same way, also taping tubes together and also realizing that their contraption would be too short. But they got creative at this point. They realized that, rather than the egg going through a tunnel, which is how they first described it, the egg was sliding down a chute. The top of the tube was not necessary. So they cut the tubes in half length-wise, yielding two chutes. This doubling of the length meant they had enough to get the egg from the wall to the target. Of course, they also had to figure out a way to get the egg up to the top of the wall. Still, this bit of creativity contributed to resolving the engineering challenge. The action of cutting the tubes in half length-wise was available to every team. Most teams never thought of it though, because they thought of the cardboard tubes as tubes, not as chutes. That transformation remained inconceivable to most teams.

Most engineering teams transformed their thinking more gradually than the sudden "tubes to chutes" insight. For example, a common action was to try to tie the string around the egg. But tying a string tightly around an egg is difficult. One group shifted from tying the string around the egg to tying the string to a box and putting the egg in the box. At this point, another team member who had put a cardboard tube on top of the wall got excited. This team member tied a longer string to the box with the egg in it, looped the string over the tube, and showed everyone how the tube could serve as a pulley, lifting the egg in its box. Now the team had a way to get the egg to the top of the wall, using their cardboard-tube-and-string pulley system. Then they got stuck, uncertain about how to get the egg from the top of the wall down to the target. They talked about the string, someone else talked about a rope-and-pulley system, and another person thought of a cable, at which point they realized that the egg in a box tied with string was sort of like a cable car. They realized that more string could be tied from the top of the wall down to the target, and the box could slide down the string to the target. Now the wall was less an impediment than a reason to get an egg up high and let gravity help it travel the distance to the target. After this bit of excitement wore off, they realized that they needed a way to get the egg out of the box attached to their tube-pulley and into the cable car box. The initial box that worked with the tube-pulley was no longer going to work. They removed the box attached to the tube-pulley and instead formed a large spoon-like device out of another cardboard tube. This device was made both to carry the egg up to the top of the wall and to transfer the egg into the cable car box. This clever, gradually developed solution resulted from multiple shifts in how the team thought about their materials and the challenge they faced.

For the teams working on the egg challenge and for the engineers working on the Shinkansen trains, the creative process was an extended journey of changing and building new ways to think about the issues at hand. These changes took the stories in new directions, built pathways forward where no pathway had existed before, resolved subplots, and collectively changed the nature of the endeavor in which people thought they were engaged.

The account of the creative process from these engineering stories turned out to be the same as what we heard from artists and accountants, musicians and mathematicians, plumbers and physicists. Everyone we spoke to about what they do when they are creative described a long process of fitfully coming to think in new ways, and then further new ways, and then still further new ways, about what was right in front of them. The changes to their thinking meant that they could now think about what had been inconceivable. As a result, they often learned something new. They also often generated new kinds of solutions. In short, when we asked everyone about creativity, they told us it was a long story.

CREATIVE PRODUCTS:
INSIGHTS, INVENTIONS, AND ENLIGHTENMENTS

Often, stories are told for a reason. The creative process has consequences. People may occasionally engage in the creative process out of curiosity or playfulness, with no end in mind. But every creator we spoke with had a purpose in going through the creative process most of the time. The nose of the Shinkansen train advanced some goals. The painters and musicians we spoke with were communicating something with their creative products; they were not primarily acts of self-expression. Typically, as creators, we are interested in attaining some kind of product. Our stories aim toward good endings. This is probably the main reason why a better understanding of the creative process matters. If we can increase our skill at navigating the creative process, we might become more efficient and more effective at generating creative products.

In examining the stories of the creative process and cataloguing the creative products of the creators we interviewed, it became clear that there were different types of products. We often heard people talking about ideas when we spoke about creativity. There are many common intuitions about being struck by an idea, or generating a new idea. Creators also spoke about making things. They might be writing a song or designing a video game. Both ideas and things seem to be noteworthy products of the creative process, but they do not seem the same. They seem different in how they emerge and how they are used. In working to generate a clear distinction between these two, the idea and the thing, we noted a third type of product that also emerged and was used in a distinct way. Thus in the end we found it helpful to distinguish between three kinds of products and found that they provide three different views of the creative process. We call them insights, inventions, and enlightenments.

Insights are ideas for changing how we as creators are thinking and so changing what is possible for our stories. Usually, our thinking advances our stories in predictable ways. We think to improve a train using the knowledge about trains we typically use. We think to use cardboard tubes in ways we already know about and can expect to apply in this story. Insights are inconsistent with these assumptions about what to think. For example, when Nakatsu formed the analogy between the train entering a tunnel and kingfishers entering the water, he was forming an insight. He was changing how he was thinking about the train entering tunnels. The egg challenge team's realization that they did not need tubes but chutes was also an insight. It changed how they thought about the tubes. Insights are like plot twists in our stories. They change how we are thinking about our stories right now, they can change how we think about what happened previously in our stories, and they can change where we next take our stories. Insights typically form over fairly short periods of time. They do not usually end our stories but instead redirect our stories.

Our stories usually end with the formation of some specific thing, which when creativity is involved can be called an **invention**. Usually, we resolve our stories using ordinary methods, yielding predictable endings and standard resolutions. We get up, get dressed, and tie our shoes pretty much how we did yesterday. We can even solve new problems in ordinary ways. For example, in the egg challenge, many teams formed padded carriers in which to place their eggs so as to protect them from bumps along the way. The stories for making the egg carriers are ordinary. Teams take a small box, crumple newspaper around the egg, place it inside the box, and tape the box shut. Yet sometimes we either do not use or do not know any ordinary way to advance our stories. Sometimes, we form insights that redirect our stories, which is what allows us, eventually, to generate inventions. The new nose on the Shinkansen was an invention. The tunnel boom story could not be resolved until the new nose invention was instantiated and shown to work. The egg cable car was an invention. Inventions resolve stories. They typically form over fairly long periods of time.

Insights and inventions are related, but they are not the same. The insight of an egg cable car was an idea, whereas the invention of the egg cable car was made of cardboard, tape, and string. Nakatsu's analogy between the train entering a tunnel and a kingfisher diving into water was an insight but not an actual new front end of a train, which was the invention. Insights are generally far short of inventions, just as a plot twist is generally far short of a full story. Insights can fail. A new way of thinking could turn out to be wrong or infeasible. Insights are usually incomplete. For example, even the simple "chutes not tubes" insight was incomplete because the cut cardboard tubes were unstable and tended to twist. A complete invention required more thinking as well as more work to stabilize the chutes. It was more than four years of effort between the insight about owls flying silently and the invention of the new pantograph for the Shinkansen. An invention can require many insights and a considerable amount of ordinary thinking. Thus an insight is a shift in thinking, whereas an invention is something we make or do, something we patent, or something we might go on to develop commercially and sell.

Insights occur within stories. Inventions resolve stories. The third type of creative product, an enlightenment, goes beyond stories. **Enlightenments** are new knowledge that change how we can think going forward. The insight of an egg cable car resulted, eventually, in an egg cable car invention. But it was not general new knowledge that transformed the teams' engineering capacities beyond that problem. In contrast, the "owls fly silently" insight Nakatsu had, even before it resulted in the invention of the new pantograph, resulted in an enlightenment. The engineers' discovery of how the serration feathers on the edge of owl wings function led them to knowledge about how shapes can break up soundwaves. The engineers could use this vortex generator enlightenment in many other stories, not just the pantograph story. Enlightenments can emerge at any point in a story. They usually take a long time to generate. Their effects are not temporary or singular. They are not shifts in how we are thinking about a specific story (insights). They are not instantiated to resolve particular stories (inventions). They are changes to our knowledge, and so can apply to any story.

Separating out insights, inventions, and enlightenments helps to clarify what the effects of going through the creative process might be. We might work to break out of our current way of thinking about something and generate an insight. We might work toward a solution and generate an invention. We might work toward new knowledge and generate an enlightenment. Insights, inventions, and enlightenments are all creative products, just different types, all of which take work.

THE CREATIVE PROCESS: FROM CUES TO PRODUCTS

The Shinkansen and egg challenge examples are illustrations of the creative process. They show the creative process as a break from ordinary thinking. We are cued to consider shifting our thinking, we work to identify an alternative way of thinking, and then we integrate any alternative we find back into ordinary thinking. The creative process extends from and returns to ordinary thinking. To become more effective at going through the creative process then, we have to start by learning about ordinary thinking.

Talking about ordinary thinking might make it seem as if we are not doing anything special. For this reason, let's call this ordinary thinking process craft as a reminder that ordinary thinking is the result of considerable learning and effort. Craft thinking involves skill and expertise. The word *craft* is also a reminder that there are strong links between thinking and acting. We work with our bodies and our minds in real time to get things done. When creativity shifts our thinking, we often have to work to reconnect our thinking and acting. In the short run, creativity can reduce our ability to get things done because our new thinking can require new ways of acting. For this reason, most of the time we are not adjusting how we think and act. Most of the time, we rely on our hard-won knowledge to think about what we are doing, take action, and perceive what resulted. Most of the time, we practice our craft.

Practicing our craft involves using the knowledge we have in a way that is consistent with how we have used it in the past. In any given situation, while we have available our entire store of knowledge, skills, and abilities, we actually use only a small subset to think about what is happening. For example, imagine that we were starting the egg challenge task. Although we might know something about the neighborhood where we live, about our grandmothers, about popular music, about how to make toast, and countless other things, only a tiny amount of our knowledge might seem relevant to getting an egg over a wall and to a target. We pull together the tiny amount of knowledge that seems relevant and start thinking and acting. Maybe we put the egg in a box with some crumpled newspaper to help keep it from breaking. The craft process involves drawing on a tiny fraction of our knowledge and applying that knowledge in ordinary ways to guide our thinking and action so as to advance our stories.

Pulling together a tiny amount of relevant knowledge is central to the craft process, because it provides us with an interpretation of what is happening and gives us the necessary focus to take a course of action. The tiny amount of knowledge that we use to understand the situation and form our stories is called a **perspective**. When an engineering team takes a cardboard tube and decides to roll the egg down the tube, they have taken a perspective that includes the beliefs that eggs roll, that tubes can guide where eggs will roll, and that putting an egg in a tube and having the egg roll down the tube is a way to transport the egg some distance without the egg breaking. This ordinary, basic information is not something any of the engineering teams had to figure out. They knew it already. This was craft thinking at work. Their perspective on the problem made it easy to think of possible actions to take. However, their initial perspective on the problem made them see cardboard tubes, not chutes. Their initial perspective on the problem also made them see string and boxes, not cables and cable cars. As a result of thinking about the materials as tubes, string, and boxes, chutes and cable cars were, at first, inconceivable.

What makes something inconceivable is that it does not fit with our perspectives. For example, here is a riddle: "What gets wetter the more it dries?" Riddles often invite us to take an unhelpful perspective, and that perspective makes the answer to the riddle inconceivable. This is why riddles can be frustrating, because they seem contradictory or nonsensical. Until we change our perspective, the answer is inconceivable. But once we change our perspective on a riddle, the answer is clear. The inconceivable becomes thinkable.

In this case, the riddle invites us to take a perspective that puts "wetter" and "dries" into correspondence. This correspondence leads us to interpret the riddle as "What gets wetter the more it gets dry?" We interpret "dries" as an intransitive verb: something *becomes* dry. But how can something become dry and become wetter at the same time? If we do not force "wetter" and "dries" into correspondence though, we can interpret "dries" as a transitive verb: something *makes something else* dry. With this change in perspective on the verb "dries" we have a way forward. What gets wetter as it dries something else? A towel.

Riddles capture in miniature a portion of the creative process. We try to interpret the riddle. Our craft process results in forming a perspective, but not one that allows us to advance our story. Instead, we get stuck. The feeling of getting stuck is a **cue**. Cues trigger us to consider changing our perspective. After all, if our initial perspective was working, we probably would not be stuck. Our craft process normally works, which is why we use it. Normally, we do not consider all manner of interpretations. Usually, the knowledge we bring to bear, the perspective we form initially, works and allows us to act sufficiently effectively that we do not question it. But riddles are designed to force us to hit a wall, and so be cued to consider alternative perspectives. We are not so lucky most of the time, as in most real tasks we do not hit a wall even when we long should have tried to be creative. In most real tasks we are not cued to be creative. Absent a cue, we are unlikely to be creative, as cues are usually the starting point for the creative process. Part of learning to navigate the creative process more effectively involves becoming more sensitive to the cues that can trigger us to launch into the creative process.

If we take a cue and consider a pause from trying to advance our stories so that we can instead turn to changing our perspectives, we confront another challenge of the creative process. Often, we feel a bit lost. We are not sure how or what to think. We think something about our current perspective is not right, but we do not know what it is about our current perspective that is unhelpful. It all appears helpful and even necessary. In the towel riddle, it is not usually immediately evident that "dries" has two interpretations. Wanting to change our perspective raises a large challenge. Our perspective was formed with the tiny amount of knowledge we thought was relevant. If we move away from what we think is relevant, we are confronted by an enormous amount of information, all of which has a small chance of being relevant. Part of learning to be more effective at going through the creative process involves developing ways to identify possibly relevant knowledge that we can use to change our perspectives.

If we do identify knowledge that we can use to change something specific about our current perspective, then we can conclude this portion of our creative process and return to craft. The new perspective allows us to think in ways that were formerly inconceivable. Whether the new perspective and the avenues for thinking are useful for advancing our story is unknown until we actually try. Thus, having changed our perspective, we return to craft to try to advance our story. Part of learning to be more effective at going through the creative process involves exiting the process and returning to craft. We do not want to get stuck considering endless possible alternative perspectives. We need to get back to craft and to advancing our story.

What riddles do well is indicate how the creative process might work to produce an insight. We stumble into a cue, we change our perspective, and we arrive at an insight, which is one kind of creative product. Riddles are less helpful for thinking about the creative process needed to generate the other two kinds of creative products though, inventions and enlightenments. To understand the creative process leading to these two creative products, we need to broaden out to consider not just how we think about one situation right now, as we do with riddles, but how we think about long stories. This is the point of the Shinkansen and egg challenge stories. Those stories are examples of how we often cycle back and forth between craft and creativity on the way to generating inventions and enlightenments. We engage in craft, get cued to consider our perspective, identify a way to shift our perspective, try using that shift to advance our story, and then see where it takes us. Later, we might get cued again. And it repeats and repeats. There is a detailed interweaving between craft and creativity. That interweaving is the result of two separate developments happening alongside each other: a craft process of advancing our stories, and a creative process of changing our perspectives.

To generate an intuition about the difference between craft and creativity and so learn how to navigate the creative process more effectively, two metaphors can be helpful. One metaphor is to think about the egg challenge task a little more literally. We can consider the set of materials, the string, boxes, newspaper, and tubes, to be like a perspective, and the contraption we build from those materials to be like a story. If we stop building a contraption and instead change the materials themselves—perhaps we change a tube into a chute—then we can now generate different kinds of contraptions than we could before. Creativity is like changing the building blocks (perspective) that we have on hand, and craft is like making things (the story) from those building blocks. The creative process of changing our perspectives means we have different resources on hand to think with, and that new set of resources allows us to generate different kinds of stories than we could previously.

The building block and contraption metaphor is helpful in clarifying the roles of craft and creativity. The distinction between creativity and craft is about what we are trying to develop. Are we trying to form a contraption or more generally develop our stories? That is craft. Are we trying to change the set of building blocks we have to work with or more generally change our perspectives? This is creativity. There is no contraption without building blocks. Craft is necessary. The contraptions we can generate are limited by the building blocks we have available. Craft is limited. Changing the building blocks we have available in itself does nothing. Creativity without craft is unrealized potential. We can think about building blocks, and we can think about contraptions. Both craft and creativity are about thinking, but what we are thinking about is the key difference between them. The building block and contraption metaphor offers helpful ways of thinking about craft and creativity.

Another helpful metaphor for thinking about the craft process of developing our stories and the creative process of developing our perspectives comes from imagining we are driving. Most of the time when we are driving, we just continue straight along the current road. Most of the time we are using craft. But sometimes we turn. Sometimes we get creative. Without making specific turns, there are specific places we will never go. Without creativity, our craft is bounded. This much is fairly similar to the building block and contraption metaphor.

What the driving metaphor adds is a sense of the longer process for generating inventions and enlightenments. We do not know before we turn and then start driving straight again where a new road will take us. Creativity, by changing the perspective we use to guide craft, changes where our stories can go and so changes the products we might generate. But we do not know where the change in perspective will lead us or whether it will end up being helpful for generating inventions or enlightenments. Any given turn, though, is not helpful on its own—we had to drive to that point and continue driving afterward for that turn to be of value. Creativity without craft does not result in creative products. It takes a set of turns, not just one, and quite a lot of going straight, to get anywhere of interest. Craft and creativity together, applied repeatedly over time, is necessary for forming the creative products we care most about, inventions and enlightenments. The trip we started out to take might, if we discover new turns, become an entirely different adventure than we expected it to be. Creativity can change not only where our stories are going but also what we think the story is about and why we think we are telling it.

The driving metaphor helps us to see creativity as having effects that accumulate over time. Small amounts of creativity set among large stretches of craft can come to be seen as much more important than all the craft because it is the creativity that established the direction that craft merely developed. It is easy to take craft for granted. It is also easy, after the journey, to forget about every turn we had to navigate along the way to reaching our destination. Our view of the creativity needed to generate inventions and enlightenments is often partial and often hard to summarize.

A final aspect of the driving metaphor to emphasize is that we often drive around the same neighborhoods repeatedly. This means that once we do learn a certain set of turns, we expand the places to which we can drive in the future. We learn a neighborhood, and traveling around it becomes routine. Once we have been creative, our craft is more comprehensive. Our knowledge is more developed. Our perspectives are richer. A history of creativity expands our capacities for craft in the future.

The expansion of craft due to a history of creativity expanding perspectives is the reason why the novices we interviewed felt more creative than the experts did. For novices, each new turn is a new creative moment. For experts, they have already learned the neighborhood. Driving all over some parts of town is now just craft for them. For example, experienced music producers have learned how to navigate some musical neighborhoods. They can produce new songs using their existing perspectives to make songs similar to the ones they have made before, but that appear new to novices.[12] As Ed Catmull from the film studio Pixar noted, when people in creative professions "merely cut up and re-assemble what has come before, it gives the illusion of creativity, but it is craft without art. Craft is what we are expected to know; art is the unexpected use of our craft."[13] Generating products that did not exist before is not enough for creativity. Expert craft can do that. As sound engineer and producer James Thane Robeson put it during an interview, "created does not mean creative."

THE CRAFT OF CREATIVITY

If our aim is to learn to generate creative products, then our task is to improve our ability to navigate the creative process. The creative process is crucial because it is primary. When we are going through the creative process ourselves, when we are the creators, we are engaged in the craft process of developing stories and also engaged in the creative process of changing our perspectives so as to change what our stories can be. When we form an insight, an invention, or an enlightenment, we do so relative to our own understandings. When we focus on the creative process, creativity is relative to the creator. If something is within the perspective of the creator, it is craft. If something is not within the perspective of the creator and so inconceivable to the creator, then it takes creativity for the creator to think it. The focus of the discussion thus far and the discussions to come are on the process of creative storytelling.

The clarity we get when we focus on ourselves as creators going through the creative process is gone when we focus on other people's products. When we start from other people's products, we are in a more difficult position. It is tempting to talk about a product as being creative or not being creative. But what does that mean? When we say a product is creative, we usually are not talking about the creative process that led to the product because we usually do not know about the process that led to the product. And it does not make sense to say that there is some inherent quality of the product that makes it creative. Whether a product is perceived to be creative is an evaluation. Whether something is perceived to be creative is a question of the perspective the evaluator forms of the product and the relationship between that perspective and the evaluator's background knowledge. If evaluators form perspectives of a product that indicate the product is just like other items they have experienced before, the evaluators will not find the product creative. And evaluators could always do so. What strikes one of us as creative may not strike another one of us as creative because we can form different perspectives and we can have different background knowledge.

It is common to talk about creative products, so the expression must mean something. For example, we might see a painting, a video, or a gadget, and think, "That's creative!" One meaning for the expression is that when we are evaluators and perceive a painting to be creative, we are forming an interpretation of the painting that represents a change in perspective from the interpretations that we would normally form. If a group of evaluators tend to have similar background knowledge and tend to form similar interpretations, then many in that group could have very similar reactions to the same product. Because people in the same community often share beliefs, many of them might agree that a particular painting is creative. Calling a product creative could be shorthand for the typical experience typical evaluators have when first perceiving the product. The limitation of course is that different kinds of perceivers often disagree. People from different backgrounds, people with different knowledge, people from different cultures, and people who live in different eras can and frequently do disagree on what products strike them as creative.

A second reason we might call a product creative is that we are getting some kind of signal from the world that the product is the type of thing we often call creative. We often think of art as a creative activity, for example, so we might tend to assume a painting is creative to some degree just because it is a painting. Or maybe the product has stereotypical hallmarks of something innovative, such as being high tech and made by someone with funny hair. Signals from the world that a product is creative indicate a complicated set of processes for why we call a product creative. Both reasons, that evaluators experience a change from their typical perspectives and that evaluators get external signals that a product is creative, play important roles in why we describe products as creative, as Jennifer Mueller's book *Creative Change* discusses brilliantly.[14]

There is a still more complex reason we might call a product creative, which is that the product is successful. For example, we might consider famous paintings, widely sold consumer products, or highly cited patents to be more creative than unknown paintings, unsuccessful consumer products, or ignored patents. However, it is a complicated measure to interpret. "Examples of once prominent but later obscure creations abound across disciplines—consider the 'science' of phrenology, 'hot pants' from designer Mary Quant, and the early Oscar winner *Cavalcade* (which won Best Picture and two other Oscars, and is currently unavailable on DVD)."[15] The reverse is true as well. Outcomes that are now prominent were not necessarily successful at the outset, including work by Van Gogh, Franz Kafka, Nicolas Copernicus, and Emily Dickinson, among many others. The social impact of creative products is important and interesting. But there are a large number of reasons products are and are not socially successful that have little to do with the creativity that went into generating the product. For example, the creator might be someone important. The creator might have many influential friends. The creator might have generated an exciting way to talk about the product. The market might be ready to receive such a product. There are many other reasons too. A product's success is an interesting and important outcome. But it is influenced by far more than just whatever creativity might have gone into the product's creation.

We must give up the fiction that we, as creators, will know with certainty if our creative products are sufficient for our needs when they first emerge. The assumption seems to be that we will. Yet a great deal of research on real-world creativity across fields and people shows that a creator's success at predicting the social impact of his or her outcomes approximates chance.[16] Consider the success rates of people who invest in new ventures. Nine out of ten investments in entrepreneurial ventures fail. If people who make their living picking inventions fail nine out of ten times, and if creators' own estimates of how successful their outcomes will be are also no better than chance, then it seems unhelpful to condition decisions about creativity on predictions about the products.

The conclusions we draw from work on why people evaluate some product to be creative are that evaluation is a complicated and important process, and evaluation is not the first process that occurs. To evaluate a product for creativity there first has to be a product. Thus we emphasize that the place to start when it comes to creativity is not with whether a person has generated many products that others perceive to be creative, and not with whether a product is widely perceived to be creative. Rather, the place to start when trying to understand creativity is with the process of generating creative products.

Generating ordinary products requires craft. Generating creative products requires craft and also creativity. We have identified the possibility of learning to notice cues that could prompt changes in perspectives. We noted the possibility of developing skill at changing perspectives. We suggested that there are opportunities to learn to manage the interweaving of craft and creativity over the long periods of time needed to form inventions and enlightenments. What that means is that people have the potential to develop specific ways of thinking and acting to help them navigate the creative process. People can develop craft at going through the creative process. This is what we mean when we say that there is a craft of creativity.

GETTING CREATIVE ABOUT CREATIVITY

The aim of this book is to explain what the craft of creativity involves and what we know about how people can improve their craft for creativity. Part of that process is acknowledging that this might involve changing some of the ways to think about creativity itself. In our own experiences studying creativity, we have had to change our perspective about creativity. We have gotten stalled in our stories about creativity and needed to change our perspectives to make satisfactory progress. We had to get creative about creativity.

The account of creativity that we have been describing might already have changed part of your perspective on the subject. Perhaps you tended to focus on the traits of creative people. Perhaps you tended to focus on the success of creative products. Those are fascinating topics to examine. The reason we are exploring the craft of creativity is because we have worked with large numbers of people who felt that creativity is not a skill they could develop. They not only felt uncreative, they did not think there was a way to improve. We think there is a way to improve, and we hope that what follows provides guidance for why and how all of us can improve.

We have also worked with large numbers of people who felt that creativity was not something they wanted to improve upon, because they were too busy getting important things done. Creativity is sometimes viewed as frivolous, inefficient, and optional. The thought is that special people can be creative, and everyone else should do useful things. We could not disagree more.

Our view of creativity is that if we can think about it, we can think creatively about it. And who wants to be a limited thinker? Take a topic that many people assume requires the opposite of creativity—accounting. Bill Foster, a tax accountant, told us that one year when working on a complicated tax filing he took a break and picked up a tax trade journal. As professors, we could relate—procrastination in the form of doing something that we can feel justified in doing is tempting. In this case though, Foster read an article detailing a power company's successful attempts to extend the time period in which it could claim fiscal losses because of extenuating circumstances. He realized that the power company's situation was like the situation of one of his clients, the Long Island Railroad. Mapping the analogy from the power company to the railroad changed his perspective on the railroad's accounting situation. It was an entirely legal bit of creative accounting that allowed Foster to save the railroad company $50 million.

Creativity is not just about exciting new opportunities. It can take creativity to identify misunderstandings and find ways to reconcile them to reduce conflict. Jeanne Brett, in her wonderful book *Negotiating Globally*, shows the costs of misunderstandings driven by a failure to change perspectives. For example, she wrote of a conflict arising because one person seemed to be making excessive demands of others.[17] The root problem turned out to be a simple translation error: a French speaker used the English word "demand" thinking it was a cognate of the French word "demander," which is typically translated as "ask." Asking and demanding are starkly different, but no one on the American side noticed the possibility of interpreting "demand" from a native French speaker to mean ask. Another reason to be creative is that it can take creativity to appreciate a risk that could make a project fail or an action that could ruin our reputations. Max Bazerman and Anne Tenbrunsel's important book *Blind Spots* documents many examples of people failing to notice ethical traps because they were thinking rigidly, locked into their perspectives.[18] It can even require creativity to be efficient. As Amos Tversky said, "[Y]ou waste years not being able to waste hours."[19] If we refuse to stop advancing our stories long enough to change our perspectives, we are unlikely to get much better than we are now. For many reasons then, we all need to be better at navigating the creative process. We could all stand to improve our craft of creativity. This may well mean that we all need to be a little creative about creativity itself, so we can think about improvements that are currently inconceivable.

Even academics studying creativity can stand to be creative about creativity. As one recent scholarly review of creativity research put it:

> [W]e are struck by the relative lack of theoretical advances across the creativity and innovation literatures in the past decade. . . . Although a whole morass of valuable empirical studies has appeared over the last decade, relatively few distinctively theoretical advances have been published within this sheer volume of studies. To invert the title of one article—"stagnant fountains and sparkling ponds"—characterizes, perhaps marginally unkindly, our impression of this situation.[20]

These are pretty strong words for academics. But these words point to a shared dissatisfaction in the community of creativity scholars with the scholarly frameworks for understanding creativity. For example, we were sitting not too long ago with a prominent creativity researcher talking about brainstorming. He said that he tended to use a brainstorming framework to think about creativity because that was the available tool, despite all its flaws and limitations. He knew there was more to creativity than this, but this is what he had to work with and so he did. Focusing on the creative process of changing perspectives is an avenue for reinvigorating creativity research as well as practice.

To reinvigorate our own thinking about creativity, we gathered fresh observations. After all, when people take seriously that they may not understand something very well, they are obligated to stop focusing on what they think they already know and start taking a harder look at what is happening.[21] This led us to discussions with 77 people, for one to three hours each, about their practices and beliefs with respect to creativity.[22] The interview approach has led to a great many insightful works about creativity.[23] In contrast to some approaches though, we did not start with those who had produced widely successful works of creativity and then try to reverse engineer the process they used to create their works. That would have made it difficult to know whether those processes were actually helpful. After all, those same creators or other people might have used the very same processes to generate many large failures. Instead, we simply asked about the process the creators relied upon when they were trying to be creative, or found themselves being creative. People spoke about their successes and their failures.

The people we spoke with ranged widely in eminence. As we were interested in what people might learn about the creative process, speaking to people across a range of skill levels was important. We talked to people who have achieved at high levels in their fields, winning Grammy awards, Emmy awards, scientific awards, and more. We spoke with experts who worked in relative obscurity, but who made a living from their creativity. We spoke with people who were amateur creators, whose creative endeavors were not their livelihood but a regular part of their lives. We also interviewed novices, such as college students engaged with their first research projects. Interviewing people ranging in skill gave us a window into what expertise in creativity might look like and what the learning process in developing that expertise might look like.

Because we have argued that if we can think about it, we can think creatively about it, we interviewed people working in a wide range of domains. We interviewed dancers, composers, painters, and other "pure" artists. We interviewed game designers, advertisers, product designers, and others applying aspects of art and design to their work. We interviewed people in technical fields such as mathematicians, IT network builders, mechanics, accountants, and engineers. And we interviewed people in many other areas as well, including medicine, law, management, anthropology, tailoring, lobbying, and more. The variety of domains allowed us to understand if domain matters to developing one's craft of creativity.

We used the responses from these interviews in several ways. We sought out repeated observations and claims to get a sense of creativity as these people understood it. We examined whether there was general convergence or divergence in what people said. Then we examined where the picture of creativity that emerged from the interviews supported, contradicted, or were about issues ignored by the scholarly literature on creativity. Then at the end of the process, after we had formed our best guesses about creativity, we returned to the interviews to see whether our best guesses were a good fit and brought out more in the interviews than we had at first noticed or were in fact contradicted by comments we initially failed to appreciate.

Complementing the interviews as a basis for thinking about creativity, we drew on research findings about creativity and about cognitive science. The reasons we drew on creativity research are straightforward. We drew on cognitive science because the creative process we heard described repeatedly is largely about how people change their thinking, and the cognitive science research community is the primary scholarly community studying thinking. The most important work for us was research describing the content of thought. The more we listened to people trying to talk about changing their perspectives, the more we realized that they spoke about specific changes to specific thoughts they were having, like the realization in the egg challenge that it was not cardboard tubes that they needed but chutes. Few people could articulate the generalization that they were changing their perspectives, let alone tell us much about what a perspective is and what it means to change one. For that, we turned to research from cognitive science.

The discussion of creativity that follows in this book is informed by our interviews, our reading of the cognitive science literature, our reading of the creativity literature, and our own primary research. The interpretations that we present inevitably will disagree in places with some of the scholars on whose work we drew. We also expect that there will be research that would have been useful but that we did not find. We are confident that none of us are fully correct, and we hope that our areas of both agreement and disagreement are opportunities for improvement. That is the nature of research. But we are finding the novel integration that we present here to be useful for our own thinking and to our students. Thus our hope for the student or practitioner is that we provide a useful, usable, and desirable framework from which you can learn to improve your skill at creating. But we also hope to provide you with new insights, inventions, and enlightenments that allow you to generate new knowledge about creativity itself.

Our current view of creativity is centered on the creative process, rather than on creative products or creative people. The creative process is about making the inconceivable thinkable. Specifically, we use the following definition:

> Creativity is a process of following cues to generate insights that change our perspectives, which with craft we can use to form inventions and enlightenments.

THE STORY TO COME

This book is intended to help you develop a deep understanding of how creativity works. That is the foundation for learning the concepts and methods to improve your skill at being creative. To this end, exercises are provided at the ends of the chapters for exploring those concepts and methods. To add to the pragmatic goal of the book, there are discussions of what science tells us about creativity. Knowing how and why creativity emerges takes longer to understand than simply which skills make creativity more likely. But such knowledge provides dividends. It provides a foundation of knowledge upon which we can build and refine our skills beyond what this book can provide.

This book strives to be thought-provoking, even for those already quite knowledgeable about creativity. It offers new views on how creativity works. By the end of this book, you may well understand creativity differently, and hopefully be able to leverage that understanding to be more creative in whatever you do. That might even mean developing your knowledge about what creativity is or how it works even further with a new technique or new research. No matter your objective, creativity can help.

This claim is based on one of the biggest surprises from the interviews. People across disciplines described their need for and use of creative thinking in ways that were almost identical. Everyone used their tradecraft most of the time, everyone had times when they needed to change how they were thinking to make the inconceivable happen, everyone used a creative process to do this, and the result was usually something they were proud of. In addition, creativity happened across professions and people in remarkably consistent ways, at least in terms of their thinking processes. In hindsight, it was clear why they gave such similar descriptions of creativity. People are all working with the same kind of cognitive machinery and going through the same kind of cognitive process. The first half of the book is thus dedicated to understanding how that cognitive machinery works to produce creativity.

Chapter 2 starts where most people are when it comes to creativity—at the level of ideas. The creative idea is the insight, which is a product of thought. Chapter 2 explains some fundamentals of thinking—how we develop ideas that are often craft but are sometimes creative. Ultimately this means understanding how our cognitive machinery operates. The chapter examines why we have to form a perspective as we try to make a story for what is happening in our present situation. Perspectives provide great flexibility in the directions a story can go, but they also impose limits on what we can bring to mind. Thus, to generate insights, we need to change our perspectives. Doing so will change what we can imagine happening in our stories. Changing our perspective is different than continuing or building upon our current perspective. But successfully navigating a change to our perspective, successfully producing an insight, allows us to imagine stories for what is happening that were previously inconceivable.

Chapter 3 shows that insight is the beginning, not the end, of creativity. Having an insight changes the direction of our story, but we still have to resolve our story. That resolution will be an invention. Invention requires more than just ideas, it requires action. We have to apply our ideas to the world so that we can transform the current situation into the situation we desire. Often this takes many actions. Thus not only must we produce ideas about what to do, we must also take action, evaluate what has happened, update our beliefs, and act again. We are advancing our story in an attempt to resolve it, and sometimes the world does not comply. So in addition to the thinking processes discussed in Chapter 2, Chapter 3 integrates a discussion of action, as we need to transform our situation to meet our goals. Our perspectives guide this process, which means that insights provide new guidance. Insights can beget further insights, and many insights may be required for a single invention. If we understand how our perspectives guide our actions, we can understand how many inventions are in reach, if we could only think to pursue them.

Chapter 4 discusses enlightenments. Inventions are not the only end product of the creative process. As we tell our stories we learn new things about our world. These are the enlightenments, the new knowledge we could not have imagined until we formed new insights about the world from our interactions with it. There is a tight relationship between creativity and learning, although the two tend not to be discussed together. This is probably the most important gap to fill in how we think about creativity. Creativity has a critical role in learning new ways of thinking about the world. Most learning is craft of course, just as most thinking is craft; we just improve on what we already know. Yet we can also generate new kinds of knowledge that do not follow from what we already know, and will change what we believe. Forming enlightenments means creativity has an even larger impact than we at first think, because it is our knowledge that is the basis for all our action. And because we can share our knowledge, this means creativity is the source of most human achievement.

Understanding the process of forming insights, inventions, and enlightenments prepares us to learn how to go through the process more efficiently and effectively than we do now. Thus the second half of the book is devoted to improving our craft of creativity. Chapter 5 discusses the cues that can signal when it is likely to be useful to begin the process of changing our perspectives. There are four main cues: impasse, dissatisfaction, surprise, and crosstalk. The chapter explores why we experience each one and what that signals about our perspective. When we understand what cues are indicating about our perspective, we can learn to better identify when our perspective could be changed.

Thinking that our perspective needs to change is just a start. We still have to think of a way to change it. Chapter 6 looks at the **cognitive tools** that help us change our perspectives. We call these activation, analogy, combination, and recategorization. Each tool operates in its own way, so they have different uses and different results. All of them help us with the most challenging part of creativity—finding a way to think differently from how we do now. In examining all four tools, we will understand why there is more than one way to help ourselves be creative. As a result, we can learn to try different tools to generate more insights and to avoid getting stuck.

Chapter 7 discusses the villain in the creative process, uncertainty. Uncertainty threatens the creative process in many ways. We have feelings of uncertainty regarding whether creativity is worthwhile. We are uncertain we can think of anything better or even different from what we are already thinking. We are uncertain that a change in perspective will actually turn out to be fruitful. There are many points in the creative process at which uncertainty weakens our resolve to go through the creative process or even to begin the creative process. Thus, in Chapter 7 we learn ways to handle uncertainty. We also revisit some of the unhelpful assumptions people may have about creativity so that unnecessary uncertainties can be avoided. Part of the craft of creativity is a willingness to go through the creative process and the persistence to stick with it.

Finally, we close in Chapter 8 with a big-picture view of the creative process and the craft of creativity. We also examine the implications of our discussions for how you can better evaluate creative products, better communicate about creative products, and better support others through the creative process.

Improving the craft of creativity is long journey. In an interview, Schell Games CEO Jesse Schell drew an analogy between learning to go through the creative process and learning to run competitively: "Everyone knows how to make new ideas . . . [and we] all know how to run. But if you want to win races? Now we got stuff to talk about . . . we have training to do." Rather than being fixed, our skill at being creative can improve if we learn more about the process. The scholar Teresa Amabile, one of the leading creativity researchers of her generation, incorporated creativity skills as an influence on the creative process,[24] and new research is starting to show that our capability to be creative can be improved.[25] When we think of the creative process as a process of changing our perspectives, we are in a better position to appreciate what those "creativity skills" are, why they work, and how we can learn them. We can develop our craft of creativity.

GAINING INSIGHT

The real voyage of discovery consists not in seeking new landscapes,
but in having new eyes.
—Marcel Proust

In his career as an acting teacher, Hayes Gordon, founding member of the Ensemble Theater and School for Acting in Sydney, Australia, came up with a nice insight: "Amateur art is about self-expression—professional art is about communication."[1] For Gordon, this statement captured an important lesson that acting students needed to internalize. When telling it to students, he found it was memorable, poetic, and effective. This statement then became part of Gordon's standard repertoire when he taught—it became part of his craft. And though it was craft to him, the statement typically triggered insight in those who heard it. It changed their perspectives about acting and then became part of their craft. Creativity is generative because of this cycle. Our creative ideas of today become our trusted craft tomorrow. To understand this process, the first task is to understand perspectives.

Ordinary intuitions about perspectives are close to how we use the term here. A perspective is commonly understood to be a viewpoint, a way of interpreting, a taking of a particular angle on some topic or event. The critical distinction is between the external world and thinking about that external world. We will use the word **situation** to refer to the external world. We use the word **perspective** to refer to the interpretation of a situation.[2]

As situations extend over time, people use their perspectives to form stories about what has happened. As time goes by, not only do their stories develop but so too do their perspectives develop. We have found that the idea of a perspective is quite natural, but it can be less natural to think about perspectives as emerging and developing over time.[3] It is tempting to think of perspectives as fixed, with only the stories developing. But in fact both stories and perspectives develop over time.

For example, consider the following situation:

> George is about to get rid of an old chest of drawers. As he is taking it to the curb, Jane comes out yelling, "What are you doing? I love that piece." George responds, "It is a piece of junk. You never use it anymore and it is taking up space. I am bringing it to the curb for pickup." "The hell you are!" Jane retorts.

When we perceive situations, we form a perspective about what is happening. In familiar situations, perceiving and forming a perspective is automatic and effortless. We do not have to ponder on what a chest of drawers might be or consider why Jane is getting angry. We recognize aspects of this situation as familiar and use these starting points to recall further relevant knowledge. It is actually rather remarkable. Our perspectives give us the illusion that we are perceiving situations as they are and in their entirety.[4] This process is typically automatic. We are hardly aware that we are interpreting anything. We just think we are perceiving what happened.

We are actually perceiving some of what happened, and we are making interpretations about it. For example, perhaps one person thinks Jane is being unreasonable, whereas another thinks that George is being thoughtless. We each have different experiences and knowledge, so our perspectives and the stories we form about situations can differ. All of us are recognizing aspects of the current situation that fit with our knowledge and using that perspective as a starting point for forming a story.

We have only a starting point on a story because we have limited information and time. We have only perceived a small amount of activity. Our ability to predict what will happen next is limited. We may feel certain that George and Jane are arguing about an old piece of furniture. We might assume, because of the way that conversations tend to involve people taking turns speaking, that it is George's turn to respond to Jane. What George will say is hard to imagine with any confidence, but we could make some guesses based on what we have already perceived.

Our perspectives and stories provide starting points for guessing. We are probably not going to wonder if there are any other pieces of furniture about which George and Jane can argue. Instead, we are probably going to wonder about the tone George will take in response to Jane's aggressiveness—if our perspective is that she is being aggressive, that is. We try to form stories that make sense to us, and so we try to extend our stories in ways that are reasonably internally consistent. If we assume Jane is being unreasonable, then we are probably going to be less likely to assume George is being thoughtless. If we assume George and Jane are married, then we will not assume they are only roommates. As George was about to bring something to a curb, George is probably not about to go get a sandwich, let alone jump out of an airplane.

To continue:

> George looks at Jane and then says calmly, "You don't need to snap at me. We talked about decluttering, and you agreed we should." "Yes, I did." Jane replies icily. "But that does not give you carte blanche. There are many other things we could get rid of, and it would be nice to be consulted before you do this. You never use that exercise bike, and it takes up space. How about we get rid of that?" George then pleads, "Come on Jane, you promised! Please can we get rid of this?" Jane just continues to glare at George.

After this paragraph, we are likely to have more confidence that, even if Jane is not bossy, she is strong-willed. We might think that George is the weaker of the two. This may seem more like the kind of argument that happens between people in a romantic relationship than between roommates. The perspective that we are forming about the situation is largely generated without explicit reasoning. We recognize patterns that are like ones we have seen before, which leads to, for example, "feeling" that this is a couple arguing, not two roommates arguing. When we first started reading, we might not have been able to determine who might win this argument. By now, we might be looking ahead and predicting that Jane is in control of this dispute.

Our perspectives are not just forward looking. We also project backward, using our perspectives to fill in parts of the story leading up to this situation. We would probably bet that this was not the first argument between George and Jane. We do not know their history, of course, but we have knowledge of similar people and similar relational patterns, and we guess that knowledge is relevant here.

Over time, what might have started as tentative conjectures about a situation become much more. We have formed a perspective and started building a story about what is happening, what happened before, and what might happen next. Parts of our perspectives and parts of our stories are tentative. We are aware of some of the assumptions that we are making. But large parts of our perspectives and stories we simply assume are true. We believe we saw Jane being aggressive, or even that Jane is aggressive. We commit to our perspectives and expand on them as we seek to make sense of what is happening and predict what might happen next. The benefit is that we can better understand what is happening in the situation and better anticipate how we might react.

Our stories, our perspectives, and the situation each have different patterns of change. The situation changes like the frames in a motion picture—incrementally altering conditions in the world. It might be that later that day George is at the bar and Jane is angrily emailing friends, conditions that emerged from this situation but bear no resemblance to it. Our stories can connect across time though, as we can bring past events back to mind from memory. If George ends up at a bar, we can review our story and remember why George is drinking. This would give a different meaning to those activities than if the dispute had ended amicably. Our perspectives shape our stories and lead our memories of what happened to seem more similar and consistent than they probably were. We become more committed to our assumptions about what happened in the story because we draw from the same perspective as we consider different points in the story. Our perspectives and our stories build upon each other and reinforce each other as we continue to perceive what is happening in the situation. We might have thought at the outset of the story that George would stand up for himself, but by now this seems out of character.

Perspectives both narrow and deepen our stories. Perspectives lead us to rule out some future possibilities and make us forget some past possibilities that our stories might have taken. In addition though, perspectives allow us to expand on what we believe we experienced. We can form a large number of stories from this narrow starting point. Earlier there was a metaphor that perspectives are like building blocks and stories are like contraptions we construct from those blocks. If so, then perspectives limit the kinds of contraptions we can build because they only provide us with some kinds of blocks and not others. But with no building blocks, we are unable to form any contraptions at all. And even a fixed set of building blocks can be used to form a large number of contraptions.

Continuing with the tale:

> Their neighbor, watching the exchange between George and Jane, comments, "Hey, I think that chest is an antique." "Really?" says George. As the neighbor is explaining why she thinks the chest is an antique, a junk collector drives up because of a yard sale nearby and stops to listen. He then says, "It's not an an-

tique, I would know. But I can do you a favor and take it off your hands. That will save you the garbage collection fee."

The situation has provided new elements that can become part of the story. We were not talking about the neighbor, and we probably did not expect a junk dealer to arrive. But our perspective allows us to integrate these changes to the situation into our story. We make new assumptions about new things—junk dealers, antiques, and neighbors—but we can assimilate them into our existing perspective. If we saw George as weak before, the neighbor might make him change his mind and the junk dealer might be a threat. Or, Jane may seize on the neighbor's comments to justify her love for the chest and may be aggressive or dismissive of the junk dealer. The assumptions that we make about our perspectives and the way we draw on them to form stories depend on our experience. We may like junk dealers as being resourceful or we may think they are barely above thieves. Our stories are a product of the situation and the perspective we have formed, drawing on our knowledge. The history is important, as we try to build on what is there already. We would get nothing done if every time new information came to light we had to rebuild our perspective and restart our story.

We tend to continue to expand our stories as we also continue enriching our perspectives. This is not just about an argument between George and Jane. That was just a beginning to a more interesting story about a chest and its potential worth. As we learn more, we expand our capacity to imagine what might happen. Oddly, even though we are now more limited by our knowledge of what has happened, at this point we can probably imagine far more directions in which this story might go than we could after just the beginning, even though this is just one of many possible stories that might have resulted from that beginning. The more we have to work with, the more work we can do to expand and continue in the direction we are headed.

All of the expanding and developing that our perspectives and stories have undergone to this point are craft. We have started and grown a perspective while also developing a story just by recognizing aspects of a situation that seemed familiar and plausible. The story has elements of novelty, as we have not experienced this particular story before. But we have made it familiar by adopting a perspective and applying the perspective in an ordinary way to form our story. By committing to our perspective and believing our story is an apt account of the situation, we have overlooked other possibilities. As long as we maintain our current perspective, then other possibilities are not conceivable.

For example, imagine the story ended like this:

George and Jane walk into the house, smiling. "Great idea, setting the junk dealer up that way, Jane. That whole fake dispute worked brilliantly. Tell our neighbor thanks and we owe her a beer. I told you that old piece of junk could fool people as being a real antique. Now we saved the trash fee and made $100."

This information cannot be incorporated into the story we were telling unless we abandon some of our perspective. Abandoning some of what we had assumed as part of our perspective will mean that we have to restructure our perspective into one that is incompatible, at least in part, with what it was before. When we change our perspectives, it changes our stories—past, present, and future. Now we see that there was no real conflict between George and Jane. We reinterpret the story we had told. This was not a story about an argument, it was about a con. The junk dealer was conned rather than the reverse. The original perspective makes this ending not just unlikely, but impossible. We *would not* have imagined this ending because it is inconsistent with the perspective we had built about the situation. It was inconceivable.

The story about George and Jane provides an illustration of how perspectives and stories co-evolve. It also illustrates the difference between craft—telling a story that maintains its consistency with our initial perspective and goes where we think it might—and creativity—changing our perspective so that we can redirect our stories to go where we had not imagined they would. Perspective changes are like plot twists that allow stories to develop and resolve in ways that were inconceivable before. Perspective changes are the center of the creative process.[5]

The primary limitation of the George and Jane story for understanding the creative process is that it is someone else's story. We were reading a story formed by someone else rather than developing our own story. We could interpret what was stated, but we had no capacity to take action. The portion of our perspective that we had to change was not assumptions we were particularly committed to in the first place. The implications of the change were easy to use to reinterpret what was happening, and could be done without much further activity. To understand the creative process so that we can develop our ability to navigate it more effectively, we need to build our understanding of how we form perspectives, how we typically make use of them, and what it means to change them. Why we have perspectives is simple enough: we need a perspective to think.

WE ALWAYS HAVE A PERSPECTIVE

The need for a perspective is a simple fact of the way our minds work. We can only think about so many things at once. The joke is that we are lucky if we can walk and chew gum at the same time. The research shows that this is not all that far off. We can only think about—or hold in what psychologists call *working memory*—about five to seven ideas at a time.[6] Perspectives are necessary to reduce the complexity of the world to something manageable.

What allows us to think intelligently even though we can only think about a few ideas at a time is that ideas are not of a fixed size. For example, we can try reading the following four letters, then looking away and writing them down on a piece of paper from memory: n, i, m, a. Four letters can be considered four ideas. Four ideas is less than five to seven ideas, and so this is within our working memory limits. We can remember them.

How about with these four letters: ي ق ى ت ? Unless you are familiar with Arabic letters, this was probably harder. The first four letters were easy because we know the letters of the Roman alphabet quite well. The letters are part of our vast catalogue of patterns that we permanently store in what psychologists call *long-term memory*. We know that the pattern of marks that count as an "a" or an "i" go together, allowing each letter to count as one idea. Unless we know Arabic, we would have to remember each Arabic letter as a pattern of squiggles and dots set in relation to one another. Each letter can require several "ideas" to remember if we do not have patterns stored in long-term memory already.

Our next task is to try to remember and write down a longer list: n, i, m, a, e, s, y, m, d, m, u. That was probably harder than the first list because there are eleven letters. If one letter equals one idea, then eleven ideas far exceeds our five to seven idea capacity. Yet we can use the same principle of making patterns that we saw with the individual dots and squiggles of the letters to be able to remember the full list of eleven letters. If we interpret the list as a sequence of random letters, we will have difficulty remembering them all. But we can group the letters into familiar patterns in the form of words: name, is, my, mud. We now have just four ideas to remember, and this is within our limits. We can continue to make still larger patterns, arranging the words into a phrase: my name is mud. Now all eleven letters become one idea to remember, provided we are familiar with that turn of phrase (that is, provided it exists in our long-term memory). Organizing information into meaningful patterns allows us to think about more at a time because the pattern can become one idea rather than having to be a set of ideas, one for each part.

There is a cost of thinking about information as one idea. It makes our thinking rigid. We used one particular structure to put together the list of eleven letters into one idea, "my name is mud." That helps us remember the letters. Yet it also makes it unlikely that we will consider other patterns for the eleven letters. We might never realize that those letters also spell "emu dynamism" (our new favorite band name). The pattern "my name is mud" is one perspective on the eleven letters. The benefit of adopting that pattern as our perspective was expanding our capacity to remember all eleven letters, and the cost of adopting it is limits on our ability to conceive of the eleven letters from another perspective.

The patterns that we store permanently are called *concepts*, following widely used language in psychology.[7] Concepts are mental representations of categories that we expect to see again and again in different forms. Our "N" concept is a collection of patterns about how the letter N can look regardless of the font, size, capitalization, and so on. The concept also includes knowledge about "N" sounds, that it is a consonant, and many other pieces of information. It was long-term memory providing us with concepts about letters that helped us remember the initial four-letter list (n, i, m, a), concepts about words that helped us remember the four-word list (name, is, my, mud), and concepts about phrases that helped us remember the one-phrase idea (my name is mud). We have concepts for things (chests of drawers), collections of similar things (furniture), events (arguments), actions (yelling), relationships between things (married), properties (old), and more. Anything that we can name and understand by itself can be a concept. We form concepts even of things we know only a little about (perhaps quantum physics or Sufi poetry) or things we just put together as a group in an *ad hoc* fashion (favorite fall recreations, things to do with our grandfather). Concepts focus our thinking and facilitate the storage, recall, and application of knowledge relevant to the concept. As a result, concepts are the foundation of our perspectives and our stories.

When we perceive a situation, we generally assimilate what we perceive into concepts we already know. It is why putting the letters together as "dm muyi sm ean" is not nearly as memorable as "my name is mud." The first way does not draw on the words and phrases we already know. Concepts store and organize what we have learned from our prior experiences, so when we encounter a situation, we are not starting from nothing as we attempt to understand what is happening.[8] In a typical situation, we draw on the vast library of concepts we have in long-term memory to interpret what we perceive, and decide how these things should fit together.[9] If we go to a friend's house and see a large furry thing sitting on our friend's lap and purring, we are not confused. We can identify the thing as a cat and know that it will have all the properties of a cat that our "cat" concept includes. We know that some cats can be large and others can be small, where large means perhaps twenty-five pounds and small means perhaps five pounds. A thirty-pound furry thing would be a notable cat, but a thirty-thousand-pound furry thing would be something else entirely. We can guess whether a cat is friendly from patterns in the concepts we perceive—the cat did not run away when we came in, it is on our friend's lap, and it is purring. All of these interpretations of the situation (running away, lap, purring, and so forth) are concepts, and all of them are associated with friendly cats. Of course, if we have been to our friend's house before, we may have a particular concept for this particular cat based on our prior experience with it. In all cases, our library of concepts stored in long-term memory is the knowledge from which we draw to form a perspective. The particular concepts that we bring to bear to interpret new situations constitute our perspectives.

Our perspectives are the product of the particular concepts we are using to think about the situation as well as the way we put the concepts together. For example, we can consider the following sentence: A married couple are having an argument about whether to discard an old chest of drawers and go furniture shopping for something new, and all their yelling has scared the cat. If we had to write down all that we know about the concepts in that sentence (married, couple, argument, old, shopping, and so on), we could fill pages. But this particular arrangement of the concepts focuses us on a small fraction of these properties that seem to matter now. The chest of drawers is the point of contention, and the chest's value is probably in question because it is old. The arrangement also tells us what we should and should not assume in terms of what is happening overall. It is not an argument about a cat, nor is the married couple yelling at a chest of drawers. It is not just that we make assumptions about which concepts are present in a situation, we make assumptions about how they connect to one another. Saying, "married couple, chest of drawers, cat, argument, yelling, shopping, furniture, scared, new, old" has the same concepts but without any structure in their arrangement, and so the information is much less meaningful. A perspective is thus a *pattern* of assumptions about which concepts are relevant to the situation and how these concepts are put together.

Our perspectives are patterns of concepts. What is conceivable and what is inconceivable is a matter of the pattern of concepts constituting our perspectives. The concept *piano* can be a musical instrument, or an indication of the volume at which an instrument should be played. The concept *player* can mean an important person, a womanizer, or a person participating in an activity. *Piano player* limits which of these meanings are appropriate, while *player piano* implies something else entirely. As we saw with the letters we formed into the phrase "my name is mud," the pattern "player piano" imposes a cost by limiting alternative interpretations in return for the benefit of allowing us to compress the information into one idea to make it manageable for our thinking. Patterns keep our working memories from becoming overwhelmed, at the cost of rigidity. Patterns of concepts—our perspectives—allow us to think sensibly about situations, at the cost of leading us to think in only some ways about those situations.

To see the value of perspectives, try to explain what is going on in this situation: *Jim wants to go home but is afraid to because there is a man wearing a mask waiting at home holding something round.* Most people have a hard time generating a story to explain what is happening. It is not because they are hemmed in by a perspective. It is because they do not know what perspective to form to account for the situation. The "freedom" that comes from the ambiguity of the situation makes it very hard to assemble concepts into a coherent pattern that fits the situation. Without a perspective, we are unable to start forming a story. In this example, if the description had read, "Jim wants to go home but is afraid to because there is a man wearing a mask at home holding something deadly," we would be more constrained as to which concepts could describe the situation and how those concepts relate to each other. And precisely for this reason, it would be easier to make sense of what is happening. We could probably think of many different concepts that would work in many different combinations, and thus we would have no shortage of perspectives to take or stories to tell about what is happening.

Our perspective is the interpretive framework we apply to situations to form stories. So when we lack a perspective, we are unable to make sense of the situation, and we are unable to make sense of new information we perceive as the situation develops. For example, here are more facts about Jim's situation:

> Jim actually ran away from home not long ago. Now he is coming back. After he departed from home he made two lefts, now he is about to make another. There were a lot of witnesses to this event; he even went past a few of them. But even if Jim called the cops they would not do anything to the man with the mask. Jim might need to stay where he is, but he may not be able to stay there very long. If he stays too long he might never go home.

This new information is almost certainly unhelpful for making a coherent story because we have no basis for determining its meaning in this situation. We understand what the words say, but we do not know what concepts they represent or how to fit them together into a coherent pattern. Who are the witnesses? We do not know how the new elements relate to the ones we already have in mind. Why does staying where he is too long keep him from going home? Nor can we understand what the significance of an element is. Why are we talking about making lefts? It is like having a pile of Lego blocks with no idea what we are supposed to build. Adding more Lego blocks does not clarify what we are supposed to make.

The purpose of this riddle is to illustrate that thinking requires a perspective. Without a perspective to restrict our attention to certain aspects of the situation, to limit the number of possible meanings we can form, and to direct what knowledge we recall from long-term memory, we have no hope of making progress with forming a story. We need a perspective made of concepts that fit together into a reasonably coherent pattern. Once we have this, we can make guesses and explain what is happening. For example, if we tell you that Jim is playing baseball, then we can gather concepts that we can assemble into a coherent pattern. We can now form a perspective on the situation and begin a story. Jim is on third base. We now understand that home is a plate, not a place to live. The man with the mask is no villain but a catcher. We now understand how to structure the information in the situation. If we asked, "Why is Jim afraid he'll never go home" it is easy to bring the right knowledge about baseball to mind and to speculate: "Maybe there are two outs." Once we have a perspective, our memory limitations will not seem so severe. Once we have a perspective, we can develop our stories.

A perspective on a situation allows us to develop our stories because it indicates how concepts fit together in a larger pattern. Absent a perspective our working memory quickly becomes overwhelmed. Without a way to limit the number of ideas we are thinking about, we will not make headway. A pattern allows us to limit the number of ideas. In addition, a pattern allows us to fill in missing information. We can make guesses about information we do not have concerning the present. We can make guesses about the past that we did not experience. We can make guesses about the future so that we can anticipate and act. As a simple example, imagine that we walk into a room and see numbers flashing on a screen, one by one: . . . 14, 15, 16, 17. Then we turn away for a moment to look around the rest of the room, but it is dark. Then we turn back and see . . . 21, 22, 23, 24, 25. We can guess that we missed 18, 19, and 20. We can guess that before we entered the room, the numbers 11, 12, and 13 flashed on the screen. We can guess that the numbers 26, 27, and 28 are about to flash on screen. This trivial little bit of predicting is trivial because it follows so clearly from a perspective that numbers are being presented in order on a screen. The perspective takes advantage of a simple pattern to fill in what we do not directly perceive. Every perspective serves these same functions, just usually with more complex and varied patterns.

We need to take a perspective on the situations we experience to guide our thinking and acting. Further, our perspectives are more useful to us the more we commit to a pattern of concepts for interpreting the situation. We make assumptions about which concepts fit which situations and how to organize those concepts into a pattern, and we commit to those assumptions by building on them with our guesses about the past, present, and future. This allows us to develop stories. That is the bargain we make as a result of our limited capacity to think. We have to adopt perspectives, and we have to commit to the assumptions we make when we do so. Otherwise, we would hardly be able to think and act. The cost is that our perspectives will channel our thinking and acting toward just some possibilities, and it will make other possibilities inconceivable.

USING, ADDING TO, AND CHANGING OUR PERSPECTIVES

Our perspectives provide the means for developing our stories. Most of the time, that is what we do with our perspectives. We use our existing perspectives to advance our stories. As noted earlier though, we sometimes develop our perspectives too. Sometimes we just need to add to our perspective, keeping the existing perspective intact. But at other times, we have to change our existing perspective. The craft process is about using and adding to our perspectives. The creative process involves changing our perspectives as well.

To illustrate each of these processes, consider what we would do if we were in the following situation:

> We are standing in front of a circle of stones that contains logs, ash, and dirt. Behind us is a picnic table. We are in northern New Jersey on the Appalachian trail at 6:03 p.m. on September 30. We have in our possession a plastic bag with "7-11" printed on it that contains a bag of Doritos and a bottle of Diet Coke. Behind us is a pack, which contains clothes, a folded-up tent, and related supplies.

Before we can use a perspective, add to it, or change it, we first have to form it. When reading this vignette, we will probably form the perspective that we are *camping*. This was almost certainly an effortless inference, even though the word *camping* does not appear in the vignette. What happened when we formed a perspective of this situation is that we recalled concepts from long-term memory to interpret what was described in the vignette. Further, though each word in the vignette has multiple possible meanings, the meanings that actually became active are those that relate to how these words fit together. The circle of stones is encoded as a *fire pit*, not a mosaic, in part because of the location. Meaning also emerges from combinations of what we perceive—the Doritos and Diet Coke are probably encoded as a *snack*. Because the plastic bag is marked by the brand of a convenience store that is commonly found near highway exits, and because it contains a drink normally consumed cold, we probably inferred that we *purchased* the snack *from a convenience store on our drive up to the trail*. This is why, even though Doritos and Diet Coke have no necessary relationship to the concept "camping," we can easily assimilate them into our perspective by filling in all manner of other missing information, such as the high likelihood of a car, money, and a recent "trip to the store" event in the past that connects them all together. It seems to fit fairly well together into a coherent pattern. We are forming a perspective and starting to develop a story.

Our ability to form a perspective is conditioned on our knowledge. Forming a perspective of the camping vignette, and doing so quickly, required substantial prior learning. It is easy to underestimate the number of concepts that we recall from long-term memory and the elaborateness of the pattern we use to structure those concepts as we form an interpretation of the vignette. That is why it is useful to slow down so much when examining this vignette (and the earlier ones). It helps make evident what normally happens without deliberation or notice. For that matter, this entire discussion takes for granted that we are recognizing that words in a book are characterizing a hypothetical situation which exists independently of what we are actually doing. We are synthesizing black squiggles on a white page into letters, words, and sentences to imagine the hypothetical situation. Any one of these tasks would be a challenge for three-year-olds, because they would not have the knowledge or skill to assimilate all this information and form it into a pattern. Yet adults do this without effort or conscious deliberation.

What allows us to form a perspective of the vignette so readily is the way that concepts are structured together in long-term memory. The concepts we have in long-term memory are not just piles of knowledge. They are vast organized networks of knowledge about what things are, what they do, and how they relate to each other. When we perceive that some subset is relevant, we limit our thinking to the attributes and connections of that subset. For example, *camping* and *fire pits* might make us think about *fire*, in the sense of *keeping warm*, *cooking food*, and perhaps *being burned*. We probably would not think about fire in the sense of what happens to bad employees. Depending on what we think about when we think about camping we may or may not think about fire in the sense of shooting a gun. The massive amount of knowledge in our networks of concepts in long-term memory is built from extensive experience.

Our experience also organizes our concepts because it groups concepts together if we tend to use them together. This means that our networks of concepts are largely grouped together in *domains* of activity, such as camping or photography or family life. The more time and effort we put into a particular domain, the richer and more complex the network of concepts we have to form perspectives in relevant situations.[10] This makes the forming of typical perspectives automatic, as we experienced with the camping vignette. And it gives our perspectives considerable depth. We know stones are not soft and do not burn in campfires. We know that Doritos are not health food, that Diet Coke pairs well with Doritos but not, say, breakfast cereal or orange juice. The word *know* here means "our concepts lead us to assume it is generally the case that" rather than that we somehow have perfect and complete understandings of situations. We may not deliberately think "Doritos are for eating" or "Packs are for carrying things," but these assumptions follow from our domain knowledge. They are embedded in our perspectives because they are part of the knowledge we have in long-term memory about these particular concepts that we recognize in the situation. Once we noticed some aspects of the situation and started recognizing them as instances of familiar concepts, then both our domain knowledge and the situation influence what the next concepts are that come to mind and how we assemble them into a perspective.

Using Our Perspectives

Having started to form a perspective, we waste little time putting it to use. We use the pattern of concepts constituting our perspective to **perceive** the situation, **recognize** what is happening, draw **inferences**, and select a **response**. In the camping vignette, perhaps we decided to start a fire, rather than set up our tent or go to view the sunset. Our perspective allows us to leverage our knowledge about starting campfires to draw our attention to aspects of the situation that might be relevant. As the expression goes, when you have a hammer, many things look like a nail. Well, when we are in a campground situation and thinking about starting a fire, we start looking at items for their relevance to that goal. We would probably focus on the logs in the fire pit more than we would focus on the Diet Coke. We would notice that the logs are thick, because that is relevant to the task of starting a fire. We probably would not notice or consider the kind of tree the logs came from, absent specific knowledge about wood types and flammability. While we might be aware of the possibility of setting up our tent or getting a better view of the sunset, having made our decision we would now recognize that these are distractions and not part of starting a campfire. Our perspective filters our perceptions of the situation and is a basis for forming evaluations.

Recognizing initial items in the situation, such as logs, leads us to think about concepts related to logs in our perspective. These then lead to drawing inferences about the situation that nudge our stories forward. For example, if we recognize that the logs are thick, we might infer that they will be difficult to light. This in turn leads us to think about what would be easy to light that could then ignite the logs—what is sometimes called kindling. We may recall that we brought a newspaper. We can weave these inferences together into a burgeoning story—*we could get the newspaper and use that as kindling to light the logs.* We are using our perspective to advance our story.

There are two aspects to perspectives that are helpful as we make use of them to advance our stories. One aspect is the assumptions embedded in the pattern of concepts we have drawn from our knowledge. For example, we assume that the thick things we perceive are logs, and that logs are the kind of thing that will burn. The second aspect is the inferences we draw from the assumptions. We infer that we need kindling, and we infer that getting our newspaper would be a useful action because the newspaper could fill that need. In general, we presume that our assumptions are correct and that our inferences are tentative. The assumptions in our perspective provide what we believe *is* true about the situation, whereas our inferences tell us what we believe *might be* true.

We can modify our inferences or even reject them as we bring more knowledge to mind. It is why we can revise the story we are creating as we think more about it. For example, thinking about using our newspaper as kindling brings the newspaper to mind, at which point we might realize that we have not yet read it. We might decide that reading the newspaper is less important than using the newspaper as kindling to start a campfire. In this case, we could go get the newspaper and proceed to use it as kindling to light a campfire. Our story would continue, as we were able to use our perspective effectively to perceive and respond.

Using our perspectives can involve setbacks though. For example, we might decide that we want to read the newspaper, so we should not use it as kindling. This leads us back to needing to find something to use as kindling. We are using our perspective to advance our story. This is true even if some of our inferences fail. We can typically use our perspective to make sense of the failure and to generate another possibility. We are still trying to light the campfire, it is just that the story for how we think we should do it is now a little different than we at first thought. Maybe we will gather some dead leaves or some twigs to use as kindling. We will continue to perceive the situation, recognize aspects of it, draw inferences about what follows, and select a response to advance our story.

Using our perspectives can be quick or slow, automatic or deliberate. When a situation is very familiar, we can perceive, recognize, infer, and respond without deliberation. If we were experienced campers, for example, this situation might be so familiar that we have routines that we would execute. We might be aware of the response we selected, because we had to act on it, but not aware of what we perceived or inferred that led to the response.[11] Alternatively, each aspect of the process of using our perspectives may be the product of deliberation. We may struggle to perceive what is happening in the situation. We might consider what it is we are recognizing in the situation. We might reason explicitly through inferences. We could deliberate over a response set to select a response. We can even loop back if we do not like any of the responses we identified, to seek out other inferences, to see what else we can recognize as occurring, or even to work harder at perceiving the situation. We can do all of this in our efforts to make use of our current perspective.

Whether slow or fast, using our perspectives is concerned with responding to the situation and so advancing our stories. Using our perspectives is action-oriented; perhaps in this case we gather some dead leaves and twigs to use as kindling. Then we continue our stories, using our perspectives to generate entirely ordinary responses that fit the situation.

Adding to Our Perspectives

Using our perspectives enriches our stories, whereas adding to our perspectives enriches our perspectives. Sometimes we realize that our perspective is lacking, that we do not have enough of an understanding of the situation. The story we are telling does not fit the situation well enough. In such a case, we typically shore up the perspective by **recalling** additional concepts from long-term memory. By **assuming** further concepts to be relevant, we can **elaborate** on our perspective. This extends the pattern of concepts composing our perspective, providing more starting points for drawing inferences and generating responses.

For example, perhaps when we look for twigs and dead leaves, we notice the ground is wet. This is not what we thought. It is not already part of our perspective. To respond to the situation now, we have to do more than just use our existing perspective. The lack of fit with the situation means we need to bolster our perspective to advance our story. We have to fill in the gap. We did not think about the ground being wet, the logs being wet, the leaves in the area being wet. This observation adds to what we know about the situation. Importantly though, this information does not contradict our perspective; we certainly know that rain is possible. As a result, this observation fits with our existing perspective. It just was not noticed until this point, and so we have to enrich our perspective to include it.

Adding to our perspectives indicates that there is more to a situation than we had originally surmised. The situation may have details that we overlooked or have not yet experienced. Something makes our initial perspective insufficient. But new details pop up. And usually, the situation is still mostly like what we have experienced before, just with an additional aspect. We go camping and start campfires. But we usually go camping in nice weather, not rain. While we can easily imagine camping after it has rained, we might not have already thought through that possibility. If we are nudged to do so now, then we can add to our perspective to accommodate it.

We typically realize that we need to add to our perspective when we are in the middle of trying to use it. Typically, we experience a gap after we perceive the situation, as we recognize elements in the situation that were not already part of our perspective and the need to accommodate them before we draw inferences. Recognizing new elements means we need to recall further information from long-term memory to expand our perspective. Further concepts are usually easy to incorporate because they typically will have some connections to the concepts that are already part of our perspective. Thinking about logs is readily updated to thinking about wet logs. It is not hard to move from recalling knowledge about starting fires to recalling concepts about starting fires in wet conditions. We are extending the pattern of concepts, which means adding new concepts and also adding new relations to link the new concepts with the existing concepts. Because our semantic memory is a vast network of concepts with multiple connections, we rarely lack for concepts to incorporate or ways to relate them to the pattern of concepts constituting our perspectives.

Adding to our perspectives means that we are making even more assumptions than we were before. Every perspective relies on assumptions about which concepts are relevant to the situation, the particular interpretations of the situation that these particular concepts offer, and the relations among the concepts. Adding to our perspectives builds more such assumptions onto the ones we already have. If we can incorporate the added concepts, including the new relationships, then the assumptions pay off in the form of added guidance. If we think "Where will we find kindling?" it can be hard to generate possibilities, but a richer perspective involving assumptions about the presence of other campers nearby, a campground store, and an emergency pack in the car will give us opportunities to draw inferences about possible responses. Adding to our perspectives enriches our perspectives to give us more possibilities for continuing our stories.

Like using our perspectives, adding to our perspectives can happen quickly or slowly. If we are experienced campers, we probably have a great deal of knowledge about camping in wet conditions. In this case, once the wetness is perceived, we may barely need to deliberate to enrich our perspective and resume our story. "Oh, I didn't see it rained, well, that means I better . . ." If we are less experienced though, then we may need to work through what it means. "The logs are going to be even harder to light than I thought, and kindling is going to be even harder to find, so let me think through everything I brought with me again . . ." But whether adding to a perspective is fast or slow, we are building on our existing perspective, further committing to what we already believe.

Using our perspectives and adding to our perspectives are both efforts to advance our stories in predictable ways. If we have enough of a perspective to continue our story, we generally will. If we do not, then we will try to add to our perspective so that we can continue with our story. Using our perspectives and adding to our perspectives are craft processes. They are products of our expertise and skill. The more expertise and skill we have developed, the more often we can use our perspectives. And the more often adding to our perspectives is sufficient to fill in any gaps. There is always an opportunity though, even if we do not notice it, of shifting away from craft. We could get creative.

Changing Our Perspectives

The creative process requires changing our perspective. Sometimes rather than just using our perspective or adding to our perspective, we revisit our assumptions about the pattern of concepts we have in place serving as our perspective and we change that pattern. For example, perhaps we look around our campsite and see that everything is wet. We think more about what we have with us, and we are unable to think of or find anything else we can use to start a fire. Worse, there are no other campers nearby, there is no campground store, and it is a long drive to any other resources. So for the sake of argument, let us assume that we have tried using and adding to our perspective and we are still not able to generate a productive response to advance our story.

Instead of trying to generate inferences to form responses, and instead of trying to recall information to build onto our existing perspectives, we can seek out alternative concepts and alternative ways to relate concepts into patterns that might yield different kinds of inferences. We can turn our thinking to changing our perspective. Perspectives focus our attention and provide interpretations of the situations we experience. These interpretations tell us what is and what might be relevant as well as what is not true or relevant. A different perspective can allow us to shift our attention, reinterpret what we experience, and draw inferences about responses that are currently inconceivable.

For example, as we are thinking about how to start a fire in the wet campground situation, we can review the situation. We have a tent, a pack, clothes, a newspaper, Doritos, a Diet Coke, a lighter, a chair, and a car. We have tried using our perspective, and we have tried adding to our perspective. At this point, we often have a grasping feeling of not knowing what to think. This is because we are trying to think beyond our current perspective. We bump up against our assumptions, but as we are committed to them it does not seem to provide any avenue for progress. We realize that newspapers are made of paper and that paper burns, but this conflicts with our commitment to read the newspaper later. That is of no use. We know that we have a tent, a Diet Coke, Doritos, and other things, but we have assumptions about what those things are for and are committed to using them in those ways. We are not going to try to burn our tent. Diet Coke is obviously not fuel. We might think about the plastic bottle the Diet Coke is in or the plastic bag we carried it in—plastic burns. But we probably do not want to pollute the woods by burning plastic. We would probably burn the newspaper first. This feeling of flailing against dead ends and frustration over noting the obvious is common in the creative process. We are inquiring into alternative possibilities but continuing to hit walls put up by our current perspective.

Just as we move from using to adding to our perspectives when the story seems to have gaps we can't fill with our current assumptions, we move from adding to changing perspective when the perspective itself seems to have gaps we can't fill by elaborating on our current assumptions. Changing our perspectives makes us able to consider possibilities that would have been inconceivable if we stayed committed to our prior assumptions. These new assumptions provide new ways of advancing our stories as a result of the new inferences that can now be brought to mind.

The first part of changing our perspectives is **inquiry**. Inquiry is the search for concepts that are inconsistent with our current perspective. Inquiry can be contrasted with recognition and recall. Recognition when we use our perspective is guided by our perception of the situation and its fit to concepts in long-term memory. We look at a log, and we recognize it as an instance of our concept "log." Recognition is normally that straightforward. Sometimes we perceive a complex pattern and we have an intuition about what is happening that we cannot fully articulate. This too is recognition at work. As Herbert Simon has indicated, intuition is recognition. We perceive patterns and recognize them as familiar.

Whereas recognition involves reacting to what we perceive, recall involves probing long-term memory for something we do not perceive. Still, recall is also guided. When we think about the logs being large and about a need for kindling, we can recall from memory items we have used for kindling in the past. One item commonly used as kindling is a newspaper. This leads us to recall that we have a newspaper in our bag that we were planning to read. Recall involves seeking concepts in long-term memory that are associated with what we are thinking about right now.

Inquiry is like recall in that we are seeking concepts in long-term memory. However, inquiry is only barely guided. We are not starting from a specific set of concepts in working memory because we are trying to get outside of the very thing that would provide such concepts—our perspective. We are not certain about what concepts in our perspective should be the starting point. We have little sense of what we are seeking. This is what we mean by inquiry needing to go beyond and being inconsistent with our perspectives. When we question the assumptions that make up our perspective, we are putting ourselves back in the state of not having a perspective. Anything is possible, and this is confusing if not overwhelming. One pair of metaphors is that recall is like searching a large warehouse with the lights on and inquiry is like searching the warehouse in the dark.[12] Inquiry reduces us to fumbling for possibilities we cannot see coming, and it can feel as if we simply have to hope we stumble into them.

The warehouse metaphors and the notion of stumbling in the dark indicate that bumping into something is not enough. For example, we might think about the bag of Doritos. What good are they? We have to recognize the value of what we find. After all, we are likely to bump into all kinds of things. Inquiry is therefore just the beginning. We not only need to find perspective-inconsistent concepts, we also need to believe that such concepts could be relevant for re-fashioning our perspective. We call this **discovery**. Discovery is the identification of seemingly promising concepts that are inconsistent with the current pattern of concepts constituting our perspective. The point of discovery is typically where we have our first inkling of how perspective could change. But it may only be an inkling. Could the bag of Doritos burn?

It can be tempting to think that once we have identified a discovery, we will know how to use it to advance our story. But there are still other steps that must take place before we can understand how to make use of what we have discovered. Often these other steps are executed so quickly and automatically that we take no notice of them. But figuring out how to use a discovery may take more effort. To continue with the warehouse metaphor, sometimes after we bump into something in the dark, we know what to do with it. Other times it takes more thought to figure that out. Is the bag in which the Doritos are packaged flammable? Are Doritos flammable? Like use and add, change can be executed quickly or slowly.

Once we discover concepts that we feel might be applicable to the situation, then we need to **restructure** our perspective. Because what we discover will not fit with at least some of the existing perspective, we will need to modify at least some of the pattern of concepts constituting our perspectives to make way for the discovery. We have to integrate the new concepts somehow. Unlike elaboration, which maintains what is there, restructuring requires that we remove some existing assumptions about which concepts apply to the situation and how those concepts relate to each other. We may retain many if not most of the concepts. But when we dismantle part of the perspective, it often alters the meaning of the whole as well.

Our initial interpretation was probably that Doritos are food, not flammable, disposable objects. But Doritos are made mostly of corn and oil, both of which burn well. These properties of Doritos were probably put into the background by our Doritos concept. The role of Doritos in starting fires, this particular positioning of our Doritos concept in the pattern of concepts constituting our perspective, was not conceivable while Doritos were assumed to be snacks. It only becomes thinkable if we change our concept of Doritos as kindling rather than a snack and also how it relates to the other concepts in our perspective, as playing a role in a fire-building activity rather than in an eating activity. Perspectives are not just individual concepts, but systems of concepts in which the relationships among the concepts are critical.

If we can complete the process of changing our perspective, having inquired, discovered, and restructured, then we are on our way to generating an **insight**. We are not yet done though. Often once we have a new perspective, it will require or suggest further assumptions. At this point we have completed the change cycle, but we still need to elaborate on the new perspective (completing the add cycle). Having made more assumptions, we still must make inferences so that we can productively respond to the situation (completing the use cycle). Insight is what emerges when we complete the full use-add-change cycle.

The insight is a new way to perceive and respond to our situation that comes after the new, previously incompatible concepts have been successfully reintegrated into the ongoing story. This is important because discoveries can be abandoned if we cannot rebuild a coherent and usable perspective afterward. Even a coherent and usable new perspective may be abandoned if we cannot use it to continue the story in progress. Changing our perspective "works" because we can add to and then use the new perspective. Creativity includes rather than stands apart from craft.

THE STOPLIGHT MODEL

The discussion of using, adding to, and changing our perspectives is a new synthesis of research on how people think. We call the synthesis the "stoplight model" because the three interlocking processes reminded us of a stoplight (Figure 2.1).[13] Then we realized that the resemblance is useful, because it helps provide an intuition about how people's engagement with their perspectives relates to their ability to advance their stories. The stoplight model indicates that craft can lead to rare ideas and altered perspectives through the add cycle. Yet no amount of adding will produce creative change. The model also indicates that creativity requires craft, as it relies on both the use and add processes. Insight is the product of the full use-add-change cycle.

When stoplights are green, we do not pause but keep going. *Using* our perspectives (the bottom part of Figure 2.1) allows us to continue advancing our stories. Normally we want stoplights to be green so that we can keep going. And normally we just want to use our perspectives to get things done. As a result, we have an inclination toward interpreting situations in typical ways. Doing so lets us leverage the knowledge, skills, and abilities that we already have so that we can quickly form rich perspectives, generate explanations, and respond. Using our perspectives is generally efficient and effective for meeting our objectives. People tend to think only as much as they have to in order to meet their goals.[14] When we are in a situation and our explanation for what is happening makes sense to us, there is no reason to deviate from our perspective on the situation. We have the green light to generate a response and so advance our story.

When stoplights are yellow, we might slow down. We might end up stopping. Or we might be able to speed up again and proceed. This is a bit like the process of *adding* to our perspective (the center of Figure 2.1). If our explanation

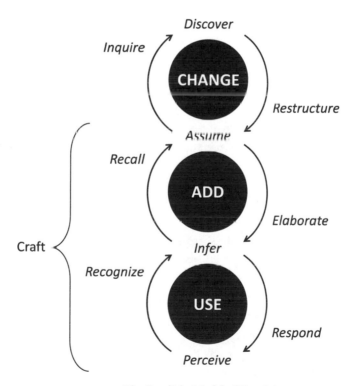

FIGURE 2.1. The Stoplight Model of Creativity.

seems faulty, we need to slow down and reconsider what we think is happening. Typically the gap between our explanation and reality is, itself, understandable and predictable given our current assumptions. Thus, while thinking about our perspective and our assumptions slows progress on our story, it is typically only a brief delay while we add more concepts to our perspective. Then we can continue using our perspective and advancing our story.

Sometimes craft alone is not enough. Stoplights turn red and we have to stop. The process of changing our perspectives involves turning away from advancing our stories and instead reconsidering our perspectives. Sometimes we are unable to add concepts to our perspective as a way to resolve the misalignment between the situation and the perspective. In such cases, we stop advancing our stories while we attempt to *change* our perspectives (the top circle of Figure 2.1). If we are successful, then we can proceed with our stories in a direction that was previously inconceivable. If we are unsuccessful, we might turn around and backtrack, we might take a break, or we might abandon the story altogether. The tough part about the creative process is that, in contrast to stoplights, there is no guarantee the light will ever turn green again.

The stoplight model implies that creativity is rarely a first choice. We usually do not question the fit of our perspective to the situation. We usually are less interested in the fit than with simply moving ahead with our story. One of the costs that the creative process imposes on us is that we have to stop advancing our story and instead turn our energies to our perspective. It is a bit like the choice between driving and changing the tires. We nearly always wish to keep driving. But when we decide to change the tires, we have to stop driving. We can either eat a Dorito or light it on fire as kindling. And either we can use our perspectives to advance our stories or we can stop our stories and try to change our perspectives. As we do not know how long it will take to change our perspectives or whether we will be successful, we often stick with using and adding to our perspectives instead. Craft is more predictable than creativity.

Earlier we used riddles to illustrate the process of changing perspectives to generate an insight. We can consider another riddle to illustrate using, adding to, and changing perspectives. Here it is: "A man has married twenty women in this town, he has divorced none of them, and they are all still alive, yet he is not a polygamist. How is this possible?"

Reading the riddle, we recognize the concepts. We know what *man, married, twenty, women,* and so forth all mean. We also recognize from the sentence much of how the concepts fit together into a pattern. At least, we do until we run into the last phrase. The description seems to be describing an unusual situation—we infer that this is a story about a man with twenty wives—and then it seems to deny that this is the case—if he is not a polygamist, then he cannot have twenty wives. If you are like most readers of this riddle (about three out of four readers in our experience), this process will lead you to realize that your developing story will not fit the situation.

When we talk to readers of this riddle, we hear all manner of responses. Some readers try to use their initial perspectives. For example, one told us that all the women died. We replied that it does say that they are all still alive, but we understood the challenge. Perception is not perfect. Details that seem unimportant at first can easily be dismissed.

Most readers acknowledge the lack of fit between the situation described by the riddle and their perspective. They think that they must be missing something. So they seek to add to their perspectives to establish a fit. For example, readers have told us that "the marriages were so short they did not count" (modifying the concept "marriage") and that "it was one woman with twenty personalities" (modifying the concept "women"). The readers are not usually satisfied with these solutions, but are often tempted to rationalize them as sufficiently good solutions such that they can say they have a story that explains the situation.

If we do not find expansions of our perspective that are satisfying responses to the riddle, then we need to change our perspective. Just as in the campfire example, we may feel stuck. The light is red as we move into inquiry. We grasp in the dark for some further concept that can allow us to explain the seeming contradiction. Any of the assumptions we made can be questioned. Maybe there are definitions of polygamy we do not understand. Maybe "this town" is important. There are more possibilities than we can think about at any one time. Usually the answer arrives quickly, with inquiry providing a discovery that quickly restructures the pattern of concepts constituting our perspective and moves on to a response. The man is not the husband. The man is not married to the women. The man performed wedding ceremonies for the women. Pick your preferred wedding officiate; the classic solution is that the man is a priest.

The priest riddle, like most riddles, illustrates that changing our current perspective is what makes creativity challenging. The new perspective is entirely ordinary. A priest performed marriage ceremonies for twenty women in town, he has divorced none of them, and they are all still alive. Of course he is not a polygamist. The difficulty posed by this riddle and nearly all creative processes is not that we have to imagine something outlandish. The difficulty is that we have to change some of the pattern of concepts that we assumed to be an apt fit to the situation. The difficulty is that the way forward is inconceivable. Our stories seem to be stalled, because using our perspectives has failed and adding to our perspectives has failed. As indicated by the stoplight model, most of the time when we are creative, it is because craft has failed us and we do not have an acceptable way to advance our stories.

Riddles are challenging when they lead us to adopt a perspective that prevents us from advancing our story. Riddles illustrate that inquiry is difficult because our perspectives make an answer inconceivable and they make it difficult to identify the concepts needed to restructure our perspectives. The stoplight model indicates the typical pattern of escalation that precedes changing our perspectives. It also indicates that, even if in the case of riddles the resolutions tend to happen all at once, we can break down the process and see its components. To generate the insight, we have to inquire, discover, and restructure so that we have a changed perspective, then we need to elaborate on it and form a response. And the stoplight model indicates many ways we can fail to generate insights. We can never inquire or inquiry can fail to yield a discovery. We can fail to restructure the concepts in our perspective to accommodate a discovery. Our restructured perspective need not lead to inferences that provide responses that turn out to help advance our stories. There are many perspectives we might form for a situation. None of them need take us where we wish to go.

INSIGHTS ARE JUST A BEGINNING

The stoplight model illustrates how craft and creativity are related. In applying the model to simple situations, such as a brief deliberation over a campfire or a riddle, it helps us examine the process of generating insights. As insights are necessary for creativity, this is a useful starting point. Insights can be the biggest hurdle to advancing important stories. For example, one of the most famous stories in the study of creativity is an insight by the eminent mathematician Poincaré. He was trying to prove a set of mathematical relationships (the Fuchsian Equations) and had been struggling to advance his story. In frustration, he stopped working on them and took a trip. It was on his trip that he generated the breakthrough insight. He described it this way:

> At the moment when I put my foot on the step [of the bus] the idea came to me, without anything in my former thoughts seeming to have paved the way for it, that the transformations I had used to define the Fuchsian functions were identical with those of non-Euclidean geometry. I did not verify the idea; I should not have had time, as upon taking my seat in the omnibus, I went on with a conversation already commenced, but I felt a perfect certainty. On my return to Caen, for conscience' sake, I verified the result at my leisure.[15]

This account of the production of an insight has been widely influential. It has been taken to mean that insights are produced through unconscious processes outside of awareness. We see that it could fit the stoplight model too. We assume that before the trip, Poincaré was trying to use his perspective and was getting nowhere. We imagine he also expanded his understanding of the Fuchsian functions by adding to his perspective, but again because of his perspective he could not find appropriate concepts to let him prove the relationships and so advance his story. He left for his trip with his proofs in whatever state they were in; his story stopped. At the point of getting on the bus, inquiry (for reasons we will consider later) identified concepts that he discovered were a fit to the situation and allowed him to restructure his perspective. He elaborated on the restructured perspective with the now illuminated non-Euclidean geometry concepts, which yielded a new kind of response. He later used this new perspective to finish his story.

This retelling of Poincaré's story in our own terms is to reiterate that having an account of insight is important because arguably there are major advances that hinged on single insights. The second purpose we have in retelling the story is to emphasize that even in this idealized account, the insight changed but did not finish the story. For while Poincaré had the insight about the correspondence between the two domains of mathematics, what resolved his story was his completion of the proof. He had to use the changed perspective to form a number of responses—the multiple steps in the proof—until he completed the story. Had he not done so, he would not be credited with the advance. Had he realized in the course of using the changed perspective that it would not actually be able to complete the story (despite his initial confidence), then this would be an anecdote about the dangers of overconfidence and the limitations of foresight. Many eminent creators have been unable to tell their influential ideas from their failed ideas.[16] They do not often talk about their failures though. Poincaré's insight is a wonderful anecdote, and it must have been a dazzling moment to experience. The stoplight model indicates that we should not trivialize the rest of the process needed to go from an insight to the invention or enlightenment that can follow.

As we noted in Chapter 1, an **insight** is like a plot twist. A plot twist does not end a story. It may make the pathway to resolution clear, but that pathway still needs to be followed. Because of the struggle to generate an insight and the taking-for-granted of craft, we often think that accounts of insight eclipse the importance of the subsequent thinking.

That subsequent thinking is routinely overlooked. Let us reconsider what is probably the most famous (and possibly apocryphal) creative insight: the story of Archimedes, the gold crown, and the bathtub. Apparently Archimedes was asked to assess whether an irregularly shaped crown was made of pure gold or if some of the gold had been replaced by less valuable and lighter silver. He could not figure out how to do this with simple measurements—the crown was too oddly shaped. He went to take a bath, still puzzling over the problem, and upon entering the bath was struck with an insight that led him to shout "Eureka!" and run naked from the bath (so the story goes). Archimedes's insight (apparently) was that the crown, when placed in water, should displace an amount of water equal to the volume of the crown.

It is common to think that whatever Archimedes needed to do after that insight was trivial. He needed to find a graded tub and compare the displacements of the crown and a lump of gold. Yet given the probable size of the crown and the difference in mass that substituting an unnoticeable amount of silver would make, simply submerging the crown and comparing it to a chunk of gold that was the same weight as the original would likely raise the water level about one-twentieth of an inch.[17] This is a difference that would not be detectable to the naked eye.

Our view is that Archimedes's insight was undoubtedly crucial to resolving the crown puzzle. But the insight is not in itself the invention that was necessary to resolve the puzzle. There is a gap between the insight and the invention. This gap is not one we can fill just by recalling concepts from memory or inquiring after further concepts. The next challenge is to apply craft repeatedly to make use of the insight so that we can resolve our story. We turn insights into inventions and enlightenments by using and adding to our changed perspectives. Doing so advances our stories in previously inconceivable directions.

PRACTICE

It takes practice to update our knowledge. Even when ideas seem clear and understandable, old knowledge can interfere with applying the new knowledge. So at the end of each chapter, there are exercises to reinforce the lessons and the vocabulary of the chapter.

Vocabulary

If we intend to think purposefully, we use input from three sources:

1. **Situation**: The objective conditions of the world

    a. **Situation (momentary)**: The conditions of the world that we perceive in our immediate surroundings

2. **Perspective**: An interpretation of the assumed true features in a situation

    a. **Perspective (momentary)**: The network of assumptions about which concepts are instantiated in a situation, as well as how they are structured in relation to each other

3. **Story**: A subjectively coherent explanation for what has happened, what is happening, and what might happen in a situation

    a. **Story (momentary)**: An account of the current conditions that presumes the past and probable future

In developing ideas to be incorporated into a story, we have three functions related to perspective.

1. **Use**: The process of developing a story that is based on our perspective; use contains four processes:

    a. **Perceive**: Sensing the situation

    b. **Recognize**: Identifying the concepts that fit what we sense

    c. **Infer**: Making guesses about the nature of what has been perceived given the concepts that are active

    d. **Respond**: Choosing what to think or how act given the current state of our story

2. **Add**: The activity of enriching a perspective by incorporating other assumptions consistent with those that already exist in the perspective; add contains three processes:

   a. **Recall**: Locating additional conceptual knowledge in long-term memory that is not yet in working memory

   b. **Assume**: Drawing conclusions that will be believed true *de facto*, and that we intend not to revise

   c. **Elaborate**: Synthesizing our new assumptions into the existing perspective so as to enrich the perspective

3. **Change**: The activity of altering the perspective that renders some assumptions in the new perspective incompatible with those in the former perspective; change contains three processes:

   a. **Inquire**: Indirectly guided search of long-term memory

   b. **Discover**: Identification of promising but perspective-inconsistent knowledge

   c. **Restructure**: The removal of prior assumptions that were embedded in the existing perspective

Two additional terms are important:

Inconceivable: What our current perspective limits us from thinking

Insight: The product of changing our momentary perspective

Exercises

1. Look at Figure 2.2. Try to explain what is happening. Then write down what elements make up the situation, the perspective, and the story.

2. Sam asked his class to come up with creative uses for a cardboard box.[18] One of his students, Anu, suggested a solar oven. "That idea will never work!" Sam said. "How could you even think of such a thing!"

   "Actually," Anu replied, "these are in use all over India. We used to have one."

   At this one of the other students, Pat, chimed in, "I bet if you insulated the box really well it could get very hot, too."

   Sam, now somewhat embarrassed, conceded the point.

Which person chiefly experienced the use cycle, which one the add cycle, and which one the change cycle?

FIGURE 2.1. The Rider.

3. Imagine you are camping but have the same kind of "no tinder" problem discussed earlier in the chapter, and this time you have no Doritos. You decide to use what is in your backpack. Consider each of the following as to whether it represents an unusable item, a craft (use or add) item, or a creative (change) item in this situation with respect to lighting the fire.

   a. A book
   b. A magnifying glass
   c. A rain poncho
   d. Sterile wipes
   e. Band aids
   f. Beer
   g. Old Grandad whiskey
   h. An auto flare

4. Bill was putting away leftover ravioli, baked beans, and chili. He went to find some Tupperware containers but saw that there were none. He looked in the dishwasher but found only a few in there,

not enough to hold everything. Then he looked in the sink, but none were there either. Where could they be? He looked in the fridge and saw that most were being used. He thought about throwing out what was in these, but the food was still good. Bill looked around for something else to hold food. He saw Ziploc bags, but thought they would be messy. Finally it dawned on him: use mason jars. Which of these responses represent using, which adding, and which changing? Why?

5. Inquiry problems—you are misled by your initial assumptions.

   a. The red house is on one side and the blue is on another. Where is the white house? Hint: not all the concepts are related to each other.

   b. There is a fire in a twelve-story building. A man panics and jumps out of the window. How does he survive? Hint: The height of the building is irrelevant.

   c. What is so delicate that saying its name breaks it? Hint: "Delicate" is a misleading way to describe what you are breaking.

6. Discovery problems—you have in front of you what you need to solve the problem, you just need to find the right concepts for the symbols and relationships among them.

   a. |R|E|A|D|I|N|G|

   b. C C C C C C C

   c. GROUND
      feet feet feet
      feet feet feet

7. Restructuring problems—you have to change the assumed relationship between the concepts presented.

   a. Two mothers and two daughters went out to eat, everyone ate one burger, yet only three burgers were eaten. How is this possible? Hint: change the way you structure the relationships between the people, and throw out your assumption that there are four people.

   b. How many three-cent stamps in a dozen? Hint: Structure some of the concepts into units.

   c. You throw away the outside and cook the inside, then you eat the outside and throw away the inside. What is it? Hint: you need to appreciate that the relationship of outside to inside changes as you modify the food.

8. What occurs once in a minute, twice in a moment, and never in one thousand years?[19] To get this answer, you have to restructure what you are looking at, then discover what you see.

Answers

1. We cannot tell you the story you made, obviously. But no doubt you had a perspective on what the objects you perceived were and their relationship to each other. Was it a horse or a mule? Was it the sun or the moon? Were the people friends or enemies? Where was the rider going, and what was the other person doing at the cactus (assuming you interpreted the figure as a cactus)? Try to articulate your assumptions, though it may be difficult because you simply take them for granted. What is even more challenging is to determine the objective situation. At one level, it is the shapes that you perceived in the drawing as well as their positioning in the picture. But you could also say that the situation was made of printed marks on a page in a book.

2. Use: Anu   although the solar oven was unknown to the others, he was merely recalling something rare that he knew very well.

   Add: Pat   given the concept, Pat thought of an improvement concept that, while not part of the original concept, is connected to ovens and consistent with their construction.

   Change: Sam—Sam could not conceive that such a device could be made from a cardboard box.

3. Unusable: Beer, rain poncho (will only melt).

   Craft: magnifying glass (focus the sun, but that would be difficult), band aids (just use the paper they come in), auto flare.

   Creative: Old Grandad whiskey, sterile wipes (both contain alcohol).

4. Most of the responses are use responses; these are all typical for putting away leftovers. It may have been add to get rid of the other food (deciding that food was past its prime expands on that concept), or possibly to think about Ziploc bags (which are for food, just not

usually that kind of messy food). The mason jars are change because we have the educational commitment that mason jars are for preserves.

5. (a) Washington, DC; (b) He was on the first floor; (c) Silence.

6. (a) Read between the lines; (b) The seven seas; (c) Six feet under ground.

7. (a) They are grandmother, mother, and daughter; (b) Twelve; (c) Corn on the cob.

8. The letter m.

TURNING POTENTIAL INTO INVENTIONS

A problem well stated is a problem half solved.
—Charles Kettering

We left Archimedes running naked from the bath after having an insight. The insight was that water displacement could help determine whether an irregularly shaped crown was made of gold alone. Stating the problem this way, we could say that the problem was half solved. We are off to a great start, but there is still a gap. The gap was how to get from that change in perspective to some kind of invention that could determine whether the crown was pure gold—an actual apparatus that could measure a small difference.

Making that invention required even more knowledge. And it required actually making something to do the measuring. The invention that ultimately emerged required, as far as we can guess, the crown, gold, a balance scale, and a bathtub. Place the crown and an equal weight of gold on the balance scale to match the weights. Then submerge the crown, gold, and scale in the bathtub. If one object occupied less volume—for example, if the crown was partly made of silver—then it would have a greater volume than the gold on the other side of the scale, pushing the scale out of balance. This invention required synthesizing ideas about levers and buoyancy, and it required interacting with the actual world.

We cannot be sure about what actually happened to Archimedes, of course. Perhaps having thought of displacement, Archimedes immediately realized the utility of using levers and buoyancy. Perhaps he added these to his perspective later. Or perhaps he experimented with other displacement solutions before having subsequent insights that culminated in his invention of this use of a balance scale. It has to take time and action in the world though—and probably further revisions—to form an actual invention.

When we think about creativity and why it matters, we are often interested in more than the conceptual. We are interested in more than an idea for a good meal; we are interested in actually eating. We are interested in actual paintings, scientific findings, and technological devices. When we think about tangible inventions, it is particularly hard not to notice the large gap between an insight and an invention. Look at just about any crowdfunding campaign for a new design or technology project, such as on Kickstarter or Indiegogo, and there is likely to be a picture of the many designs and prototypes the team tried along the way to getting to their invention. Somehow, an insight that arrives in an exciting moment is often not enough to get all the way to an invention. There must be more than verification. There must be a slower process, a longer timescale over which creativity unfolds.

Bridging the gap between insights and inventions is the focus of this chapter. The last chapter focused on a moment or two of thinking during the interpretation of a situation. It showed that even in one moment in a simple situation, we can draw from all that we know to form different perspectives and take our stories in different directions. Although the discussion considered the selecting of responses, there was no emphasis on what happens when we actually do respond. As we extend beyond a momentary situation to consider the broader episode to which that moment belongs, we have much more to think about. We can think about what might happen now. We can think about what we are going to make happen. We can think about what is happening in the world. We can think about what happened previously. This is far too much to think about at any one moment. We therefore form stories to understand episodes. There was this king, and we had to figure out whether this crown was solid gold, and we dunked it in the bathtub to test whether it was. The story is our way to put together all the specifics.

We form stories by drawing from our general knowledge to arrive at interpretations of a particular episode. We come to an episode with knowledge in long-term memory of generic concepts, such as "crown" and "bathtub." Psychologists call these *semantic memories*, or general meanings unattached to any particular episode. In this particular episode, we are not thinking about crowns in general, we are thinking about some particular instance of a crown—this ornate gold crown right here. We weigh it on this scale, and we submerge it in that bathtub. This particular crown gets wet. The emerging story about these specific items and activities is then something we think about and remember. Remember that time we put that gold crown in the bathtub? Thus, in addition to our semantic memories of generic concepts, we form what psychologists call *episodic memories*.[1]

Differentiating between generic semantic knowledge and particular episodic knowledge is important for understanding the process of generating inventions. As we think and act over time, our perspectives and our stories grow larger and become thought worlds in themselves.[2] We talk about getting lost in a story, being transported by a book, and feeling as if we are in a movie. Over time, as we develop our stories, we lose track of the difference between our story and the episode itself. We lose track of the difference between our story and what we know in general. The particular past, present, and future of our current story tend to dominate our thinking. This means that to form an invention, we have a large task. When we were just thinking about a moment of thought, some momentary situation such as a riddle, the task of changing our perspective was pretty small. We just had to restructure a few concepts that were used in interpreting one situation. When it comes to generating inventions by telling whole stories, the task of changing our perspective is much larger. We have to restructure concepts that we may have been using to interpret many situations over long periods of time. We have to revise the past as well as the present, and we have to reimagine the future.

To illustrate how quickly perspectives can narrow stories about episodes, we will embarrass ourselves with some fifth-grade math problems.[3] The task is to identify a single formula that can take four inputs and transform them into four outputs. It starts out fairly easy and then it gets harder; these examples have stumped plenty of MBA students and professors. The reason why people can get stumped illustrates a key part of why the process of forming inventions is challenging.

The first set is not too hard (Figure 3.1). In this set, the challenge is to identify a single formula that will take a 0 as input and return a 5 as output, take a 5 as input and return a 10 as output, take a 2 as input and return a 7 as output, and take a –3 as input and return 2 as output. When perceiving this situation, we are bringing knowledge about mathematics into working memory. Our goal is to produce a formula that transforms the input in some way to generate the output. We probably start by perceiving the first pair. We recognize that we have to do something to the 0 to generate a 5. We infer that we can add 5 to the input. That is probably the simplest possibility. Then we try using this perspective to think about the remaining pairs. It happens to work for all of them, so without much trouble at all we have Input + 5 = Output.

	Input	Output
Pair 1	0	5
Pair 2	5	10
Pair 3	2	7
Pair 4	−3	2

FIGURE 3.1. I/O Problem Set 1.

Now we can try Set 2 (Figure 3.2). Our perspective from Set 1 largely carries over to Set 2. We are still trying to solve math problems, and in particular, identify a formula to transform inputs into outputs. We might think that because this is a different set the formula from Set 1 likely will not work here. But we will probably need a similar formula. We will probably take the same approach to finding the formula for this set as we did for the last one. We perceive the first pair, recognize the difference between the input and output, and see if we can generate a simple rule for transforming one into the other. This time, the output is not a larger number than the input but a smaller number. We infer that we have to subtract. The straightforward inference, reduce the input by 7, is plausible. We try using this perspective on the remaining pairs and it works, resulting in the formula Input − 7 = Output.

	Input	Output
Pair 1	12	5
Pair 2	4	−3
Pair 3	−3	−10
Pair 4	7	0

FIGURE 3.2. I/O Problem Set 2.

With Set 3, as with Set 2, we are applying what we have learned in the previous two sets (Figure 3.3). Perhaps we see the first pair and think that the output is once again greater than the input, as in the first set, and so we look at the difference and posit that we should be adding 4 to the input. Using this perspective fails on the second pair. We seem to have a somewhat different pattern. We consider the discrepancies to add to our perspective and so guide us toward an alternative formula. We have to recall additional information, assume further operators are possible, and elaborate on the perspective to accommodate new concepts. In short order, by adding multiplication to our perspective we find that Input * 3 = Output.

	Input	Output
Pair 1	2	6
Pair 2	5	15
Pair 3	−4	−12
Pair 4	0	0

FIGURE 3.3. I/O Problem Set 3.

Now we can try Set 4 (Figure 3.4). On perceiving the first pair, two inferences probably come to mind. We could add 4. Or, we could multiply by 5. Yet both of these responses fail on the second pair. We will try to add to our perspective. Perhaps we guess that division will be involved, as we have added, subtracted, and multiplied. But this does not seem to provide a straightforward answer. Perhaps we consider other mathematical operators (square roots?) and maybe this leads us to wonder what a fifth-grade student is expected to know these days. Many people at this point find that they are unable to find anything to add to their perspective that allows them to identify a working formula as a response. They realize that they have to change their perspective.

	Input	Output
Pair 1	1	5
Pair 2	5	1
Pair 3	7	−1
Pair 4	−3	9

FIGURE 3.4. I/O Problem Set 4.

In contrast to the riddles and other examples we have examined previously, there is nothing we have to retrieve from semantic memory for this math problem. There is no obscure mathematical operator at work that we need to identify. The difficulty is in episodic memory. The difficulty is the perspective we formed over the course of the first three sets.

What was readily apparent as we worked on the second and third sets was the change in the operator. We added, subtracted, and multiplied. What was probably less apparent was how similar our perspectives were across the first three sets and how similar the final formulas were. The similarities allowed us to make assumptions about what kinds of things might change and what kinds of things might stay the same across sets. Using those assumptions repeatedly over time in each situation leads us to commit to those assumptions ever more strongly across the episode. We do not commit to them deliberately. We did not think, "The formula Input <operator> Number = Output will apply to every set." Instead, our commitment to our assumption that this formula structure would apply to all sets increased precisely because we did not think deliberately about it. It became part of the pattern organizing concepts in our perspectives that we used repeatedly. We took it for granted.

Having just noted that this formula structure may not be right provides an indication about what to change about our perspectives to generate a response that fits the situation. Although it is helpful to know what might be wrong about our perspectives, this does not mean we can readily identify what should replace it. Most people who encounter the problem tend to think about making the formula more complicated, usually like this: Input <mathematical operator> Number 1 <mathematical operator> Number 2 . . . = Output. As noted in the last chapter, we find it easier to add to our current perspective than to change our perspective. We seek to keep what we are currently thinking the same and try to elaborate on it to make it work.

One way to change our perspectives is to identify concepts outside our perspectives. We inquire into long-term memory to locate concepts and discover whether they fit the situation. A second way to change our perspectives does not require identifying further concepts. Instead, inquiry can identify an alternative pattern for organizing the concepts that are already included in our perspectives. In this case, for Set 4, one of the simplest restructurings is to reverse the formula. Instead of Input <operator> Number = Output, we could try Number <operator> Input = Output. It hardly seems as if it would matter. And yet if we elaborate on this restructuring, we will quickly find a working formula as a response to Set 4: 6 − Input = Output. Changing perspectives to invent a satisfactory response is not easy. As noted at the outset, many MBA students and professors stumble on Set 4.

To be successful at advancing stories, we have to apply craft. Yet a perverse effect of craft is that it generates the possibility, even the need, for creativity. An initial perspective seems to work well at launching us into our story. It allows us to respond effectively for a while. Yet our progress through the episode may rest on assumptions that, while at first arbitrary, quickly become commitments as we come to take them for granted. Committing to these assumptions closes off possible inventions. Creativity is then needed to reach them.

For example, the company Vicks has spent over a hundred years making and selling cough and cold medicines, such as NyQuil. NyQuil was invented in 1966[4] to help people who are sick minimize their coughing and sniffling so that they can sleep. While the drowsiness brought on by NyQuil was an important part of the product's success, it was also a limitation, as it meant that people could only take the product at night and not during the day. Fully ten years later, Vicks offered another product, DayQuil (or at first DayCare), so that people who liked and needed NyQuil could take the product during the day and not fall asleep. It was another thirty (!) or so years later that people at Vicks realized that consumers were using NyQuil to help them get to sleep even when they were not sick. It was yet another six years until, in 2012, Vicks introduced ZzzQuil, which only has the ingredient for making people sleepy. It is the same ingredient used in other over-the-counter products, including two competing sleep aids that had been available for over thirty years, Unisom and Sominex. Still, within two years of launching, ZzzQuil captured about 30 percent of the sleep aid market, generating about $120 million in annual sales. Why, then, did it take so long to introduce ZzzQuil if similar products existed for thirty years?

Vicks had been selling NyQuil, which included the sleep aid ingredient, for forty-six years before introducing ZzzQuil, and over thirty years after removing the sleep aid ingredient for DayQuil. We do not know why the invention of ZzzQuil took as long as it did. It could have been because the Vicks brand was strongly associated with cough and cold medicine, not sleep aids. It could have been because when we generate new products we usually try to add more functionality, not remove functionality (ZzzQuil removed two of the three key ingredients in NyQuil). But the parallel to the Input-Output math problem may well be critical. The story and perspective around NyQuil had existed in the same way for a long time. They might have committed to the assumptions underlying Vicks's perspective.

Our commitments to our assumptions build over time. Our immediate situation is the result of where we have been. What short puzzles have difficulty capturing, but that is indicated in the ZzzQuil story, is that we form and use perspectives over long periods of time. We do not just make assumptions, we rely on them extensively and commit deeply to them. In this context, changing our perspectives is no small act. It can be world changing, if not universe changing.

One way to appreciate the influence of the past on the present is to consider a plot twist in a long story. To avoid ruining a new story, we will examine an old one. To avoid having to retell a long story, we will examine a fairly popular one. This pretty much reduces us to the Bible, the Harry Potter books, and the original *Star Wars* films. As gluttons for punishment, we will discuss *Star Wars*.

The *Star Wars* films are a sort of intergalactic morality tale. They revolve around a pitched battle between good and evil, emphasizing the need to remain good rather than succumb to the temptations of evil. On the good side, we have Luke Skywalker, Princess Leia, Obi-Wan (Ben) Kenobi, and the rest. On the evil side, we have Darth Vader, the Emperor, and endless storm-troopers. Through a large variety of plots and subplots, direct fighting and indirect conflicts, these two sides are kept in tension. There is some within-group jockeying for position and some personal growth in the character of Luke Skywalker. But most of these developments support the larger tension between the good side and the evil side. Most centrally, Luke's uncle, aunt, and mentor Ben Kenobi are all killed, directly or indirectly, by Darth Vader. Luke Skywalker is set up as the one person who can fight Darth Vader. Luke is trained by two wise figures, Ben and then Yoda, for this task. At the climax of the second film, Luke gets his chance.

To reach the climax of the second film, viewers of the films spend hours forming, using, and adding to their perspectives of the extended episode. Viewers get immersed in the fictional universe of the films, understanding its assumptions about its customs, technologies, locations, creatures, and other novelties. As at least some of these are unexpected, including its handling of the mysterious "force" that will be central to Luke's development and his special role with respect to Darth Vader, there may well be some changes in perspective that viewers experience. Yet the pitting of Luke and Darth Vader against one another is a constant, central concern.

This steadily building perspective is what makes the outcome of the climactic duel noteworthy. Our hero, Luke, loses the duel. In our morality play, Luke is then tempted as Darth Vader asks Luke to join him by turning evil. Luke then confirms our sense of his character, indicating in effect that he would rather die. At which point Darth Vader says to Luke, "I am your father." This plot twist leads to a change in perspective on the relationship between Luke Skywalker and Darth Vader. This in turn implies a need to revisit a host of prior discussions and scenes involving and about Darth Vader, as well as sparks thoughts of a host of new future possibilities for where the story might go.

We raise the story of *Star Wars* and emphasize this famous plot twist to illustrate a point about assumptions and people's commitments to them. For those who know only a little bit about *Star Wars*, the plot twist is easy to accept. Villains have close, secret relationships to heroes in many stories. But for millions of fans of these movies, the revelation was difficult to accept. The writer, producer, and director George Lucas was apparently worried enough about whether the public would accept the plot twist that in the next film a trusted authority (Yoda) confirms it. Examining why there is such a difference between viewers about this plot twist indicates an important fact about the creative process.

The difference between viewers is driven by the depth of viewers' commitments to the assumptions in their initial perspectives. *Star Wars* certainly generated a passionate fan base. But it is not just general passion for the films that produces this effect. Rather, when we form perspectives, we are making assumptions about how to interpret episodes. We make assumptions about what is right and wrong. Critically, we reinforce our assumptions repeatedly over the course of extended episodes, as we saw in the fifth-grade math problem sets. Finally, we have no choice but to reinforce our assumptions. Today we can watch the *Star Wars* films on our own devices and pause them as needed. But in general, episodes continue on. If we stop to consider an assumption, we might fall behind. It is beyond our capability to hold every assumption tentative while we await further evidence. Instead, we reinforce our assumptions by using and adding to the assumptions within our perspectives. Thus, if viewers reinforced assumptions central to the story repeatedly throughout watching films and when discussing them with other fans, it should be apparent why they might have been strongly committed to their assumptions about the relationship between two of the main characters in the films. Those assumptions were foundational to their perspectives on the *Star Wars* films. Assumptions are necessary for forming perspectives and advancing stories. Changing assumptions is the center of the creative process. Our commitments to our assumptions are a central reason why creativity is difficult. If we change them, then we change what we think we can do right now, where our stories can go in the future, and our understandings of what happened in our stories in the past.

CREATIVE POTENTIAL IN AN EPISODE

Each momentary situation is an opportunity to change our perspective. But if we take every opportunity, we will never advance our stories. The world will move on without us. Instead, we tend to take an insight we have generated and use our new perspective to respond and advance our stories. In the discussion of the stoplight model, it was noted that we have a tendency first to use our perspectives if possible. We tend not to stop to change our perspectives unless we feel particularly compelled to do so. Our bias toward advancing our stories means we have a bias away from changing our perspectives.

For example, in the previous chapter we examined a riddle about a man who marries twenty women. We have given this riddle, the priest riddle, to hundreds if not thousands of people. But it was not until recently that someone replied, "Oh, the man is their father." To which we exclaimed, "What?!" The person replied, "No! *He married them off.*" This alternative perspective had never occurred to us. Having identified the priest insight, we did not think, "There must be many kinds of insights." In contrast, we figured that we had noticed all there was to notice about the riddle. Despite there usually being many directions in which people can turn, many opportunities to change our perspectives, we usually stop at one change. We go back to using our perspectives. Yet there is often far more creative potential in an episode than we imagine when we encounter the first situation.

For example, we can consider one of the most prominent puzzles in creativity research, the *nine dot problem.*[5] First, draw nine dots in a three-by-three grid, like the one pictured in Figure 3.5. The problem is to try to connect all nine dots using up to four connected straight lines, without picking up the pen or backtracking.

FIGURE 3.5. The Nine Dot Problem.

Usually when we present this problem to people, we find that some have already seen the problem before. When this happens, one of two things occurs. Either they draw out the classic solution to the problem from memory and then stop, or they struggle to remember the solution and then stop and tell us they do not remember it. That is, when people have experienced something before, they have a tendency to recognize it and to try to use their prior perspective to respond. They try to retell a known story. If that fails, they might take the part of the solution they recall and see if they can get from there to a solution. But then they typically stop. We have never given anyone the problem, had them tell us they had seen it before, and then had them say, "I'll try to generate a new kind of solution." People do not typically take the opportunity to be creative if they think they can just recall an episodic memory.

For those who have not encountered the nine dot problem before, though, they typically begin by drawing lines and failing to generate viable responses. The nine dot problem is often described by those who study creativity as an insight problem. We think it is an invention problem. The classic solution is not often found with one insight. The insight that is associated with this problem is that to solve the problem, people have to "think outside the box." This problem is the origin of that expression.

The idea behind the expression is that the grid formed by the nine dots can appear to be a box that we can assume has to contain all the lines we draw. And if we make this assumption, then we cannot generate the classic solution to the problem. Abandoning this assumption is necessary. However, the insight that lines can be drawn outside the box does not actually appear to help people generate the classic solution. At least, people who are told to draw outside the box do not tend to do any better on the problem than those told nothing.[6]

The insight that we can draw lines outside the boundaries of the box formed by the dots means that we are now trying to solve a different problem than the one we faced originally. Our perspective on the problem changed. The variety of potential inferences grows, as there are now many more lines we could try. The directions in which our stories can develop have expanded. What usually happens after this insight is that people use their new perspective to draw some longer lines. They see if it helps get them closer to a solution. But it usually is not immediately apparent why drawing outside the box helps. Our perspective has changed a bit, and as a result we can advance our story a bit, but more is needed.

The next assumption that people need to address is about how lines connect. Many of us as children completed "connect the dots" puzzles in which we drew lines to connect a series of dots to make a picture. This might explain why many people assume that they have to connect two lines at a dot.[7] This assumption was not easy to notice when we were drawing lines inside the box formed by the dots. When we were doing that, there was really no sensible place to change direction other than the dots. But once we realize that can draw a line outside the box, this assumption about where we connect lines becomes important. The generalization is that often, changing one assumption that is part of our perspective only matters after we have changed a different assumption. Put another way, one insight is often helpful only after we have had an earlier insight.

Once we have both insights, we can form an invention to resolve this story. When we make both changes to our perspective—we can draw lines outside the box and we can join two lines anywhere—then our capacity to make inferences about possible responses changes. At this point, using and adding to our perspective is sufficient to generate an invention. This does not mean it is easy. It can take quite a few minutes to make use of these two insights to generate a response that works. This is because insights give us a new array of possibilities to try. Insights can even generate so many possibilities that can overwhelm working memory. But this is a small enough problem that in this case it usually can be done fairly quickly. The classic solution to the nine dot problem, capitalizing on these two insights, looks like Figure 3.6.

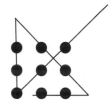

FIGURE 3.6. The Nine Dot Problem—Classic Solution.

If you have never seen the nine dot problem before and arrived at this solution now, it is an invention for you. That many other people have already generated this solution is irrelevant to whether you in particular go through a creative process to generate this invention. If you did not try to generate a solution but just read along or watched as someone else solved it, then you may not have experienced a perspective change at all, and would not find this to be an invention. It just looks like craft. You did not know the solution, and now you see the solution. But if you have not formed much of a perspective on the problem initially, then the solution is just adding to your initial, vague perspective. It is like asking middle school students to memorize a set of facts about the U.S. Constitution rather than giving them the challenge of developing the principles for forming a governmental system and guiding them through the insights behind the constitution. The key question when it comes to the creative process is, what is happening in the mind of the creator? If an individual made changes to her perspective and then made use of those changes to generate a response that was previously inconceivable, then she has formed something that is, for her, an invention.

Generating inventions is a process of making the inconceivable into something thinkable, and then something actual. It is a process of using, adding to, and changing our perspectives repeatedly over time to develop stories. These accounts are different and perhaps more complex than another way people have described the creative process, which is as a process of searching a maze.[8] For example, in a maze it is difficult to look far ahead. We do not know what lies around the next corner. Sometimes we think we are making progress and then find ourselves confronting a dead end, arriving back where we started, or simply getting lost. Other times, we know an answer is nearby, but there is a wall in the way. And once we find our way out of the maze, the next time we enter we try to remember the pathway through it that we found before to avoid getting lost again. The more we learn and remember about a maze, the better able we are to move rapidly, without taking wrong turns, through the maze. Drawing and redrawing lines as we work on the nine dot problem can feel a little like searching a maze.

More precisely, the maze metaphor is a helpful account of *using* our perspectives. Searching a maze is a reasonable way to describe what we were doing after we had both insights in the nine dot problem. We know that we can use our perspective to draw such and such line. We know that we can walk down this pathway in the maze. We do not know whether drawing that line will help. We do not know if this pathway will lead us toward the exit of the maze. We have strategies for how we go about testing lines. We might generate an approach for searching the pathways of the maze. The sequence of attempts at drawing lines is like the sequence of pathways in the maze down which we travel. The difference between knowing and not knowing our way around the maze is the difference between having developed craft knowledge and not having done so.

The maze metaphor also helps us refine our understanding of what changing our perspective does in the course of the creative process. Changing our perspective means that our interpretation of the situation is different than it was before. The limitation of the maze metaphor is that it conflates the actual situation with our perspective on the situation. In the maze metaphor, if we see a pathway forward, there is a pathway forward. If we see a wall, there is a wall. But we do not act on the world. We act on our interpretations of the world. The challenge of the nine dot problem is not the drawing and redrawing of lines, it is realizing that lines can be drawn outside the box formed by the dots and that lines can be connected anywhere, not just at a dot. The challenge of the maze could be realizing that something we thought was a wall was really a doorway, and something we thought was a pathway is really a trapdoor to somewhere else. This is one way to think about what it means for possibilities to be initially inconceivable. But even this is only partly effective as an adjustment to the maze metaphor.

To see why we need a more radical adjustment to the maze metaphor, we can consider a simple reinterpretation of the nine dot problem. Perhaps we will try to find a solution to the nine dot problem that uses only three lines instead of four. We are trying to form a new invention now. We can apply craft and creativity, just as we have so far with the nine dot problem, but this time we have to produce a different kind of solution. To do that, we have to think about the problem as a different kind of problem. We have to think that maybe we are not in a maze at all anymore. In the maze metaphor, everything is still just a wall or a pathway, and we are still looking for a series of turns to reach an exit. But changing our perspective can generate larger transformations; other interpretations of the world are possible. Perhaps we are not looking for an exit but have some other goal instead. Perhaps we are not really in a maze, but are involved in a different kind of event. A change in perspective can alter not only what we perceive and what possible responses we might have, but where we think we are going, what we think we are doing, and even who we are. The creative process is harder than searching a maze (craft), not because searching mazes (craft) is easy, but because creativity introduces a sort of challenge entirely different from searching a space of known possibilities. Creativity allows us the unbounded opportunity to reinterpret everything.

Which reinterpretation to form is the challenge. The immediate reaction we usually get when we ask people to form a different kind of solution, such as a three-line solution to the nine dot problem, is uncertainty. Just as the first solution might have been inconceivable to them at first until the two insights made it thinkable, they are now once again confronted with the same feeling that a second solution is inconceivable. Having been creative once does not mean they somehow are granted complete understanding. Every perspective is limited. Every perspective makes assumptions about how to interpret the situation, what is possible, and what is not possible. In addition, and this is the crucial part for creativity, every perspective also makes some interpretations and reactions inconceivable.

The first solution to the nine dot problem required all four lines. So what has to change to make a three-line solution? If we are using our perspectives to advance our stories, we might not know exactly where each response will take us, but we have a sense of what might happen. This was the idea behind comparing using our perspectives to searching a maze. We know that we are searching a maze. Likewise, we know that we are trying to advance our current stories. However, when we are changing our perspective, we are engaged in a different kind of process. We are not searching some known space. We are considering the possibility that any aspect of our perspective could be changed. Not just that this wall might be a path, but that this wall might be a trampoline or a weapon or something else inconceivable within the maze interpretation of the event. The process of changing our perspective is difficult because absolutely anything we know might become part of our new perspective. When we are inquiring to try to identify ways to change our perspectives and have no direction, it is particularly challenging. One way to capture the feeling of this distinctive mode of inquiry is to describe it as "going into the void."

When we question the assumptions we have made to form our perspective, we are creating a void. We are trying to think beyond our perspective. But our perspective is our guide for thinking. In the void, we do not know where we are. We do not know where we should go or even where we can go. Normally we use our perspectives to advance our stories. But if we are inquiring into alternatives for our current perspective and we have little or no starting point for that inquiry, then anything is possible. For example, if we do a microphone check with an experienced sound engineer, she will say, "please count to five" or something like that. And it is easy to count to five. If we are doing a microphone check with an inexperienced person though, he will ask us to "say something" and we will pause, stumped, unsure what to say. That we could just say anything, including counting to five, is obvious in retrospect. But at that moment we are paralyzed, not freed, by the absence of direction. Going into the void is a little like that. When we remove our perspective and drop the assumptions we are making, it is usually thought freezing, not thought freeing. We have no idea what to think because we could think anything. Making some assumptions allows us to think. When we step away from our assumptions, when we go into the void, it is often confusing.

To address the confusion and get us unfrozen with respect to forming the three-line solution to the nine dot problem, a hint would be helpful. A way forward follows from closing a gap between our perspectives and what is possible in the episode. If we look back at the classic four-line solution to the nine dot problem, we might notice something that we have probably been overlooking. The lines do not go through the entire dot. They do not even go through the centers of every dot. Some of our students have noticed this but figured it was just sloppiness in the graphic design (they must know their teachers well). But what if instead of ignoring this or viewing it as being sloppy, we viewed this as being intentional? This is usually the third insight we form about the nine dot problem. This insight does not matter for the four-line solution. But it is key to the three-line solution.

Once again, after this change in perspective, we are not done. We do not yet have an invention. There is still some much-needed craft to do. It will take some using and adding to our revised perspective to find the three-line solution. Often the addition to our perspectives, if not a fourth insight, is that if the lines do not need to go through an entire dot or even through the center of the dot, then this means that a line that goes through a row or column of three dots could be angled (Figure 3.7).

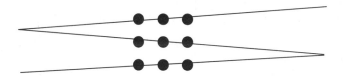

FIGURE 3.7. The Nine Dot Problem—Three-Line Solution.

PAGES OF POTENTIAL

A three-line solution to the nine dot problem is not the best we can do. What about a one-line solution? This probably seems inconceivable right now, just like the three-line solution and four-line solution appeared inconceivable at first. Does it matter anymore if we draw lines outside the box? We no longer know. What if we learn that there are multiple one-line solutions? Does that help? It usually only makes people feel worse! We know our current perspective is not helpful, but we do not know which assumptions in our perspective to revise. We do not know which aspect of the episode to investigate. We are going back into the void.

The last time we went into the void with the three-line solution, there was a hint. But that hint (about lines going through different parts of the dots) was specific to the nine dot problem. That hint helped us find the three-line solution, but it is of little use now. This time, we will develop a general framework that we can use as a guide any time we are going into the void.

To develop this framework, we have to learn more about perspectives. Thus far, we have treated perspectives as a pattern of concepts. It reminds us that the choice of which concepts are included in our perspectives matters, and it reminds us that how we think the concepts fit together also matters. Another consideration is to identify the role of the individual concepts in the larger pattern.

Concepts play roles within the pattern of concepts composing our perspectives. It is a little like how words play roles in a sentence. For example, we can consider the sentence, "The cat chased the mouse." In that sentence, "cat" is playing the role of the subject, "chased" is playing the role of the action, and "mouse" is playing the role of the object. Of course, the roles might have been different. The mouse might have been the subject, and the cat might have been the object: "The mouse was chased by the cat." When it comes to perspectives, there are five main roles into which we cast concepts.[9] These roles are **Parts**, **Actions**, **Goals**, **Events**, and **Self-concepts**, or PAGES.

For example, imagine that we are in our supervisor's office for our annual review. We might be thinking about the person sitting across from us (our *boss*), the stack of paper in front of us (*feedback reports*), the piece of furniture between us (our *boss's desk*), and other such items. These concepts (boss, feedback reports, and desk) are examples of concepts playing the role of **parts** in our perspective. There can also be intangible parts, such as our *anxiety* or our *relationship* with our boss. Our stories usually involve many parts. The parts do not just sit there, though. In our stories we do things with and to the parts, we transform them in some way using **actions**. For example, we might *look* at the reports, we might *smile* at our boss, or we might *calculate* in our head what percentage raise we want. We do not usually take actions on parts randomly. We usually have a purpose or motivation. We are trying to achieve things. These are **goals**. For example, we might want a *15 percent raise*, or we may simply want to *leave this meeting* because we do not like performance reviews. We probably also want to *maintain a good relationship*. We organize concepts using more than just our goals. The individual actions and the goals are typically predicated on being in a particular type of episode. These are **events**. For example, we might think of this meeting with our boss as a *performance review*, a *chance to negotiate*, or a *waste of time*. Each event implies that we are involved in a different kind of story. Finally, we ourselves have a particular role to play. This is the **self-concept** we have formed to account for how we see ourselves in this episode. We could see ourselves as an *employee*, as a *negotiator*, or as *someone who must feign concern* in this event. Altogether then, when we form a perspective, we are assigning concepts to the relevant parts, actions, goals, event, and self-concept, or PAGES.

PAGES gives us a window into how we use, add to, and change our perspectives. When we are using our perspectives to advance our stories, we (self-concept, S) are taking actions (A) on parts (P) in an effort to attain our goals (G) within some event (E). Understanding PAGES gives us a way to reflect on our perspectives more deliberately. To return to the annual review example, considering more directly what we (S) think we want to get (G) out of this meeting (E) can be a means for us to bring assumptions to mind that we might otherwise take for granted. It might help us to realize that rather than make this meeting a waste of time (E), we should leverage (A) the good performance review (P) to get our 15 percent raise (G). We just need to be careful not to harm (A) our relationship (P) in doing so, as we (S) would not be happy (G) if we did. PAGES can help us surface assumptions in our perspectives so that we can consider them deliberately. Once we find these assumptions, we are in a better position to think about how to change them. As a result, PAGES provides a guide to what our current assumptions are, which we can use to generate alternatives. PAGES provides a guide to going into the void.

With PAGES as a guide, we can return to the nine dot problem to see if we can generate new inventions, beyond the first two we generated. If we inventoried the problem, we would probably start by identifying some of the obvious parts. There are dots. What do we know about the dots? When students make their own versions of the nine dots on their own pieces of paper so that they can try to generate solutions, some of them draw tiny points, some draw circles, some fill in the circles just like the dots in our picture. When we thought about the three-line solution, we noticed that the lines went through different regions of the dots. These observations about the dots are intended to be ordinary, now that we have been thinking about the problem for a while. But these observations do imply that the dots, like many physical parts, have a size. When we started the problem, we probably assumed that the size of the dots was fixed. But must it be? What if we redrew the figure with big dots? This modest insight is a modest change to our assumptions about one part in our perspective. That change, in turn, has a larger effect. The parts in our perspectives are organized into a pattern, so a change to a part can change the larger pattern. In this case, the dots make up the figure (the box of nine dots). Making the figure and dots bigger would not change anything much. Yet keeping the figure the same size and making the dots bigger so that they overlap might open up new opportunities. For example, if we do not change the size of the figure but make the dots bigger, then we change the relationship among the parts. This might lead us to change the assumption that the dots cannot touch each other. We can redraw the figure with nine, big overlapping dots. If they are big enough, we can connect them all with any line that goes through the middle. In this example, we focused on one obvious aspect in our perspective, one obvious part, and that led us to one obvious assumption to consider changing. This in turn led to identifying further new assumptions that we probably were not considering previously, all because our concepts in our perspectives are linked together into a larger pattern.

We can go through this exercise repeatedly. For example, we can decide that we do not want to allow overlapping dots because maybe we feel that this is not the way the figure was intended. We could consider another part. Other than the dots, the other obvious part is the line. If dots can be big or small, then perhaps it is no great leap to imagine that the line could be thin or thick. Perhaps we could draw (action) a thick line (enriched part) that goes through all nine dots in one swipe.

These very simple solutions to the nine dot problem followed directly from considering obvious aspects of PAGES directly. Rather than going into the void with no guidance and being overwhelmed by possibilities, we used PAGES to guide us toward changes to our perspectives. If we press harder, we can generate still more interesting inventions. The parts that are in focus (the dots, the lines) are not the only parts there are. For example, when we thought about the thickness of the line, perhaps that made us think about whether we were using a pen, a marker, or a paintbrush to form our lines. Our pen was not an obvious part of the problem. What other parts are there? Usually it takes a few minutes for people to realize that the paper on which the dots are drawn or printed is also a part of the problem.

What if we break the assumption that the paper should remain in the background, uninvolved in the problem itself other than providing a surface for writing? The question that arises next is what actions can we take on the paper? Making the paper larger or smaller, thinner or thicker, might not be of much use for advancing our story. But there are plenty of typical actions we normally take on paper that we have not considered in this problem. For example, it is fairly common to fold, rip, and crumple paper. Each of these actions can yield a one-line solution to the nine dot problem.

Thinking about folding the paper leads the story in one direction. For example, we might think about how we can align the dots by folding the paper in thirds so that the three columns of dots are on top of one another, then folding it again in thirds so that each stack of dots is on top of one another. Then we use a different action, to poke a hole through the dots, drawing a line downward through all nine dots. This solution started with thinking about the paper but also required using a different set of actions to get to the invention. There are other ways to fold the paper too.

A different direction for our story would involve rolling the paper into a tube. If we did this and then slightly tilted the edge, we could draw a line around the paper in a spiral that goes through a different column of dots on each pass, as if we were tracing the coils of a spring. This is a very different kind of invention than the one we generated as a result of thinking about folding the paper.

A third direction for this story came from one of our daughters. She drew the dots on paper, tore each one out, put each little ripped piece of paper in a line, and drew one line through all nine dots. Like the other inventions, this one followed from changing assumptions related to the parts (that the paper must remain intact, that the relationship between the dots is fixed). It probably also breaks an assumption about the "rules" in these kinds of events—that destroying the materials in the puzzle is not allowed. Our daughter, the future lawyer, responded, "There was no rule that said I couldn't."

In our experience with the nine dot problem, we tend to find that students have two main reactions to these demonstrations. One reaction is surprise at the variety of assumptions that they made without realizing it, as well as the variety of solutions that could be found when they broke them. We are excited when students react this way. Beyond the first lesson from the first solution that insights lead to inventions (that they often have to change their perspectives to solve problems), the idea that there is not one but a great many possible creative inventions to resolve episodes is a crucial lesson. As the stoplight model indicated, people have a strong tendency to use their perspectives rather than change them. This means they are generally creative on demand. But they could be creative repeatedly if they simply stopped to consider multiple changes to their perspectives. By understanding PAGES, they have a guide for going into the void. We hope this makes people more willing to try to generate multiple insights and multiple inventions.

There is a second reaction we often get to the variety of inventions for resolving the nine dot problem. Some students feel uncomfortable with these explorations and think that these are not legitimate solutions but just different ways of breaking the rules. Or to put it more bluntly, some students just find these inventions to be cheating. We are also excited when students react in this way.

We are excited because it is important to appreciate that creativity has consequences. Changing perspectives is not a neutral act. Breaking assumptions, making the story go in different directions, generating inventions of different sorts is interesting. Yet there is no guarantee the changes will be useful or will please other people. The broken assumptions might have been ones others would have refused to break. The inventions might be ones that excel on dimensions that others do not value. For example, just because there are kinds of creative accounting that we can all appreciate does not mean there are not also kinds of creative accounting that some of us think should be illegal. Thus students' reactions that some of the inventions for resolving the nine dot problem do not count is a useful reminder to consider the consequences of creativity.

We are also excited when students think that some of the inventions to resolve the nine dot problem are cheating because it indicates two aspects of perspectives that we have not yet discussed. These are the event and the self-concept. The event of the nine dot problem that most people adopt can be characterized as "working on a puzzle." The question is what assumptions we make as part of our "puzzle" event. For example, we might be relying on basic geometry definitions: a dot is a mere point, a line is one-dimensional with no width, the points are in fixed positions on a plane, and so forth. If this was our interpretation of the event, then the different solutions that were presented, with large dots, a thick line, or a rolled-up piece of paper, might not have seemed like clever explorations consistent with the given information but rather violations of the rules for this event. Our self-concept as people who are not cheaters will likely lead us to resist such violations. Such value-driven notions are reasonable to adopt and to commit oneself to, but we do have to ask ourselves some questions. Is this really the right and only interpretation of the event? Is this really the right and only interpretation of our self-concept?

It might seem surprising that the nine dot puzzle can raise such strong concerns. Yet because our perspectives are composed of PAGES, and PAGES include our self-concept, our sense of who we are can be brought to mind even when we work on simple puzzles. Therefore, we can have commitments that we are not willing to forgo. For example, perhaps we are not going to let go of the "geometry" commitments in the nine dot problem. There are still inventions to be generated. One of our colleagues drew three parallel lines through the three rows of dots and said, "As Einstein proved, all parallel lines connect at infinity."[10] We realize that we can argue about what it means to lift one's pen here, but the rules did say lines not line segments, so perhaps this is not a concern.

The larger concern is that creativity involves both breaking assumptions and building new ones. Changing perspectives means we are erasing some of our PAGES and rewriting others. The inventions that follow changing PAGES rest on the new PAGES, the new full pattern of concepts constituting our perspectives. We evaluate those PAGES as well as the inventions themselves, because we use and add to the changed perspective when we form inventions.

An additional important observation about our perspectives is that we are often most committed to our assumptions about our self-concept and the event. Our self-concept and the event are usually the source of our goals. These in turn guide what parts we think are important and what actions are desirable. When we change our interpretation of the event or our self-concept, many other aspects of our perspectives often change as a result. As just noted, if we think of the nine dot problem as a geometry problem event, this has a large influence on what we will and will not change about our perspectives. This means that different kinds of changes to our perspectives are likely to have different kinds of effects. Part or action changes might be quite local. Connecting to lines away from a dot did not make us rethink the entire problem. Self-concept and event changes are unlikely to be local, but instead be sweeping. The PAGES framework for thinking about our perspectives is a helpful guide to the potential for change and so the potential for creativity.

PAGES OVER TIME

There is enormous potential for creativity in a given situation, and still more over time throughout an episode. In an episode, not only does our own thinking have the capacity to change, but so too does the world change. In the nine dot problem, our perspective was changing but the situation itself was not changing much. Our stories were simple and short. Yet it is much more likely that we are thinking and acting in lengthy episodes. This means our story is advancing and growing more complex as our perspective is advancing and growing more complex. Our perspectives and our stories do not develop at the same rate. Sometimes, as in the nine dot problem, our perspective develops considerably without our story advancing much. At other times, as in the ZzzQuil example, our story develops considerably without our perspective advancing much. And sometimes, both our stories and perspectives develop.

To explore the relationship between perspective development and story development, we will use the (slightly adapted and necessarily simplified) story of a former MBA student of ours, whom we will call Nate. Nate could have crafted an ordinary story, using PAGES to tell, "How I got a job at Big Company." While that would be a fine resolution for many, Nate left an interview at Big Company feeling disinterested. He saw his peers excited by their interviews for similar positions at similar companies. Yet Nate's self-concept directed him to want to create a different kind of story. He wanted to break from the typical MBA assumptions of a high-power job in a big city and instead wanted to move back to his hometown. As he thought about who he was and what he wanted (his self-concept, once again), Nate thought about starting his own company. As he thought through that prospect, though, he did not have a burning idea for a company. Besides, Nate was not interested in starting a company, he was more interested in leading and managing a company. Nate's insight that satisfied his self-concept was that he would try to buy a small business in his hometown so that he could lead it. Nate's "buy a small company" story began.

Stories operate at several scales simultaneously.[11] There is the step-by-step progress of specific actions taking place in stories. There are also, simultaneously, larger events at play, being advanced or thwarted by the accumulation of specific actions. For example, we might think about a relatively simple story: "Last week I bought a car." This event almost surely involved many smaller events, such as thinking about the need for a car, saving up the money to buy a car, identifying possibilities by reading and talking with people, going out to test drive some cars, talking with salespeople, signing some papers, and driving away with a car. Those individual events could also be further examined. Taking a test drive might have involved allowing the salesperson to copy your driver's license, getting the keys, getting into the car, adjusting the seat, and so forth. And these events, in turn, can be further examined too. Allowing the salesperson to copy your driver's license involves them asking you for your license, you getting out your wallet, pulling out your driver's license, handing it to the salesperson, who then walks to a copy machine, and so on. Pulling out your driver's license is part of taking a test drive, which in turn is part of buying a car. The story proceeds at multiple scales at one time. A story is a useful way of thinking about the process of generating an invention because a story allows us to think about the packing and unpacking of events at different scales.

The packing and unpacking of events is critical to explaining why insights are separate from inventions and why we need to examine both perspective development and story development over time. Only very small stories, like a riddle or something similarly brief, have just one event. Most stories can be unpacked into sub-events, like a book is divided into chapters or a film is divided into scenes. To tell the full story, we have to tell all the sub-event stories too. To summarize the story, though, that is not needed. A synopsis does not get into all those details. We can just say, "Last week I bought a car." We usually need an overarching idea to write a story. We usually need at least some initial sense of what we are doing. That initial sense might be due to craft or due to creativity. In Nate's case it was an insight: "I would like to buy and run a small company." That led to the story he set out to tell.

Buying a small company is an event that can be unpacked into sub-events. Nate needs to find a business. He needs to secure funding. He needs to negotiate the purchase of the business. Each of these sub-events, in turn, raises further sub-sub-events, such as identifying a local bank from which he might secure funding. But importantly, even with this start to a story and newly developing perspective, Nate was able to start to organize this thinking and form initial PAGES. This meant that Nate could use his PAGES to decide which sub-event needed attention and action first. For example, in Nate's story, it seemed like the first sub-event he needed to address was the "find a business" sub-event. After all, the PAGES Nate set up would lead him to think that if there were no small businesses for sale, or if all the ones for sale were very unappealing, this story was not likely to continue to a happy ending. So, with this guess about what action to use to respond to the situation and advance the story, Nate started to work on the "find a business" sub-event.

Nate was almost immediately stumped. He was not familiar with buying businesses. How do you find a business to buy? There is no store where you can go to buy a business. No one comes to campus to recruit MBA students to buy businesses. How does one find those who are selling businesses? Nate could not use PAGES to advance his story, because he did not know of any actions that could allow him to address the goal of finding a business to buy. So he had to add to PAGES. Nate contacted a variety of mentors about his goal of buying a business and asked for their help. Nate learned that there were brokers who sought to match small business owners looking to sell with new entrants looking to buy. Nate had not known that small business brokers existed. This was a new part for his PAGES, and it added a new sub-event (actually, a sub-sub-event, to the sub-event of "find a business") to the story: "find a small business broker." This is what adding to PAGES normally does to stories—appends a new sub-event to the existing events.

As events can be unpacked, adding to PAGES can be a small adjustment or a large one. In Nate's case, the addition occurred within the sub-event of finding a company to buy. It could have been a much larger change. For example, if Nate found out his identity had been stolen and his credit rating was terrible, he would have a large new sub-event to address and that could have a large influence on the story. There is no clear limit to the size of an event, because unpacking an event can proceed indefinitely. It is like a set of Russian nesting dolls, where we open up one doll and there is another one inside. But irrespective of the size of the addition to PAGES, the effect of adding new events to the story is similar. Adding to PAGES means more parts to integrate, more actions to consider, and more goals to meet, because there are more events in the story. It also means that we have a new task. In addition to working on the immediate event and taking actions on parts to attain its goal, we can also think about which event to work on. In Nate's story, after learning about small business brokers he decided to pursue that sub-event and then took steps to identify a small business broker. That is, Nate used PAGES to select a sub-event and then used PAGES to select an action to take to make progress in that sub-event.

In this story, Nate found a broker and learned there was more to add to his PAGES. He learned that a broker would not assist him with acquiring financing but would be doing the negotiating with the small business owner. More generally, adding to PAGES can involve not only adding events but also refining other, existing events because of the presence of new parts that are then integrated into the existing structure of PAGES. Adding to PAGES narrows and deepens our perspectives.

After reviewing several possibilities, Nate identified a small business that excited him, a business that made and installed custom mirrors, glass windows, and doors. The business was the right size, listed at $1.9 million. It was big enough that there was really something to lead and manage, but not so big that he could not plausibly find a way to buy it. It was not so technical that he would be in over his head running it. The broker also told Nate that the owner had a health issue and so was being forced to retire. Thus Nate was using PAGES to take steps (looking for a listing, getting information from the broker about the listing he liked, and so on), and his story was advancing. His perspective was deepening and narrowing. The part "business to buy" was replaced with a specific entity, a mirror and glass company. Linked to that was a small business owner looking to sell, which was now replaced by a specific entity, an owner with a health issue. These specifics matter to the story, even if they do not make much difference in the very next steps Nate would take. They matter because they imply that the owner is probably not in a strong position and so particularly likely to accept an offer, perhaps even a low offer, from Nate. Nate got excited.

Having completed the "find a business" sub-event, Nate needed to think about which of the other sub-events to address next. Using his perspective, he decided it was time to set up his financing so that he could make an offer for the business. Nate completed this event by talking to local banks about business loans. This was an event carried out with pure craft. There was no need to add to his perspective, let alone change his perspective, so why would he? Having resolved that event, it was time to negotiate the purchase of the business. Through his broker, Nate made an offer for $1.3 million. Nate fully expected the owner to return with a counteroffer. That is what happens in a negotiation event. Nate also expected that there would need to be multiple counteroffers from both sides before this event would be resolved. Thus Nate readied his thoughts about the next action he would take to chip away at the price.

A few days later, the owner responded, thanking Nate for his interest and reiterating that the price was $1.9 million. This was not typical. Nonetheless, Nate could use what he knew about negotiation events in general to explain the new situation in which he found himself. The owner probably did not want to drop the price instantly. So while the change to the situation (that is, the counteroffer) was unexpected, it was still conceivable in this kind of event. It just meant that Nate could not use the action he intended, and would have to add to his PAGES before taking his next action. So Nate worked up a more detailed analysis, just like his MBA training led him to do. Nate offered $1.5 million and submitted that number with a detailed analysis that he thought justified the number. Nate gave this to the broker to give to the owner.

A few days later, the owner came back with an offer of $1.85 million. Nate was getting a bit frustrated. The nature of the situation was spoiling his story. Nate didn't think he could get through the next few years if he paid that much for the business. He was also annoyed by the lack of communication from the owner. Nate was dissatisfied about where the story was going. He expected the business owner to concede to a reasonable offer so as to deal with whatever the health issue was. Nate thought something in his approach needed to change. While Nate was generating one more offer, he had an insight about the process. His assumptions, embedded in his PAGES, about the "negotiate with the owner" sub-event had been that this was a haggling process with an adversary, conducted through an agent (the broker). But Nate's reason for wanting to move back to his hometown and buy a small business was not because he liked engaging in haggling processes with adversaries through an agent. He wanted to be part of a community. Nate's perspective on this negotiation sub-event had changed. So Nate told the broker that he needed to meet the owner and deliver the offer in person. Nate demanding to deliver the offer in person was taboo, and the broker was not happy. The owner, however, agreed.

The decision to meet with the owner changed the event and the relationship with the broker. This was a change to PAGES. It might have been a difficult insight to generate because Nate committed to the assumption that he needed to work through the broker. Or Nate might not have committed to the broker playing the role of a negotiating agent at the outset, and his frustration at this point led him to remove what he had always seen as an impediment. In either case, the insight was notable because it changed what events were possible to resolve and so what might happen next in the story.

In Nate's story, the owner agreeing to meet in person meant that Nate traveled home for the meeting. The story was opening up, because Nate was uncertain about what might happen in the meeting. Maybe it would be more intense haggling. Maybe it would be the formation of a meaningful new relationship. Maybe he would learn something that would call off the entire deal or even make him reconsider moving home and buying a small business. Further, it would not be until the meeting, or possibly after, that Nate would find out. Stories take time. If we are just thinking about a riddle, then our perspectives can form and change quickly. With stories, we often have to wait and manage uncertainty.

Even waiting on the end of Nate's story, we can resolve any uncertainty that there are important differences between forming an insight to change our perspectives and forming an invention that resolves a story. We often hear people say things like what mathematician Tim Sauer said to us: "Once the problem is framed the right way, any idiot can solve it." Sometimes an insight provides a change in perspective that does in fact lead to a clear path toward an invention that resolves our story. In this case, the gap between an insight and an invention seems unimportant. But as our stories grow larger, we are confronted by the challenge that it takes time to develop a perspective to frame a problem. We might not even know what the problem is at first. We can have insights about what the problem is. Nate had to generate an insight—"I want to buy a small business in my home town"—just so that there was a story to tell. We can also have insights that redirect our stories, such as Nate's insight to meet with the small business owner. These changes to our perspective may or may not lead to a resolution. The final reason to separate insights and inventions is that even if we can imagine the invention that follows from the insight, we still have to bring the invention to life. And only when we make the effort might we learn that the world does not align with our imaginations. Our confidence in our perspectives to allow us to see to the end of our story may be greater than warranted. The challenge is that our perspectives usually make that gap inconceivable.

PRACTICE

Vocabulary

This chapter extended the possible scale of thinking beyond the present moment. We still think about situations with perspectives and stories, it is just that each source of knowledge expands. Thus the chapter reiterated what was learned in Chapter 2 but also extended the definitions with what was learned in Chapter 3.

1. **Situation**: The objective conditions of the world

   a. **Situation (momentary)**: The conditions of the world that we perceive in our immediate surroundings

   b. **Situation (episodic)**: The conditions of the world that relate historically to the present conditions that we perceive

2. **Perspective**: A coherent characterization of the assumed true features in a situation

   a. **Perspective (momentary)**: The network of assumptions about what concepts are present in a situation, as well as how they are structured in relation to each other

   b. **Perspective (episodic)**: The network of assumptions about the specific elements and relationships between them as they have existed over time in a particular story

3. **Story**: A coherent explanation for what has happened, what is happening, and what might happen in a situation

   a. **Story (momentary)**: An explanation or narrative describing the current conditions that may include descriptions of the past and probable future

   b. **Story (episodic)**: A coherent explanation or narrative describing the relations between elements of a particular episode, including how they have historically transformed into their present conditions

4. **PAGES**: The roles in which concepts are put so that you may use them to guide response choices in a situation

   Parts: The elements of the situation

   Actions: Our capabilities for altering the parts

   Goals: Our interpretation of the needs we are trying to meet in a situation; generally these are met when we take action on the parts to make the situation meet desired conditions

   Event: The type of situation we see ourselves as being in

   Self-concept: The type of identity we assume in a situation

5. **Invention**: The product of resolving goals after changing perspectives such that the resolution is one that would formerly have been inconceivable

Exercises

Note that what follows are very much like riddles. PAGES should work for either situations that are fixed (like riddles) or ones that do provide feedback as you change them (like the nine dot problem). We thus provide both kinds for practice.

1. What are the parts, actions, goals in the following riddle: move one penny to make two rows of four (Figure 3.8)?

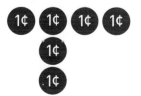

FIGURE 3.8. The Penny Problem.

Hint: Think first about the parts, and how you can make eight out of only six. Then think about the actions. Then think about if you had these physically in front of you, what action might you have trouble conceiving when working with dots on a page? You may also need to think about the part "row."

2. There is a man found dead in a circular mansion. The detective interviews the cook, maid, and babysitter. The cook said he couldn't have done it because he was preparing the meal. The maid said she couldn't have done it because she was dusting the corners. The babysitter said she couldn't because she was playing with the children. Who was lying? Hint: think about what actions are possible.

3. What do these two phrases say? Hint: try to isolate the parts, and then to think about their structural relations together.

   a. TOIMWN

   b. STRAWBERRYcake

4. There are nine pigs in a square pen (Figure 3.9). Build two more square enclosures so that each pig is in its own pen. Hint: Draw the missing parts, and then try using the action of changing their orientation (that is, turning them).

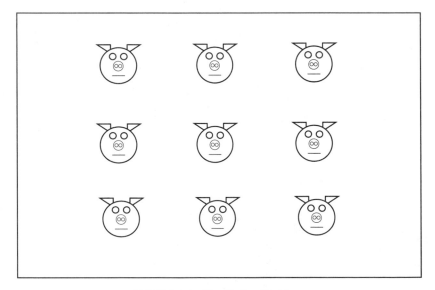

FIGURE 3.9. The Pig Pen Problem.

5. If they put wheels on refrigerators to make them easy to move, what other things should they probably be on (although they are not yet)? Hint: Wheels are parts that help with certain actions, goals, and events. Use this to decide.

6. Move two matchsticks so the olive is outside the glass (Figure 3.10). Hint: Some actions may cause the meaning of the parts to change.

FIGURE 3.10. The Olive Problem.

7. In a locked cabin in the woods are one hundred people who are all dead. The cabin itself is not burned, but the forest all around is burned to cinders. How did they die? Hint: Think about events and parts.

8. A farmer has seventeen sheep. All but nine of them die. How many sheep does he have left? If you said eight you are wrong, so go back and think about the actions you used to figure that out.

9. A girl is sitting in a house at night that has no lights on at all. There is no lamp, no candle, nothing. Yet she is reading. How? Hint: Think about the action she is performing.

10. Arrange six matchsticks so that they make four triangles (Figure 3.11). Hint: This event is easier when using physical matchsticks rather than lines on a page. Why are those different?

FIGURE 3.11. The Triangle Problem.

11. How many apples can you fit into an empty box? If you don't know, think about the goal.

12. Three girls are taking a bull to the zoo when their car breaks down. They motion for a guy to pull over. They ask to use his phone to call the zoo. He agrees, but says it would cost them $1 for every word. They only had $1. They agreed and said "comfortable" and five minutes later the zoo was there. Explain. Hint: unpack the parts in the word.

13. A woman who did not have her driver's license with her went through a stop sign without stopping, then went the wrong way down a one-way street. A cop saw all of this and did nothing. Why? Use only the PAGES explicitly stated to help you figure this out. Note that the response, "Because the cop was her boyfriend," is an *add* response, and not the right answer.

14. Move three circles so the triangle is upside down (Figure 3.12). Hint: No hint! This one is easy!

FIGURE 3.12. The Pyramid Problem.

Answers

1. Put the leftmost coin on top of the corner coin.

2. The maid had no corners to dust.

3. (A) I'm in town; (B) Strawberry short cake.

4. A square in the middle and a square rotated 45 degrees (that is, a diamond) around the middle square. The corners of the middle square touch the midpoint of the diamond sides.

5. We thought of washers and dryers, you could probably think of more.

6. Move the horizontal match half its length to the right, then take what was the left edge of the glass and make it the right edge of the upside down glass. The stem (P) transforms into an edge (P).

7. Airplane crash (event); the cabin is the cabin of an airplane (part).

8. The correct action is just to read the sentence "All but nine of them die." People often automatically use mathematical actions because of their expectation about the event. (Bonus points: What kind of commitment was that? Educational—we are used to word problems in which you have to perform mathematical operations, not simply read.)

9. She is reading braille.

10. Matches have a third dimension. It may prompt you to think about an equilateral pyramid.

11. Zero, the box must remain empty.

12. Come for ta bull.

13. She was walking.

14. Seriously, you can figure it out.

ENLIGHTENMENT AS A CREATIVE PRODUCT

By definition, a technological project is a fiction,
since at the outset it does not exist.
—Bruno Latour

We started a story about a former student we called Nate who wanted
to buy a small business in his hometown after finishing his degree. Nate's insight to buy a small business was a fiction, in the sense that it was an imagined
story. Nate worked hard to bring that fiction into reality. There is much to learn
from Nate's story. It illustrates the close relationship between craft and creativity. Nate used, added to, and changed his perspective over time as he developed
his story. The story illustrates the separate development of perspectives and
stories. His story stalled at times. There were stretches when his perspective
went unchanged. The story illustrates that insights do not lead directly to inventions. Even when Nate's perspective did change, it was not the end of the
story nor was the end of the story even in sight. Nate was waiting to meet with
the owner of the small business owner, and he was uncertain about how that
meeting would go. This part of the story illustrates another important aspect of
Nate's story, which is how much Nate learned along the way.

When the waiting was over, Nate and the owner did not start by talking about
the price of the business. They talked about the town and who they knew in common. They talked about the business and how much promise it had. The owner
talked about being frustrated by having to work less, which is information that
would not have emerged in the prior story in which all negotiation was on paper
and handled through the broker. The broker had said the business owner needed
to stop working altogether. The owner told Nate that she had a heart condition
and that her doctor had told her she needed to reduce her work hours and her

stress levels. But she did not want or need to leave the business altogether and would have preferred to continue working. Nate had made an assumption about the owner upon learning the owner's health situation from the broker, and had committed to the belief that the owner needed to leave the business entirely and soon. This framed Nate's approach to the negotiation. But now Nate realized that this commitment was faulty. (If you made an assumption—not a tentative guess, but an assumption to which you committed—that the business owner was a man, then you know how easy it is to fall into making assumptions.)

Further, the idea that the owner was stepping away from the business fit with Nate's idea that he would buy and run a company, which came along with an assumption that he would do so himself, without the owner still being involved. That is, after all, what normally happens when you buy something. So the assumption about the owner needing to leave the business was interpreted in light of the earlier assumption about the way that purchases normally work. It was interpreted as a potential sign of weakness due to a need to sell. However, because of the change in his perspective about the owner, Nate now realized that the owner could play an entirely different role in the transaction. Nate proposed that the owner stay on as a consultant to the business, introduce Nate to customers and suppliers, and advise Nate for a three-year period. The owner gladly agreed. Thus, Nate changed and replaced an assumption about a part (the owner), and that revision to PAGES allowed for new actions, new ways to meet goals, and new ways to conclude events that Nate had not conceived of at the start of the event.

The story is not over. Nate and the owner still were going back and forth on price. But with the changed perspective (the owner is no longer an adversary, there is a goal of working together, and there is more information shared on both sides), the story continued to develop. Nate had been concerned about the worst case scenario and so was offering a low price, whereas the owner was more optimistic and so insisting on a high price. So they agreed that the better the company's sales in the next three years, the more Nate would pay the owner for the company. If things went as well as the owner expected, the owner would get the full amount of money desired, but otherwise would accept a lower payment from Nate. This kind of contract is something Nate would have learned in his MBA training, but it might not have been brought to mind had the story not expanded due to the change in Nate's interpretation of the owner.

Further, Nate found out that while the owner was close to retiring, she did not need the money from the sale all in one lump sum. This allowed Nate to avoid taking out a loan from a bank and instead allowed the owner to finance the sale of the business to Nate. Basically, Nate took out a loan from the owner to buy the owner's business, and that way the owner not only got the purchase price but also the interest that would otherwise have gone to a bank. Nate would also pay out the money to the owner over time, which also would make it easier to pay the owner more when the business did better.

The invention that Nate and the owner generated is more complicated than the insights we have discussed. This is not exceptional. Inventions blend both craft and creativity. It can even be difficult to pinpoint what led to an invention because of all that happened along the way. Craft and creativity become entwined. When we change our assumptions, we alter the events that are possible in a story going forward, allowing outcomes that would have otherwise been inconceivable. We also change our understanding of the past. As Nate shifted from trying to win a low price for a business to working out a complex long-term partnership with the owner, he and the owner invented a very different resolution to their story.

Nate was a somewhat different person after forming the "business partnership buy-out" invention. Nate generated insights during the process, changing his perspective on what he was doing and why. Those were temporary adjustments. Nate generated the invention through this process, which put him in a different role, a new professional relationship, and a new starting point for future stories. But these also led to durable changes to Nate's life. He had a signed contract, he lived in a different place, and many aspects of his life changed. In addition to these products of the creative process, Nate also learned. Nate developed an understanding of what a business broker is, of the value of forming relationships in negotiations, of the potential for seller financing to align incentives, and much more. He built new knowledge that he could use in the future to form perspectives and advance stories.

In reviewing what was written about creativity, we were surprised by how often discussions of creativity were separated from discussions of learning. Both creativity and learning are concerned with the formation of new understandings. Granted, there are forms of creativity that do not seem to be terribly involved with learning. When people figure out a riddle, other than perhaps learning the riddle's answer, they are mainly changing their momentary perspective. And there are forms of learning that do not seem to be terribly involved with creativity, such as memorizing facts. Yet if we reflect on our best moments of learning, the times when we came to see the world differently, when our capabilities expanded, when we were struck by wonder, and when we felt new levels of understanding, those are surely times at which changing our perspectives was instrumental to building new knowledge. These are **enlightenments**. They are the most far-reaching products of creativity. They are changes to what we know about the world.

WINE AND ENLIGHTENMENTS

If insights are new fictions that inventions make into new realities, enlightenments are new nonfictions that we now believe to be generally true. Insights typically are bound to moments. Inventions are bound to stories. Enlightenments are bound to knowledge. This is why enlightenments are far-reaching. Enlightenments often arise in a story but then extend beyond it. By changing our knowledge, enlightenments can change any story and any perspective we form in the future.

For example, imagine wanting to drink a glass of wine, but not the whole bottle. The challenge is that once a bottle of wine is opened, the wine inside starts to change for the worse. Burt Miller and Morgan Weinberg asked themselves a question: What if we can get the wine out of the bottle without letting air into the bottle? The insight they had was that it might be possible to push an inert gas into the bottle instead of air and push out the wine. It took six years to turn this fiction into an actual device. It took six years for Miller and Weinberg to form an invention, called the Pungo, that allows people to drink from a bottle of wine and still keep the remaining wine in "just opened" condition for months.[1] Their story is both a classic tale of creativity and an illustration of how much we have to learn from creativity.

Miller and Weinberg's story began at a trade show. They were displaying a different invention of theirs, a way to keep soda carbonated. Their device slowly compressed a bottle of soda to keep the air-to-soda ratio in the bottle to a minimum. They had learned that the more air that was in a bottle of soda, the more the bubbles—the carbon dioxide gas—would escape from the liquid into the air, causing the soda to go flat. While at the trade show, Miller and Weinberg talked to another inventor about whether this same principle could be used with wine. The inventor said that he had been trying and failing for a decade.

Miller and Weinberg like tackling challenges, it is part of their self-concept, so on the way home from the trade show they tried to imagine a wine-preserving device. They started with the notion that air was the problem, like it was for soda. But their solution for soda—slowly compressing the plastic bottle—would not work with wine, because wine bottles are made of glass and so cannot be compressed. They thought that instead they had to find a way to get the wine out of the bottle without letting the air in. They thought that maybe it was possible to pierce the cork with a hollow needle that could draw out wine and replace it with an inert gas, like argon. By the time they got to their hotel, they had formed an insight about envisioning this fiction and the idea for the Pungo was born.

Thus far, Miller and Weinberg's story sounds like a common kind of story about an invention. Experience with one story prompts a possibility that launches a new story. The soda project led to a wine project. Critically, the effort seems to be concerned mainly with drawing knowledge from memories— both semantic memories about the world in general and episodic memories about specific past stories. Thus far, it is about drawing on knowledge that has already been learned.

The perspective Miller and Weinberg formed allowed them to imagine a story about how to get wine out of a bottle without letting air in. It was not a very richly developed perspective. They populated some initial PAGES with their engineering knowledge. The goal was to drink some of the wine in a bottle while maintaining the rest in good condition. The key action they imagined was replacing wine with argon gas through a needle puncturing the wine bottle's cork. While this effectively describes the invention they went on to make, at the time it was inconceivable how many more PAGES they would need to form to tell this story and produce this invention. They did not know how much they did not know about the device, about the world, and about their own knowledge. They had a lot to learn.

They began by learning. Miller and Weinberg did not start by trying to make needles. Instead, they started by learning more about air. They needed to know more about their assumption that air was what caused wine to go bad. They knew that they could buy rubber stoppers and pumps to remove most of the air from an open wine bottle. They learned that that these do not work very well. They did not know how or why air spoiled wine though. They started doing tests to confirm that air was actually the problem and to understand why it was a problem. The result was a change in perspective on what mattered, and an enlightenment about the relationship between wine and air. It was not the amount of air in the bottle that mattered. It was that once new air entered the bottle, it started a chemical process that would eventually spoil the wine. They had not known this beforehand, nor would they have figured it out just by thinking about it. They tested their assumptions by interacting with the world. This allowed them to learn something new about wine, and this enlightenment had implications for any story they might tell going forward. They were now committed to a new assumption about the world: the only way to store wine properly is to prevent air from ever touching it.

This enlightenment had an implication for their initial insight. They thought that piercing a wine bottle's cork with a needle, drawing out wine, and replacing it with an inert gas might work. Their enlightenment about air and wine indicated support for continuing to develop their insight. Had they learned something else, they might not have bothered developing their initial insight. If they tried and failed to develop their insight, they would have had a reason to try generating an alternative. Or they might have decided they were solving the wrong problem. Perhaps they needed to find new ways to commit to finishing a bottle of wine once opened. Perhaps they needed to identify new ways to gather friends and family in greater numbers so that any open bottle would get finished, or they needed to develop an app so that anyone could quickly find someone else who wanted to buy the rest of an open bottle of wine. Their new knowledge, in short, could have led in many directions.

The direction they pursued was to try to develop their initial insight. The assumption about air not touching wine led to the inference that whatever part and action would be involved in piercing a wine bottle's cork, it had to maintain the seal keeping air out. Miller and Weinberg conceived of a hollow needle to go through the cork. They constructed a thin, stainless steel hollow needle to meet this goal. When they tried pushing it through corks in wine bottles, it did keep the seal. The problem that emerged was not one they anticipated. It turned out to be difficult to get the needle through the cork without also pushing the cork into the bottle. This difficulty led them to add a new role for friction in their perspective. This was not a dramatic change in perspective, but it was an update about the relative forces involved.

After learning more about the role of friction in this particular story, Miller and Weinberg added to their perspective. They recalled that corkscrews are twisted in shape rather than straight. This led them to try forming and inserting a twisted hollow needle. It did not fully resolve the problem of pushing the cork into the bottle. Worse, it sometimes generated a new problem in the form of cracks in the corks large enough to allow air to leak in. Minor cracks in a cork are not a problem when removing a cork from a wine bottle, which is what a corkscrew normally does. But they are a problem when one is trying to preserve the seal on a wine bottle.

It was a failed attempt, or perhaps more accurately, a learning experience. Apparently the inventor Thomas Edison once said about the great many attempts at constructing a light bulb, "I have not failed. I've just found 10,000 ways that won't work." Many creators can relate. We try using and adding to our perspectives to form responses, and then we observe what happens. This might sound mundane, but it is an important complement to drawing knowledge from memory to add to and change our perspectives. In addition to drawing knowledge from memory, feedback from acting in the world and then perceiving the results is one prompt to building new knowledge. We can learn. Then we can use the new knowledge to add to or change our perspectives. Thus one reason to emphasize the link between creativity and learning is that even craft responses can, if we attend to the situation for feedback, spur changes to our perspectives—changes that we might not have considered without acting and observing.

In Miller and Weinberg's case, they learned something about the shape of the needle that led them away from considering further alternative shapes and turned instead to another aspect of the part. They considered its surface. They added to their perspective once again by recalling another way to reduce friction. They coated the straight needle with Teflon. A Teflon-coated straight needle reliably punctured corks in wine bottles without pushing the corks into the bottle. They resolved this sub-event in their story and could continue onward.

Their story stopped again almost immediately. As they were testing their Teflon-coated needle, they found that the hollow needle could either let wine out or let argon gas in, but it could not effectively do both at once. Again, they learned that their perspective was underdeveloped. They added to their perspective. They needed to use a double needle with one channel for wine and another channel for argon gas. But learning this and adding this new aspect to the design of their invention created a new, large sub-event. While Miller and Weinberg could readily buy or manufacture hollow needles, the same could not be said of a double-chambered needle. They were confronted by a larger gap in their knowledge. They did not know how to manufacture a double-chambered needle. Should they try to put two needles together? Or should they try to learn how to make a double needle? Their domain knowledge indicated that machining a double needle would be expensive and difficult. They decided they needed to find a way to put two needles together to keep production costs low.

Adding to their perspective once more, Miller and Weinberg considered welding two needles together. However, welding too often melted the needles. If the hollow channel closed or even changed shape too much, it could alter the way gas and wine flowed through the needle. A distorted shape might also cause problems with insertion into the cork.

Their second attempt at adding to their perspective was to consider brazing the two needles together. Miller said that they had to learn quite a bit about brazing in the course of working on this invention. Welding means melting the metal parts themselves and then fusing the parts together directly. Brazing is like soldering. It involves melting another kind of metal and then using that melted metal as a sort of glue to fuse together the two parts of interest. Miller told of scouring books on brazing but not finding any answer as to how to braze two hollow needles together. They had to build new assumptions by experimenting and experiencing many failures and dead ends. They incorporated a new action, a baking process (furnace brazing rather than torch brazing, for those interested in brazing technicalities). That worked half of the time. Then they developed a new part, a ceramic heat sink that they inserted into the hollow needles, to get the brazing process to work every time. They had built enough new knowledge to produce a double needle, coated in Teflon, that would reliably puncture a cork and allow wine out and argon gas in. Importantly, Miller and Weinberg were still on their way to constructing the invention they had envisioned with their initial insight. They just had no idea how poorly they had envisioned the invention at first. What they did not know was inconceivable to them, and there was much they needed to learn. And with all of that effort, learning, and creativity, they had now arrived at the hardest part.

They needed a way to release argon gas into the wine bottle through the needle and draw out the wine. The challenge is that argon gas is kept under pressure. If too much gas is released at once, it could result in wine shooting out of the bottle so fast it could tip over a wine glass. Worse, if the wine could not come out of the bottle fast enough as the gas entered, the wine bottle could shatter. On the other hand, if not enough gas was released, no wine would come out. They had to get the balance of gas in and wine out just right.

They needed to generate a new means to control the release of the argon gas. There are devices called regulators that could control the flow of the gas. However, these were too large to fit on a wine bottle. They needed a small mechanical method for controlling the flow of gas and wine. They designed a trigger that would rotate a small part, called a cam, covering the hole keeping the argon gas contained. Rotating the cam out of the way of the opening could, at least in principle, allow careful control of the release of the argon gas. Figuring out a way to control the gas's release with just the cam mechanism was a unique enough approach to get Miller and Weinberg a patent. That is, Miller and Weinberg's resolution of one sub-event within their larger story was not just an enlightenment to them, it was also an enlightenment to the larger community of inventors in the United States.

One small strand of this story was an enlightenment in itself. When Miller and Weinberg first constructed the Pungo, they made the cam out of plastic. Yet it was difficult to manufacture plastic consistently, which they did not like (both are perfectionists), and they also thought it looked cheap. Their dissatisfaction pushed them to make the cam out of stainless steel, which could be manufactured more consistently and was better looking. Yet after making this change they were surprised to find that it did not work reliably. Sometimes when they pulled the trigger to let wine out, the wine would come shooting out. They did not think anything had changed in the cam design, but they did not know why the stainless steel cam was having problems controlling the pressure. It should have worked more accurately and effectively than its plastic counterpart, not less.

Miller and Weinberg started experimenting with their computer models to see if somehow there was a problem in the shape of the cam that was causing the problem. After running about twenty different models without learning any reason why the steel cam was having problems controlling the release of the argon gas, they were stuck. In thinking more about it, they had an insight about the cause of the problem. When they were using a plastic cam, some of the pressure from the release of the argon gas was absorbed by the cam itself, as the plastic distorted and limited the outflow of argon gas. A stainless steel cam would not distort in this way. The difference in material was not represented in their computer modeling effort or in their thinking about how the part was working. That was why they hit an impasse. Their perspective needed to change to incorporate the material out of which the cam was made and the way materials can absorb pressure. They went back to the plastic cam. Miller and Weinberg had learned a lesson about hard parts.

We have provided a tiny sampling of the trials and tribulations that Miller and Weinberg went through to imagine the Pungo and turn that fiction into reality. We repeatedly found such stories of adding, using, and changing perspectives in our interviews with people about their processes of forming inventions. We described this particular example in depth because the initial insight that led to the invention of the Pungo was accurate and did not need to change. Yet clearly that initial insight was far from the whole story. As Miller put it, the

Pungo was spurred by an insight that "took fifteen minutes to come up with" and "was one of about two hundred others we needed to have to make it work." We only wrote here about a handful of those two hundred insights.

Miller and Weinberg had numerous insights and engaged considerable amounts of craft knowledge. They experimented extensively. Yet it is also clear that they learned a substantial amount as they went through the creative process. And we do describe this entire story as one creative process, not two hundred separate creative processes. All of their efforts were part of forming one invention, the Pungo. The different insights were interrelated. The way in which the needles were manufactured was critical to the way in which the release of the gas was controlled, as they had to rely on a particular-sized channel and opening in the needles to get the gas release mechanism sized just so. Consequently, irregularities in manufacturing the needles were not viable, forcing them to find a reliable way to form the needles. The reduction in friction of the needles through the cork with the Teflon could not be so great that the pressure change of releasing argon gas pushed the needle back out of the cork. That is, the different aspects of the story were only partially separable. We described them as being more independent than they really were for the sake of simplicity—we do not have six years to go through the entire story.

What we take from this story, first and foremost, is how much there is to learn from an invention that seemed on its face to follow directly from the initial insight. As they unpacked each event into a sub-event and then explored that sub-event, and unpacked and interconnected aspects of the story from there, the creative process grew and extended in ways they did not anticipate. Miller and Weinberg learned a considerable amount of new knowledge during their creative process. That learning was not incidental but central to the process: that any contact with air changes wine, that they needed a furnace-brazed, double-chambered needle coated in Teflon, and that the cam part's hardness mattered were all critical to expanding their PAGES and producing the invention. Building new knowledge is often part of the creative process.

BUILDING NEW KNOWLEDGE

Earlier, when we examined the changes in perspective needed to solve riddles and puzzles, we did not need to learn anything new about the world. We could just pull knowledge from long-term memory to change our perspectives. In examining long stories such as *Star Wars*, we saw that we had to revise some assumptions that we had committed to in the course of making sense of the story, changing from some concepts to others available in our long-term memories and in our memories of the story itself. It was only in the longer stories of inventions such as the Pungo and Nate's purchase of a small business that we noticed the role of building new assumptions about the world. To change our perspectives then, we might have to identify knowledge in long-term memory and discover a way to incorporate it into our perspectives. Yet we might also have to identify new assumptions and build new concepts around them that we can then incorporate into our perspectives. Creativity can mean building new knowledge and forming enlightenments about the world.

Building new knowledge is usually a last resort. Which is not to say that we resist making assumptions. Without making assumptions, we are unable to think. Making new assumptions allows us to think in new ways. Consequently, part of the creative process is forming new assumptions. It is just that we make different kinds of assumptions. We make assumptions about what we are perceiving in a situation, about what has happened in our stories, and about what exists. Creativity can lead us to change any of these types of assumptions and so change our perspectives on what we are perceiving, our stories, and our knowledge. Creativity can also lead us to build new general knowledge— enlightenments. Again, this is usually a last resort.

The assumptions we make about what we are perceiving rarely feel interesting. For example, imagine we go outside on a clear night, we look up at the sky, and an older man in a button-down shirt says to us, "Tell me what you see." Since we are outside on a clear night, we see small dots of light. We use our concept *stars* to interpret what we are seeing and would reply accordingly: "I see stars." This is ordinary. We constantly match concepts from long-term memory to what we perceive in a situation. Usually we draw on semantic memory—our concepts that represent all the kinds of things we can think about, such as stars.

As we perceive more in a situation, we can update our assumptions. Perhaps we notice that one of the points of light is moving slowly across the sky and blinking. We could interpret this new information and update our assumptions about what we are perceiving, as we are not committed to seeing only stars in the sky. We already have the perspective that we are looking at stars in the night sky, but we know that stars do not move slowly and blink like this light is doing. We know that this new pattern matches other concepts. We could add, "I see a plane, too."

The concepts we assign to what we perceive are the ones that we think fit best given our perspective at that moment, given our knowledge.[2] It may not be a perfect process, but we play the odds when making assumptions about what we perceive, and it usually works well enough. The light in the sky that is moving could be a satellite, but planes are more common. Up to five points of light in the sky are planets, not stars. But the fit between our assumptions about the situation and the situation itself is good enough that we do not worry about such discrepancies.

Even though our assumptions about which concepts apply to the situation are made quickly and intended for use for a limited time, we are nonetheless quite committed to them. Even though we know that there are many interpretations of situations, we believe in the one we generated. We typically have a strong sense that we know what we saw, for example. If the man in our example said that he saw *beauty, an absence of light pollution*, or *evidence of God*, we would be unlikely to exchange our commitment to our assumptions about what we saw for theirs. We might say, "I could look at it that way, too."

In addition to alternative interpretations of situations as a reason to consider our assumptions, we also know that there are times when we might be mistaken. We have seen optical illusions. We have seen magic tricks. Perhaps there is an elaborate stunt with lights on drones in the night sky. If we only saw a situation briefly or if our view was unclear because of distance, rain, darkness, our glasses being off, or some other impediment, we would not be as committed to our assumptions about what we perceived. But normally we do not second guess our assumptions about what we perceive.

Creativity can come in the form of second guessing assumptions about what is being perceived. Earlier, when we considered the nine dot problem, we reviewed many assumptions about what was being perceived. We noted the tendency to perceive the dots as a box limiting where we might draw. We noted the tendency to think of the dots as points. We noted the tendency to ignore the paper on which the dots were drawn. We made many assumptions about what might be perceived in the situation and what concepts to use to interpret what was being perceived. In the story about Nate buying a small business, we noted that he shifted from perceiving the owner of the small business as the opposition to perceiving the owner as a partner. In the story about the invention of the Pungo, we noted that Miller and Weinberg at first perceived the shape of the cam controlling the release of the gas to be important but not its material. These were all changes to assumptions about what concepts mapped onto the situation. What we did not emphasize, though, was that some of these changes in assumptions required forming new assumptions.

Forming new assumptions about what concepts map onto a situation usually feels like puzzling out what we are seeing.[3] Is the blinking light a plane or a star blocked by clouds? What do we think upon seeing 10 + 10 = 100? Is it simply a mistake? Or if we make some assumptions could it be sensible?[4] It might be difficult to identify the signal for all the noise in many situations, but then the noise may be in our assumptions due to our prior knowledge rather than anything about the situation. Situations are overwhelmingly complex or eminently sensible because of our knowledge. Just try watching a sporting event whose rules you do not know.

In addition to forming new assumptions about what we perceive, the creative process can also lead us to form new assumptions about what we stored in memory. Because we maintain a perspective over time, we remember what we have already interpreted over the course of an episode. We make assumptions that carry forward our beliefs about the past, those that we think are settled and do not need to be revised. This maintains consistency between the present and possible future. For example, to return to the discussion about the night sky, if after we said that we saw stars, the man in the button-down shirt treated us to a long and detailed explanation about the dark matter that we did not see, and how dark matter is important to the galaxy, then we might make an assumption that he is an astronomy enthusiast. If the conversation continues in this manner, we will soon feel confident in our assumed knowledge about this person, and commit to it. The more an assumption seems to hold in our experience, the more we rely on it going forward.

Thus we build knowledge about the specific elements in an ongoing story as the episode continues. Such elements might start out as being mere examples of general categories we have experienced previously (the man is an example of an astronomy enthusiast), but as we develop particular experience with them they gain their own identities.[5] General knowledge about the kinds of people who are astronomy enthusiasts give way to what we learn about this specific person. We can think about this person as an individual with a particular history, set of tendencies, and relationships. This is not just true of people. We individuate all manner of places, animals, artifacts, events, and other items. We form assumptions about what these things are, what they have done or is done to them, and what they are likely to do or have happen to them in the future. We can commit to those assumptions about what happened, and this cements how we remember the episode and its elements.[6]

For example, perhaps we continue our story with the astronomy enthusiast. That person may be prattling on about astronomy now, but when he stops, we assume it does not mean he no longer likes the subject. It just means we have moved on to another topic. If the man starts talking about the Big Bang theory, this would not be surprising, and would confirm what we have assumed about this individual. If he starts to talk about soil enrichment, it might seem less likely, but not inconceivable. We can add to our assumptions about this individual like we add to them in a perspective; we are talking to a science enthusiast or someone with a fondness for the outdoors. We form enduring perspectives on the individuals, which like any perspective is a structure of concepts. It is why, if the person started to talk about the necessity of divine creation, it would probably conflict with the assumptions we had made about the person from our earlier discussions and the general knowledge that we have. We might have to change and restructure our assumptions about this person, or even make a new kind of concept for this specific man. We build knowledge about the elements in this particular story as the event goes on.

Uncontested experience is one way assumptions become knowledge. For instance, in the Pungo example, it was the history with the original plastic cam that made Miller and Weinberg so surprised by the stainless steel cam being a problem. Their assumptions indicated that the steel cam would improve the performance of their device because it was even more precisely constructed. Miller and Weinberg's change in assumptions about stainless steel's hardness led to a change in their assumptions about the original plastic cam. The plastic cam was effective not just because of its shape, but also because its material provided some give that helped regulate the release of the argon gas. Miller and Weinberg's device had not worked in quite the way they had assumed it did. Similarly, in the story of Nate's buying a small business, the assumption that the business owner could no longer work due to ill health needed revision. In both cases, the people involved were not using knowledge from an on-the-fly assumption about which concepts were present in a situation, but from an assumption that had emerged in the past and solidified over time.

Knowledge building can happen explicitly as well as implicitly as we think about how a story should progress. Nate was constantly forming assumptions during his effort to buy a small company. He formed assumptions about his self-concept as a leader, as someone returning to his hometown, as a partner.

He formed assumptions about the events he would need to undertake, such as involving a broker, haggling over price, and traveling for a meeting in person. He formed assumptions about his goals (only paying more if the business was more successful), actions (seller-financing), and parts (small business brokers) as well. As Nate learned more about the story, he added new assumptions about what was relevant.

Forming new assumptions about what we are perceiving and what is included in our stories is central to developing our perspectives. In many situations, we recognize the situation as being like one we have seen before and adopt a perspective encompassing a large number of assumptions about the PAGES. Sometimes we have to think and even struggle to form assumptions about what we are perceiving and what is relevant. Either way, the process does not stop when our story starts. Rather, it continues throughout our stories. Forming new assumptions about what we are perceiving and about our stories is usually an ordinary act of forming and adding to our perspectives.

In contrast, forming new assumptions about what exists is a much less ordinary act. The most important assumptions that we make are about what exists, our general (semantic) knowledge, our concepts. When we form new assumptions to generate new concepts, we are building new knowledge.

The concepts we have in long-term memory have two properties that lead us to commit to them. As we noted, our concepts are interpretations that we assume account for what we perceive. Thus to use a concept to interpret a situation is, in a way, a commitment to the concept representing a kind of thing that exists. When we say something like "brokers are helpful," we are making a generalization about brokers but we are also implicitly assuming that brokers exist and are a general type of thing in the world.[7]

In addition, our concepts are interrelated in semantic memory so that part of what we assume a concept means is given by its relationships with other concepts.[8] For example, we might assume that *stars* are massive, bright balls of plasma that can have planets or other stars orbiting them. Thus when we build a new concept we integrate it with what we already know. As the concept takes part of its meaning from other concepts we already believe exist, we commit to our assumptions that this concept too represents something that exists.

When we are building new knowledge, we are making foundational assumptions about concepts. Our assumptions about what we perceive are concerned with which concepts we apply to some situation. Our assumptions about what happened previously are concerned with interpreting specific instances in specific episodes. These two types of assumption are generally about assembling a perspective. But our assumptions about concepts themselves are concerned with something much more general. These assumptions hold outside of any particular story. We build collections of concepts that together mark out domains of thought and activity. If asked what we know about astronomy, religion, or whatever subject, we would recall concepts that typically are associated with the requested domain. We accumulated these beliefs over time through experience, including formal education. We use these concepts to form our perspectives and advance our stories.

Our concepts represent commitments to assumptions about what is, what might be, what is not, and, implicitly, what is inconceivable. General knowledge about what is and is not in the night sky is critical to how we make assumptions about what we are perceiving when we look there. General knowledge is how we can interpret questions about the night sky. We do not take them to be requests for help with a tax return—that makes no sense given our knowledge. We cannot form an assumption that the person in the story with whom we are talking is an astronomy enthusiast who hates astronomy. That does not make sense. These assumptions are easy to overlook because they represent our taken-for-granted interpretations of reality. But these assumptions are actually achievements.

For example, a recent news story featured a planet made of hot ice.[9] At first, this seemed to imply "ice that burns," like dry ice. But no, the planet was solid water at 475 degrees Fahrenheit. An initial interpretation might have been something like a ball of ice that is somehow super hot. But really understanding this requires a little more effort. It turns out that the water is compressed to a hot solid by the strong gravitational forces of that planet. Picturing what the hot ice looks like or how it maintains itself is challenging. Is it crystalline? Is it clear? We keep bumping up against what we think should be true, which in this case is that the water should not be ice (or even liquid) at that temperature. We lack the concepts not just for this situation, but for this kind of thing in the world. Whereas our perspective on a moment tells us what is possible right now and our perspective on a story tells us what is possible in some episode, it is our perspective on a domain that tells us what is possible *at all*.

One way to access the challenge of building new knowledge and to form a greater awareness of how committed we are to our assumptions about our existing knowledge is to look back at seventeenth-century astronomy. Galileo Galilei famously advanced astronomy by identifying the phases of Venus, four moons orbiting Jupiter, and sunspots, as well as advocating for the Copernican view that the earth orbited the sun. In addition, Galileo first noted the odd shape that Saturn seemed to take. Saturn sometimes looked as though it had two moons, sometimes looked like an ellipse with two dark spots, and sometimes looked like a sphere. We now know that this is because Saturn has rings. To Galileo it was inconceivable. The discovery of Saturn's rings is credited to Christian Huygens, and it is often mistakenly believed that he made this discovery because he had a better telescope with higher resolution. In actuality Huygens had a better ability to reconsider the assumptions about planet formation to which astronomers of his time were committed.[10]

Huygens's proposal about Saturn's rings defied the current knowledge about planets. The idea of Saturn having a ring was inconceivable to many because planets were assumed to be spheres. All the knowledge in astronomy at the time explained how planets formed as round bodies. The proposal that a planet had a ring around it could not be generated arbitrarily. It required a person to think, "How could that happen? What would it be made of? Why would it not fly apart?" and many other questions. It would not have been accepted without substantial argumentation, as it was not consistent with the widely accepted knowledge about planets at the time. In fact, years passed before Huygens's insight became accepted as an enlightenment.[11]

A second puzzle in seventeenth-century astronomy was planetary motion. The assumption was that planets moved at a constant speed in circular pathways, or at least circular pathways around circular pathways. The challenge was to figure out how to reconcile that belief with observations of the planets' locations. The data did not seem to line up with the beliefs about planets. Johannes Kepler spent ten years pouring over Tyco Brahe's data of the location of Mars, trying to work out the logic of its orbit. He generated numerous possibilities, partially building on and partially discarding what had come before—using, adding to, and changing his perspective repeatedly.[12] Kepler discovered that speed was not constant and that instead of being "circles within circles," the orbit was an ellipse within which the speed of the planet changed depending on the distance from the sun. Eventually, Kepler took the equation that fit the data on Mars's orbit and extended it to other planets as well.

The primary challenge to identifying elliptical planetary orbits was not finding an equation to fit the data. Nobel Laureate and scholar of cognition Herbert Simon was fond of noting that college undergraduates, when given the data Kepler had available, could derive Kelper's third law of planetary motion in about ninety minutes, as opposed to Kepler's ten years. We do not think it is because college students today are vastly better thinkers than historically recognized scientific minds. Instead, we would say that Kepler had to work much more against deeply held commitments about the nature of the universe than today's college students do.

In the twenty-first century, students have no specific commitment to planetary orbits needing to be one shape or another. Kepler, on the other hand, lived in a time and culture with strong, socially reinforced assumptions about planetary orbits being circles. These came from both pillars of knowledge and education about the universe (and most other facets of life) at the time—Greek philosophy and Christian theology. There had been over two thousand years of work treating planetary orbits as circles and generating accounts of planetary motion resting on circular orbits because circles were considered perfect, and God, who made the heavens, worked with perfection. In early seventeenth-century Europe, with the Inquisition taking a strong interest in such matters, one did not blithely dismiss such assumptions about the nature of the universe. Given such strong commitments to the assumption of circular orbits, non-circular orbits were likely to have been strongly inconceivable at the time. So it is remarkable that Kepler ever generated an account of noncircular orbits in the first place, not that it took him more than ninety minutes to do so.

There is a final ironic twist to our discussions of seventeenth-century astronomy, one that reinforces how challenging creativity is. Changing our perspectives once is no guarantee that we will change our perspectives again. A willingness to build new knowledge is not an indication of a general openness. We experience that ourselves with every new solution to the nine dot problem. We see it in Galileo. Galileo was a contemporary of Kepler. He is remembered for almost being put to death for supporting the Copernican notion that the earth moves around the sun. Galileo had the strength of character and intellect to defy prevailing wisdom and contradict one of the most strongly held assumptions about the heavens because it did not fit with the data. Yet he never accepted Kepler's theory about noncircular orbits.[13] Strong commitments to our assumptions can make building new knowledge exceedingly difficult. Yet what choice do we have but to make strong commitments to our assumptions about the way the world works?

The strength of our commitments to our assumptions about what exists is exemplified by how firmly we believe the earth revolves around the sun. It is also indicated by much more mundane truths. For example, when we say that something is "empty," we really mean that we cannot see anything inside, not that it is a vacuum.[14] We do not often notice the lack of fit between our knowledge and situations. But sometimes the lack of fit blows up in our faces. For instance, consider how if a person were to toss a cigarette stub into an "empty" gasoline drum, the gasoline vapors at the bottom could catch on fire, leading to a major blaze. The assumptions about what "empty" means are not quite right.

Even when we do notice a lack of fit between our beliefs and an episode, we have so many ways of rationalizing the difference that we rarely think that it is our concepts that are incorrect.[15] We might ignore the difference. We reject it. We exclude it as an exception. We decide to wait and see. We reinterpret it as normal or an accident or as what we thought would happen after all. That is, the problem might just be our perceptions or our stories, so we do not jump to building new knowledge.

It is hard to imagine, but most of our general knowledge is the result of prior creative efforts. The knowledge that the earth revolves around the sun, that there is a number zero, and that human beings are not always rational are all achievements. People did not always think these things exist and are true, and presumably some people do not think so even now. That these kinds of ideas probably seem self-evident descriptions of the world, rather than assumptions about the world, is what so often makes creativity necessary for building new general knowledge.

When we go through the creative process, we sometimes need to be creative in this way. We sometimes build new assumptions about the world. The process of generating inventions usually involves both retrieving existing knowledge to change our perspectives and forming new assumptions. This is often in the form of new assumptions about what we are perceiving and about what happened in the past. But sometimes, and most critically, we generate new knowledge about what exists. For example, Miller and Weinberg had to build new knowledge about what air does to wine. This was not just a different understanding of what they were perceiving. It was not just a different way of thinking about something in their story. It was new knowledge about something that exists and happens in the world that they did not imagine before. It was an enlightenment.

Enlightenments are important products of creativity because they change our understandings of the world. In doing so, they become part of the knowledge we use to form new perspectives and tell new stories. There is no limit on the number of perspectives and stories they might foster. Despite or perhaps because of their sweeping influence, we lose track of enlightenments. We tend to take our knowledge for granted. We learned that points of light in the night sky are stars and planets. We learned to read English. Some of us learn to read music. Some of us read mathematical notation. Radiologists learn to read x-rays and MRI scans that the rest of us do not need to know how to interpret. Building new knowledge about the world eventually becomes a resource for craft. But at first it may well take creativity.

LOST IN THOUGHT WORLDS

The creative process might involve a few moments considering a riddle, and it might involve years of dedicated effort to understand the nature of the universe. The more PAGES we assemble and the longer the story we develop, the more encompassing the thought world is. Those thought worlds need stability and structure; otherwise we can get confused, disoriented, and lost. The insights and enlightenments that we generate can provide new ways to think about parts in the world and actions we can take. These result in new concerns to consider and new behaviors to try. Insights and enlightenments can generate new goals and so send us off in directions we did not anticipate. Insights and enlightenments can generate new events and so alter what we think we are engaged in doing. Insights and enlightenments can generate new self-concepts and so shape who we think we are. As we move through each of the PAGES, the stakes get larger and the risk of upheaval grows. A cautionary tale is in order.

The tale is the history of the would-be invention *Aramis*, drawn from an analysis by the engineer and scholar Bruno Latour. Aramis was a fiction generated by the French manufacturer Matra. The company had conceptualized a new form of public transportation that was to revolutionize how people would move about in a city. "If I take my car, I'm stuck for hours in traffic jams. If I walk, I breathe carbon dioxide and get lead poisoning. If I take my bike, I get knocked down. And if I take the subway, I get crushed by three hundred people. . . . [Matra] has come up with a system that allows us to be all by ourselves in a quiet little car, and at the same time we are in a mass transit network."[16] The system was called Aramis. It was like a train, in that it would run on rails and travel between stations carrying passengers. But it had some amazing properties. Aramis would take you from any station in the city to any other station without transfers or stopping. You would get into a small car that would seat a handful of people. That car would link up with others and get passed from train to train until it reached its destination. Aramis was a collection of insights about a potential invention.

Aramis was in some ways like the Pungo. Initial insights, when amplified with craft, yielded a fiction about a potential invention. The question was how to turn the fiction into reality. In the case of the Pungo, Miller and Weinberg broke down the overall event of the story into sub-events like so many Russian dolls, one mostly nesting inside another. How to get the needle through a cork without pushing the cork into the bottle (Event 1 or E1) was mostly a separate event from how to make a double-chambered needle (E2). That in turn was mostly a separate event from how to design a cam mechanism to release gas in a controlled fashion (E3). Digging still deeper, each of these events could be further unpacked. The Russian doll of the double-chambered needle (E2) could be unpacked into further challenges around welding (Event 2 sub-event 1, or E2.1) and brazing (E2.2), which in turn unpacked into challenges around furnace brazing (E2.2.1). But Miller and Weinberg could, for the most part, keep the different events and sub-events clustered and organized so that when they resolved one, the others were largely unaffected. And when they resolved all of them, they could pack all the dolls back up and reassemble them into their vastly incomplete but somehow still approximately on target original conceptualization. They were able to turn their fiction into reality. In contrast, the Aramis story remained fiction.

The Aramis fiction was in many ways a compelling scheme for what a city's train system might be. Its PAGES were incomplete at the start, with a plausible set of events to consider and resolve. Aramis had to have passenger cars (Event 1 or E1). The designers imagined small passenger cars (Event 1 sub-event 1, or E1.1) that would allow small numbers of people to start and end at the same stations, and allow for tighter turns in the track to fit in many parts of an old European city. The passenger cars had to be able to be passed between the trains (E2). Passing the cars between the trains meant developing a new way to connect trains (E2.1), which they proposed resolving by using magnets to hold cars together rather than the traditional metal couplings. This spawned yet more events, the need to develop the magnets, which they called a *nonmaterial coupling* (E2.1.1) and a way to control the nonmaterial couplings with computers (E2.1.2). Finally, the cars had to be guided automatically to their destination (E3). This required developing microprocessors (E3.1) to control the passenger cars, with further specifics around microprocessors for handling the cars' direction, speed, and so forth (E3.1.1–8). Within each event, there were parts to be manipulated by actions, and a goal to be met to resolve the event. Each event became an occasion for its own craft and creativity. Thus far, the Aramis story seems complex, but fairly similar to the Pungo story.

The difficulty they had with Aramis was that developments for one event had fairly strong implications for the other events. For example, as they developed the technology costs across specific events, this made Aramis's total projected costs increase. This, in turn, made it important to consider larger passenger cars so that more people could ride at once, thus increasing the economy of scale. But larger cars would mean a system that relied more heavily on hub stations where large numbers of people wished to go. It also changed where tracks were possible, affecting the original vision of what Aramis was to be. The events were not discrete problems with clear linkages to only the other relevant problems. Changing one event in the story changed many other events in the story, often through linkages at higher levels of abstraction. Such is a hazard with inventions as they grow beyond what two very smart people can do by themselves. Latour puts this poetically:

> If a project were made up of Russian dolls, everything would be simple. You would take the big doll, knowing that there are other ones inside . . . [d]ivision of labor, division of problems. A good flow chart to handle all the embeddings, and we'll be all set. Unfortunately arrangements of this sort are only valid for finished objects that need simply to be supported and maintained. The lovely series of successive tasks and embedded specializations is not valid for [these kinds of] projects. Their topology is so nonstandard that the smallest one may, from time to time and for a certain period of time, contain the larger ones. Is nonmaterial coupling Aramis' content or container? . . . In the real Aramis, precisely the one that does not exist, we see that the nonmaterial coupling becomes, for some people, the big doll that contains and justifies all the others.[17]

The challenge with interdependencies across events is that a change can ripple across the others, reordering everything all over again. What the "problem" is remains in flux as the story continues. Resolving one event in the story does not cement that event into place, for all the events are subservient to the ultimate goal, precisely the one that is still being worked out. Latour continues,

> This sudden mutation may take place at any point in the old chain. Is the eighth microprocessor that controls the movement of the trains in its turn contained by or contained in the nonmaterial coupling? Here is a new uncertainty and it grows larger as it's examined carefully, to the point of blocking the entire Aramis project.[18]

Aramis is less one story than a great many plotlines all being woven together. Yet these plotlines share PAGES. Thus the adjustments in understanding needed to fill out the PAGES for one event nearly always resulted in a need to make adjustments to the PAGES within another event. It was easy to lose track of what the story was that they were trying to tell. By the time the Aramis project was abandoned, there were twenty-one interpretations of the same situation.[19] The larger the story, the more latitude we have to fill subplots with concepts from our own narratives.[20] But if the PAGES fail to make a story that is coherent across all the events, then we are lost. The story has to put all the Russian dolls back together again, even if there are a great many, even after each one develops into its own independent figurine.

It is similar to the situation of having multiple goals. Sometimes we want to get work done and we want to attend a social function. We want to read a book and also paint pictures with our children. Sometimes our desires conflict with one another. At that point, as the early twentieth-century management writer Mary Parker Follett wisely counseled, we have to pick:

> We progress by a revaluation of desire, but usually we do not stop to examine a desire until another is disputing right of way with it. . . . We want to do so-and-so, but we do not estimate how much this really means to us until it comes into conflict with another desire. Revaluation is the flower of comparison.[21]

Not only do we have to pick, we must adapt. It is the world, not just our story, that we are trying to change. The consequence of getting lost in the thought world of the story is that the beautiful fictions we imagine never become material realities. Aramis is one such cautionary tale. It never materialized, and not for all the typical reasons we might have thought. It did not run out of money or support, prove technologically infeasible, or fall apart organizationally. The twenty-one interpretations were not twenty-one warring factions of storytellers. Aramis died because the commitment to what the story would be—the initial perspective—was too strong. The story came apart because the perspective did not develop. The authors would not let it.

At the outset of a story, our perspectives provide a vision for where that story will go. But as many authors will say, stories take on a life of their own.[22] And as the episodes advance we can learn where the stories need to change to fit the world. Our initial assumptions are often incomplete. Our initial insights can be wrong in the simple sense that they will not work. They can also be wrong in a more complex sense. They can fail to fit with other revelations that emerge as the story continues.

In the case of Aramis, this accommodation did not happen, and that was a failure of inflexibility rather than imagination. The initial vision of Aramis was a beautiful and incomplete fiction. When every aspect could be realized individually but the collection could not be realized together, there was a need to adapt the fiction to reality. Some deeply held assumptions needed to be changed to accommodate the stubborn fact that both fiction and reality could not be maintained in their original form. The authors were so committed to what they wanted the story to be that their story remained a fiction:

> They've been saying the same thing for fifteen years . . . nonmaterial couplings, small size, adaptability to the sites, no transfers. . . . Where does it get us? . . . It doesn't get us anywhere. . . . The basic concept hasn't undergone any transformation, any negotiation, except for the pair of cars and ten seats. It's held up against all comers. . . . It didn't incorporate any skepticism, any random event. . . . While everything is shifting around inside the mobile Aramis unit, outside everything is carved in stone. They don't renegotiate.[23]

FROM FICTION TO NONFICTION AND BACK

Emmy Award–winning news anchor Angela An told us that creativity was essential in her business. "The incident where 'Police are on the scene of a shooting . . .' could happen twenty-five times a day. We need to find a novel way to give it depth and connection to the viewers." Most younger producers will, she said, simply state what happened. She teaches them to take a different angle. She has the new reporters talk to people who experienced the event and get a backstory from an interesting relation so that they can find a way to make each story resonate. An had figured out a method for generating fresh perspectives on familiar episodes to create compelling news stories, and was teaching it to new reporters. An had formed an enlightenment about the craft of creativity.

An's journey illustrates a common pathway for creative professionals. We start in the realm of fiction about what might be as we generate ideas and insights. An generated insights about possible approaches to a news story. We produce inventions, moving into the realm of the actual. In An's case, that meant forming an actual news story that caught people's attention. Then with refinement of the invention and abstraction to similar situations, we generate enlightenments, and are now in the realm of nonfiction. An figured out that taking a non-obvious angle on a story drew attention, and that generally worked in the world.

If we are clever, we can form enlightenments about how to form insights. An realized that by interviewing bystanders and relatives, she could generate fresh angles on news stories repeatedly. She may not be able to predict the insights, but she can predict that they will come. Like An, we form nonfiction about generating fiction. And we share these enlightenments with others. We do not have to keep enlightenments to ourselves any more than we have to keep inventions to ourselves. An shared her learning so that others could develop their craft of creativity.

PRACTICE

Vocabulary

In this chapter, we discussed how one generates knowledge through learning. Such learning goes beyond specific situations and stories but nonetheless connects to them. Thus we round out our conceptualizations of situations, perspectives, and stories with definitions of how these can exist as organized sets of knowledge.

1. **Situation**: The objective conditions of the world

   a. **Situation (momentary)**: The conditions of the world that we perceive in our immediate surroundings

   b. **Situation (episodic)**: The conditions of the world that relate historically to the present conditions that we perceive

Situations become kinds of events—identifiable and discrete happenings that have predictable causes and consequences, as well as a predictable sequence of transformations.

2. **Perspective**: A coherent characterization of the assumed true features in a situation

   a. **Perspective (momentary)**: The network of assumptions about which concepts are present in a situation, as well as how they are structured in relation to each other

   b. **Perspective (episodic)**: The network of assumptions about the specific elements and relationships between them as they have existed over time in a particular story

Perspectives become domains of knowledge about a subject; these structure concepts and their relationships to each other both within and between domains.

3. **Story**: A coherent explanation for what has happened, what is happening, and what might happen in a situation

   a. **Story (momentary)**: An explanation or narrative describing the current conditions that may include descriptions of the past and probable future

   b. **Story (episodic)**: A coherent explanation or narrative describing the relations between elements of a particular episode, including how they have historically transformed into their present conditions.

Stories become completed episodes—specific events that have happened and can be recalled as needed.

4. **Enlightenment**: The product of changing our perspective on concepts themselves, such that those concepts rest on assumptions that would formerly have been inconceivable

Exercises

One of the biggest challenges with creativity is that it is personal. It has to be because it is you who are changing perspective. So we want you to reflect on some of the things that you have done as you have leveraged creativity to accomplish your endeavors or learn new things. We are going to give you some common ways in which creativity can bear fruit. See if you can fill in the appropriate concepts with examples from your own life.

This task is kind of like the word game Mad Libs, except that the specific example that you are trying to fit to our concepts should make the story make sense, as opposed to being silly. Fill in examples that fit within the brackets.

An example of a mundane but useful insight:

I was in the middle of [1: a routine task that you do all the time] when I realized that I should use [2: knowledge you use all the time in other situations] to [3: respond in some way]. This [4: improved how you do this task, say how] and [you benefited, say how].

1. Classify this event.

2. What was the insight? What commitments did you break?

3. What PAGES were changed?

4. What was the knowledge that you stored for future use? Could you call it an invention or enlightenment?

An example of how a step-level insight takes the story to a new kind of resolution:

One time I had to [1: name an endeavor]. I was working toward [2: name the goal] when I suddenly realized [3: name an insight]. It made me realize I was thinking about this whole thing the wrong way because [say why], and so after that I [4: say how you changed the nature of the story]. I completed it by [say how], which I had not expected given where I started.

1. Characterize the episode as a type of event (even if you have to blend concepts).

2. Did the goal resolve the story or just a sub-event? If the latter, say what it was.

3. What assumption(s) did you break?

4. What PAGES were changed?

5. What knowledge did you store? Was it an invention or enlightenment (and say why)?

An example of how insights build on each other in an endeavor:

I was trying to [describe overarching endeavor]. As I was working on it I had an insight [describe insight]. This let me [describe how capabilities expanded]. Because of this, later I [describe insight that came from the first], and that [describe how capabilities expanded]. *Repeat this until you get to the resolution to the endeavor.*

1. For each insight-capability pair, explain how your knowledge expanded.

2. Explain how the new knowledge from the prior insight led to another insight.

An example of how a series of seemingly mundane choices led you to an invention or enlightenment:

I started with [this resolution in mind] but I wound up with [this inconceivably better one]. Here is basically how it happened: It started when I took [name a use step] and that led to [an alteration in the situation that was off the expected path]. I continued along and then I [name a use step] and that [pulled you further off the beaten path] After that. . . . [repeat this sequence as many times as you need to complete the chain of events. Try to focus on the mundane actions that led to an invention or enlightenment.]

An example of how a story failed to resolve well but produced an enlightenment nonetheless:

One time I was trying to [1: name an event you needed to resolve or a goal you needed to achieve]. I wanted to come up with a better way of [2: name the goal you were trying to meet], so I had the idea to [3: describe the invention you conceptualized]. After I worked on it for a while I just could not get it to operate like it needed to. It [say what it did not do], however I learned [4: give enlightenment]. I wound up using that to [say how you used it in some other situation].

1. What PAGES were important in this event?

2. Does this goal have subgoals? If so what are they?

3. What was the insight?

4. How did the insight lead to enlightenment in the context of this story?

5. What concepts did the enlightenment change or build?

An example of how insight leads to invention then enlightenment:

I remember needing to [describe a goal]. I realized at one point when I was trying to meet this goal that I should [1: describe insight]. With this in mind, I set out to [describe invention]. *Optional*: I couldn't get the invention to work until I [2: describe second insight]. Once I got the invention to work, I realized that it could also be useful for [describe other event, action, or goal], and so learned that [describe enlightenment].

1. What PAGES were changed? (Do the same for item 2 if you have it included.)

2. What did the invention do better in terms of the goal?

3. Are there yet other stories or objectives for which this enlightenment might yet prove useful?

An example of how novice enlightenments become expert knowledge:

When I was first starting out in [your domain], I used to [1: describe how you would resolve an event]. Eventually I came to realize how this was kind of ineffective. I realized that what I needed to do was [2: describe learning]. After that I was [describe how performance improved].

1. Categorize the event using concepts from your domain.
2. What concepts did the learning change?
3. Is this more an invention or enlightenment?

CUES AS CLUES TO CHANGE PERSPECTIVE

*Some people see the glass half full. Others see it half empty. I see a glass that's
twice as big as it needs to be.*
—George Carlin

Many discussions of creativity describe it as luck, an accident, a gift from
the muses, a lightning strike—a magic moment that is not under your control.
In contrast, we have said that creativity is most often an ongoing effort, and
that some parts are under your control. A central reason why we have mapped
out a detailed view of the creative process has been to identify opportunities for
developing skill at navigating the long journey that creativity actually requires.
Such a journey will continue for a while, but it must always begin somewhere.
And beyond any lucky magic moment, it will require craft.

The view of creativity we have developed is that it requires many steps to
transform the inconceivable into the thinkable, and then into the actual. Most
often, people are not creative. We think of the conceivable and then use this to
follow well-worn routines of actions to make the conceivable actual. We write
stories that are a lot like the stories we usually write using perspectives that are
a lot like the ones we usually take. As we resolve these stories, we learn how to
better use the concepts in the roles for which we typically use them. This is
pure craft.

Cognitively, craft is our default because we draw on our experience to form
a perspective about the current situation. As the current situation extends into
an episode, we expect our perspective can develop and advance a story about
what has happened, what is happening now, and what might happen in the
future. Our perspective becomes structured into PAGES—parts, actions, goals,
event, and self-concept. We use PAGES to alter our situation in an intended

way so as to advance our story. We incorporate new information that the episodes provide by adding to the PAGES, and our story is thus enriched. We may even develop new combinations of concepts to put into our PAGES, but these concepts will follow directly from what we already learned in our story.

When we add creativity, we change our perspective on a story. This allows us to tell a new *kind* of story. Sometimes this is just telling a different but otherwise well-known story, one we had not conceived of being helpful in this situation. But sometimes it means forging a new kind of story. Often this requires multiple insights that we would not have needed had the story not taken this new direction. As we follow the new kind of story, we may resolve the various events that themselves were not predictable, or in ways we could not have conceived. If they are marked improvements to our goals, they are remembered as inventions. We may also discover patterns in the world that seem inconceivable given our domain knowledge. If we can validate these and abstract them beyond the current story, they become enlightenments. Throughout the process, the insights, inventions, and enlightenments can build on each other as the story goes on.

Cognitively, it all starts when we stop advancing our stories in the usual way. We need to inquire and ultimately change our perspective. We then may go back to craft, albeit with a different story. Or we may need to consider using our old craft in new ways to try to invent something. As we expand our capabilities we might learn something that does not fit with what we know about the current episode or what we believe altogether. We may need to build new structures of knowledge in a void where we thought none could exist. This is an extended process that both leverages existing craft knowledge and develops new kinds of craft knowledge. Thus creativity outside the moment has the capacity for development and refinement with the help of our common craft knowledge, but should creativity succeed, our knowledge will be changed. Yet even though we are leveraging craft, when we are building out into the void there is a great deal more uncertainty. Using old craft in new ways means uncertainty about what will or even should happen.

With this account of craft, of creativity, and of how craft and creativity relate to one another, we turn to the craft of creativity. For there to be a craft of creativity, a skill at navigating the creative process, there must be ways to enter and proceed through the creative process more efficiently and effectively. The beginning of the creative process is the shift away from the story in progress. We stop advancing the story and shift to considering our perspective. The question is why we shift our focus to our perspective. In addressing that question, we can then develop our skill at noticing opportunities to shift focus to our perspective and so provide ourselves with more opportunities for creativity.

STOPLIGHT TENDENCIES

We are not creative all the time or even most of the time, nor should we be. Most of the episodes we engage in are familiar, and most of the time we can tell a familiar story. We rely on craft so that we can respond to and accomplish our goals efficiently. As long as our stories seem to be advancing as expected, we have, in the terminology of the stoplight model of using, adding to, and changing our perspectives, a green light to continue using our perspectives to advance our stories. We get up, get dressed, eat breakfast, and go to work in much the same way every day. We are not necessarily looking to be creative with these tasks. Even at work, we typically are handling the kinds of tasks we handled yesterday. Usually, working on and completing these tasks using craft allows us to be productive.

In the short run, creativity is not productive but disruptive. Changing our perspective means we have a red light and need to stop our story. Further, we stop without any guarantee that we will find anything better. The new direction for our story indicated by an insight might not turn out to be the improvement we expected it to be. The invention we produce might not offer a better resolution than the one we could have produced in the ordinary way. The enlightenment we generated might not yield knowledge that is more useful going forward than what we already knew. And generating all of these products of creativity requires time and effort. For all these reasons, what we do ordinarily is the result of effort, experience, and learning. It is not foolish to practice our craft. We would hope to have a good reason to diverge from telling the kinds of stories we usually tell and disrupting our productive activities.

We are not alone in tending to stick to craft rather than consider creativity. Our stories often involve other people. The results of our stories often affect other people. We coordinate with others, work in teams with others, act in organizations with others, get permission from others, and more. All of that coordination requires considerable work to develop and maintain. Just being able to communicate with other people requires a reasonably high degree of mutual understanding.[1] If we change our perspectives, then we are at risk of being out of sync with others, misunderstood by others when we try to communicate, and even in conflict with others who believe differently. Others often say, for example, "I don't get it" or "That won't work" when we share new ideas. No one else might value the inventions or enlightenments we produce, and our ability to predict others' reactions is limited.[2] Changing the PAGES in our own perspectives can come at the cost of no longer being on the same page with others.

Sticking with craft rather than pursuing creativity is partly due to our emotional reactions to craft and creativity. People tend to prefer a sure gain to a potentially larger but uncertain gain.[3] We can be unduly averse to uncertainty, as the feeling of uncertainty itself is typically experienced as a negative emotion.[4] And creativity often generates feelings of uncertainty.[5] If we go ahead with creativity and are successful, then we get the honor of knowing that we have been wrong all along, and sometimes wrong in a very obvious and stupid way.[6] Thus the typical tally of emotional experiences tends to be positive for craft and negative for creativity.

Sticking with craft appears to require less effort. For example, the great oracle Google defines *habit* (our most typical craft) as "A regular tendency or practice, *especially one that is hard to give up* [emphasis added]."[7] When we use craft, we feel as if we understand what is happening. We feel we can track our progress toward our goals.[8] We can explain what we are doing and why. We can be confident that we will finish our stories and produce results. To the extent that we are committed to the assumptions in our perspectives and so believe, implicitly or explicitly, in the correctness of our stories, then the seeming productivity of craft is a bit of a trap.[9] If a better way is currently inconceivable, and the pressure and rewards of performing are high, then adhering to craft seems like the smart choice.[10] We will be doing what we believe is effective.

For these and many other reasons, we are not likely to perceive entering into the creative process an obvious winning move.[11] Before we turn our stoplight red, we typically want to evaluate whether the benefits will be worthwhile. But because our perspective is the tool for making this assessment, it is very hard to generate an accurate impression. Yet it is almost surely the case that we should be creative more often than we are.[12] Thus there is a need to push back against the tendencies just discussed so that we initiate creativity more often.

It might seem a bit funny to make a big deal over the need to initiate a creative effort. We might think, "We can simply choose to be creative." And we can certainly make a deliberate effort to try to change our perspective. But most of the time we do not get some clear signal to be creative. Craft usually keeps us occupied. All of us have certainly been in meetings in which leaders called for creative solutions, but such events are usually a prompt for creativity about as much as a trip to the dentist is a prompt for joy. Absent significant pain, it is unlikely. One reason for the dearth of creativity is the failure to initiate creativity, which means that part of the craft of creativity is simply getting started.

A review of the research literature as well as our interviews shows that there are four main **cues** that can indicate it is worth stopping to change perspective. The **impasse** cue is the sense that craft does not offer a way forward. The **dissatisfaction** cue is the sense that craft will only bring sub-par results. The **surprise** cue is the sense that craft did not allow for something that occurred in the episode. The **crosstalk** cue is the sense that something in one story could apply to a different story. Each of these cues presents people with a chance to change their perspective. We may not respond to the cue by changing our perspective. We may not set ourselves up to experience the cue. The craft of creativity includes practices that lead to experiencing these cues and to capitalizing on them.

IMPASSE

The **impasse** cue is the feeling that we are stuck and that there is nothing we can do to productively advance our story.[13] It could be that there are no actions that will individually or collectively work to transform the parts, or that the goal is unreachable. It might also be that we are sure that the event has no good resolution, or none that we, given our self-concept, would care to dignify. Impasse is a cue to consider changing our perspective because an impasse implies that otherwise our story will pause or end. Thus we have little to lose in considering a change to our perspective because our current perspective is not helping anyway.

For impasses to be a cue to creativity, we have to experience one. This is not a foregone conclusion. We do plenty of activities and never encounter an impasse. Even if we fail, we do not have to conclude that we are stuck. We can just decide that we were unlucky or that it is a difficult situation. For example, consider the mutilated checkerboard problem (Figure 5.1).[14] The challenge is to determine whether and how one might use thirty-one dominoes to cover a checkerboard with two opposing corners removed. Each domino covers two squares.

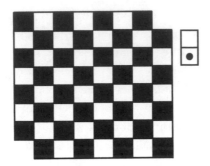

FIGURE 5.1. The Mutilated Checkerboard and a Domino

This problem does not require us to generate many PAGES for our perspective. But the few parts and actions can be combined in a great many sequences. For example, we can put a domino in one corner, and then place another after it, and work our way around the perimeter of the board. Then we can turn and spiral in toward the center. Or we can try to cover one column at a time. There are many patterns for placing the dominoes that we can try.

It is common for people to spend thirty minutes or more trying one configuration of dominoes after another. Some people have spent hours.[15] People spend their time trying to find just the right pattern for laying out the dominoes to make it work. Because we are unable to imagine all possible configurations, it is easy to think that the right one is just a few steps away. Because we do not remember everything we have tried, it is easy to repeat failed sequences of actions. Further, because we expect that events like this have solutions, it is common to conclude that even if we have failed to generate a workable solution, we might have done so. We can spend quite a lot of time just using our perspectives.

The mutilated checkerboard problem is actually a bit cruel. There are sixty-two squares to cover, and there are thirty-one dominoes that each cover two squares. So it appears that we should have all that we need to solve the problem. However, it is impossible to place thirty-one dominoes in an ordinary way and cover all sixty-two squares.[16] Could we solve the problem in a creative way? Absolutely. We could "mutilate" the dominoes, for example, in a similar way as the checkerboard. But that is only a question we can ask if we are prompted to switch from craft to creativity. If we do not experience an impasse, then we cannot count on the impasse cue to nudge us to change our perspective.

Perspectives limit our thinking about what is conceivable. This often includes limiting our thinking from recognizing that something is impossible and limiting our thinking from recognizing how narrow the set of conceivable possibilities really is. When thinking about how our stories might go, we often only consider a few choices for what might happen and ignore the rest.

It can be shocking to realize just how many possibilities we routinely dismiss. For example, if we restore our checkerboard and start a game of ordinary checkers, we might think about a handful of moves. Over the course of a game, we might consider one hundred moves or even two hundred moves if we are particularly thorough. Yet checkers offers as many possible moves (at least 10^{20}) as the number of words spoken by all the people who have ever lived (about 10^9 words * 10^{11} people). Just using our perspective on the game of checkers can provide us with more actions than we could ever attempt. We often fail to experience an impasse simply because situations provide us with opportunities to take so many actions that we run out of time before we run out of actions we can try.

We also fail to experience an impasse because we can explain failures and stoppages in other ways. If we are unable to use our perspectives to advance our stories, we can use our perspectives to explain why we are stuck. For example, we realize that there are other actions we did not take. It is easy to imagine that somewhere in a multitude of possibilities exists a sequence of actions that would have gotten us to our goal. More generally, we have many applicable concepts to help us explain why actions did not lead us to resolutions. Perhaps it is bad luck. Perhaps something is broken. Maybe we made a mistake. Maybe another person will be more receptive. We have so many ways of explaining away failures, stoppages, and other reasons we did not reach our goal that we rarely feel that our perspectives are wrong. Instead, we find other explanations for why an outcome occurred.

It gets easier to find reasonable rationalizations for failures when we have more experience. The more we have developed our craft and the more we have told similar stories in the past, the less likely we are to experience impasses. Expertise is not usually a liability, but when it comes to impasses, it certainly can be. Experts typically know how to resolve their stories. Experts typically have learned not to bother trying to fix some challenges that pop up in their stories. These triumphs of efficiency will also deepen their commitments to the assumptions in their perspectives.

To question our perspectives can be to question our sense of ourselves as competent people. That is, in addition to the cognitive challenges of realizing that we are at an impasse, there are also motivational reasons for why we do not think of ourselves as being stuck. Admitting we are stuck is unpleasant. It might signal that our craft is inadequate and, in a way, that we ourselves are inadequate. Thus we can avoid drawing the conclusion that we are at an impasse because we do not wish to admit our limits. It is more comforting to conclude that there is no way around the impasse, or that the event does not warrant the effort to overcome the impasse. Perhaps this story is not worth the trouble, or maybe we can return to this story later. There is no rule that says we have to finish every story. As W. C. Fields famously put it, "If at first you don't succeed, try, try again. Then quit. There's no point in being a damn fool about it."

Thus the challenge to leveraging the impasse cue to foster creativity is that we have to be willing to quit our current perspective. We have to be willing and able to recognize that we are stuck, that there is still the possibility of identifying actions that could lead us forward, and that it is worth trying to identify them. We have to believe that a different perspective might help and that we might generate one. The more we develop our craft of creativity, the more sensitive we are likely to be to the impasse cue.[17]

One way to advance our craft of creativity is to recognize that there are two types of impasse that we experience. One can be called a *dead end* impasse. A dead end impasse results from moving our story to a place where no further actions seem possible and therefore no good resolution seems possible. This kind of impasse is very common in the middle of a story. Dead end impasses are normally what we think about when we talk about impasses.[18]

Dead end impasses often suggest that we need to break a commitment to a current assumption, and thus need an insight, if not also an enlightenment or invention, to resolve our story. For example, master mechanic Merv DeMello told a story about a dead end impasse that resulted in creative products. DeMello and his team have been fixing cars for decades. They have well-developed perspectives for handling all manner of episodes. One common episode is fixing an air intake manifold. An air intake manifold is basically a series of pipes that deliver air to the engine. Gas engines burn gasoline, and burning requires oxygen. The air intake manifold provides just the right amount of oxygen. DeMello told us that for some cars, air intake manifolds have holes that require small plastic bushings (plastic rings or cylinders that line a hole) to seal a connection and so minimize air leaks. The challenge is that these plastic bushings wear out and need replacing. Typically, a mechanic can use one finger to gently push a new bushing into a hole when replacing one. But as car parts have become more sophisticated, they have made use of smaller and more delicate parts in harder-to-reach places. In some recent models, no mechanic can reach a hand to where the plastic bushings go. The typical craft action no longer worked. A craft resolution would have been to remove the entire air intake manifold to provide access to the plastic bushings. But this is a long, expensive process to replace a few cheap plastic parts, and it conflicted with DeMello's self-concept as an honorable and skilled mechanic. He hit a dead end impasse.

DeMello had an insight that, while a human hand could not reach the location of the plastic bushings, a long, thin spongy tool could reach the location. This was an insight for DeMello because long thin tools tend to be metal, and that would make steadying the bushing as you pushed it into a hole very difficult. But a spongy rubber material could act like a finger, enabling mechanics to do the job. Thus the dead end impasse led to an insight, which in turn led to an invention. That invention then proved useful in an array of other stories to help fix other problems. A dead end impasse led DeMello to add a new tool to his toolbox.

The second type of impasse is a *blank page* impasse. Here, instead of being in the middle of a story as in a dead end impasse, we are at the start of a new story. If you have stared at a canvas and not known what to paint, stared at a screen and not known what to write, or sat in front of a piano and not known what to play, then you have experienced a blank page impasse. A blank page impasse follows from, well, blank PAGES. We do not have a sufficiently developed perspective to guide us in identifying and selecting responses. The situation itself provides little guidance for what to retrieve from long term memory. When we can do anything, we often do nothing—having too many choices often leads to making no choice.[19] We do not have enough guidance on how to start the story.

Artists face the challenge of blank page impasses more often than most others. One approach is to begin with an arbitrary action just to have a starting point.[20] For example, producer James Thane Robeson talked about using prerecorded drumbeats to get his thinking going when writing a new musical part. The drumbeat can be modified later or removed altogether, but a drumbeat often provides enough structure for him to start building other parts on top of it. The blank page impasse helps in understanding why imposing constraints can benefit creativity.

The blank page impasse also helps explain the value of problem finding. While there are many discussions of problem solving, the idea of problem finding is less well known. Two scholars, Jacob Getzels and Mihalyi Csikszentmihalyi, realized in their classic work with art students on creativity that they could trace how effective the students were at, in our terms, overcoming the blank page impasse by considering multiple possible perspectives.[21] The two scholars provided art students with a table of odds and ends and then asked them to generate a drawing. The art students whose drawings were rated as less creative rapidly set up a few objects and the basic composition of their drawings and spent most of their time filling in their initial idea. The students whose drawings were rated as more creative spent a greater proportion of their time figuring out what they were going to draw and how they were going to draw it. More time spent formulating the problem was indicated by the number of items they considered including in the drawing, the number of compositions, and similar indications of time and effort spent developing possible perspectives. Thus a blank page impasse, like a dead end impasse, can be an opportunity for considering alternative perspectives.

If impasses are useful cues to prompt creativity, then, ironically, it could be useful to experience being stuck more often. It is not particularly pleasant to feel stuck, though. It is not fun to feel as if we have failed. It is humbling to feel that we do not know what to do. But if we are willing to entertain those costs for the sake of prompting ourselves to change our perspectives, then there are a few ways to help ourselves get stuck more often.

One way to help spur impasses, following from the Getzels and Csikszentmihalyi work on problem finding, is to force ourselves to avoid trying to solve a problem but just consider different ways of thinking about the problem. We can consider what we would do if we were starting from nothing. We can talk to someone who does not work in our area and consider what they are drawn to. We can accompany different kinds of people who are involved in the same situations we are in. We can ask questions and listen to others. The critical issue is not allowing ourselves to begin using a perspective. Instead, we just try to form different possible perspectives.[22]

A second way to identify an impasse is to track the progress toward some goal and to identify when the story seems to stall. It does not even need to be our progress. For example, operations professor and entrepreneur Sridhar Tayur was working on a way for companies to manage their inventories. The specific problem he was considering had been puzzling operations professors for about thirty-five years. Most professors had tried using various versions of a technique called stochastic dynamic programming. Tayur thought, "If no one in the field had been able to crack it with this approach, what are the odds that one more guy is going to do it? . . . I thought there must be something wrong with that approach *in itself.*" Tayur saw that though many had characterized the problem as that type of event, with such events progress was always stalled. Interestingly, his self-concept gave him both the confidence to try something new and the humility to not try the same thing and expect a different outcome. He felt equal in skill to the others who had worked on the problem, so the problem seemed like something he could tackle. Yet his equality in skill made him realize that if he attempted a solution in a similar way, he would probably get the same unsuccessful result. So he thought, "If not stochastic dynamic programming, then what?" and started his journey into the void. It was ultimately successful when he changed how he thought about the kind of event he was solving, shifting from discrete units of time to continuous flows of time. Thus, by candidly confronting the lack of progress by others when using the current perspective, Tayur realized there was an impasse and so it was worth considering how to change his perspective.[23]

A third way to experience impasses more often is to set and commit to unreasonably high goals. After all, one way to reach an impasse is to find that we are unable to reach our goals. We are less likely to be able to meet hard goals than easy goals, so setting a challenging goal can help spur impasses. An unreasonably high goal is important because if the goal is reasonable, then we will probably just try to use craft to meet it. After all, it is our current perspective that leads us to decide whether a goal is merely challenging or unreasonably high. So it is most often the case that a goal that seems unreasonably high will push us to experience an impasse that prompts us to consider how we might change our perspectives. We need to commit to the unreasonably high goal though, because otherwise we will simply give up rather than work through the impasse and undertake the effort to navigate the void.

Choreographer Dan Joyce told us of how he spurs creative performances from students using unreasonably high goals. For example, about four weeks into his dance performance class, he will say with a tone of disappointment, "People, we have been at this for weeks now and I haven't seen anyone dance on the walls. What is the problem here?" Students will of course be confused and try to accommodate. Most will fail. That is good in and of itself, as students learn that failing is a normal part of being creative, and be less scared of failing in the future. But a few students will find ways to use props to dance on the walls, or the ceiling, or something even more interesting.

Unreasonable goals are also sometimes discussed in the business world.[24] For example, Google encourages its employees to adopt goals to make products

10 times better, not 10 percent better.[25] Increasing performance by 10 percent is often a perfectly reasonable goal at their company, but because it is reasonable it can encourage people to try to use their current perspectives to attain it. In contrast, a goal to make something ten times better probably means rethinking it altogether.

There is a great deal of research about setting goals, so the recommendation to set unreasonable goals needs to be put into context. The point here is only that committing to what appears to be an unreasonable goal, when we have the self-confidence, resources, and interest to pursue it, is likely to force impasses that will then cue an attempt to change our perspective to find a way to reach the goal. This does not mean that unreasonable goals are always the right ones to generate. If we understand the story we wish to write, and craft knowledge is all we need to write it, then committing to specific, concrete, challenging goals is the best move.[26] If we do not understand very much, then a goal to learn more is helpful.[27] If we have a pretty good but still incomplete understanding, then we might commit to pursue a specific but abstract goal.[28] Or we might set an unreasonable goal. Just as creativity should be used judiciously, so too should impasses.

DISSATISFACTION

An impasse means we are stuck and do not have a way forward. A related cue, **dissatisfaction**, is a feeling that, while we have a way forward, it is not one that we find appealing. We may be at the beginning, the middle, or the end of a story. The dissatisfaction cue arises when we feel unhappy about how we are about to proceed, how we are proceeding, or how we just proceeded. Whereas an impasse involves responding to external feedback from the world that, despite our wishes, all is not proceeding well, dissatisfaction is internal feedback that our current story is not living up to our hopes.

For example, early in his career, Sridhar Tayur was given a summer project by his advisor. He worked on an optimization problem using a standard method, but he was not happy about it. "We got it to work but it was so clumsy . . . and I kept thinking 'man this is so dirty' . . . it was inelegant. It bugged me." This is dissatisfaction. It is a burr under the saddle, an irritant that can promote a desire to find a better way. It relates to elegance. As Tayur said, "Elegance is not something that should be considered discretional, but rather an intrinsic feature of a proposed solution. The tragedy in some academic circles is that they make elegance the 'whole thing,' losing sight of the problem to be solved, while the pragmatic sort do not have the luxury for aesthetic considerations. The intersection of elegance and effectiveness is the essential intellectual challenge." Often dissatisfaction comes from an imbalance.

We tend to experience dissatisfaction in relation to the higher-order aspects of perspective—the goals, events, and self-concepts. We may be able to use actions on parts, but this may not fit with our other goals. We might reach a goal but think it is not a good goal to have. We can be dissatisfied with the event because we feel like our story, the way we apply actions to parts to get to the goal, is clumsy or inefficient. We might not like the kind of events we included in the story or how the event resolved. Ultimately, though, dissatisfaction rests on our self-concepts. We want better stories for ourselves than this!

Dissatisfaction tends to result from the values that are integral to our self-concepts. The people we interviewed were just as prone to agonize over a painting as they were to agonize over a legal brief. Both the builder and the musician could fail to be satisfied with their performances even though those performances pleased those who paid for them. The reason that people can feel dissatisfied with what they create even though it counts as a resolution to their stories is that they have beliefs about excellence in the domains with which they identify. Those we interviewed used words such as *amateurish, mundane, overly technical, ugly*. We heard these applied to dance pieces as often as to computer programs.

Dissatisfaction is a signal that there should be a better way, and that we do not want to accept a mediocre way. Yet often we do not have an alternative in mind. That is, if we could think of a more satisfying way to write our story, we would. But we do not yet have such a way. This is why the dissatisfaction cue can motivate us to change our perspective. It might prod us to form better stories, stories we can be proud of generating. For example, home designer and builder Ted Daniels spent extra time and money to generate an invention that would allow a drain in a bathroom that he had designed to integrate and fit just so with the shower basin and underlying plumbing. It was a detail that his customer would never notice. But it mattered to Daniels, leading him into a creative process.

Dissatisfaction typically arises as we are using our perspectives. We perceive the current condition and evaluate it using our perspective. We inevitably are evaluating what is happening because we need to choose how to respond. We have the potential to take stock of how well we did, how well we are doing, or how well we are likely to do. If we do, then we can assess how satisfied we are.

Embracing the notion that something is not good enough yet, and hence we are dissatisfied, can be motivating. Negative emotions can spur creativity.[29] This use of dissatisfaction is an extension to the work on intrinsic motivation or passion.[30] The usual argument is that people who are passionate about a subject will spend more time exploring possibilities about the subject. As a result, they are more likely to find new perspectives interesting and new products worth the effort to generate. Dissatisfaction is the other side of the coin. The people we interviewed were bothered by inelegance, not curious and exploring, when they were dissatisfied. While intrinsic motivation can be a siren song drawing people to explore, dissatisfaction is an ugly racket pushing people away. Both can motivate the changing of perspectives.

Of all the cues, dissatisfaction is probably the one we are most likely to dismiss. There are many reasons to push it away. We have many of the same kinds of issues that we had with impasse in terms of being able to imagine that there are craft alternatives that will fix our dissatisfaction if we can just find them. We also have the same kinds of issues in terms of the omnipresent option to accept defeat and keep with the status quo. The impulse to accept the status quo is even stronger with dissatisfaction than with impasse because there is progress. We have something that is actually a way forward, a resolution. Given the demands on our time, that is difficult to overlook. Dissatisfaction can be interpreted as a fact of life—things could always be better, but resources are finite and time is short. Another story is calling for our attention, and so we decide that this one is good enough or at least not bad enough to make us stop. Addressing dissatisfaction can be hard to justify.

We can have difficulty justifying dissatisfaction to others. Our dissatisfaction is often socially tempered. As dissatisfaction stems from an internal gap between how our stories are developing and our self-concepts, others may not experience the gap. Others often think the story is fine. If others are not challenging the status quo, then perhaps we are wrong or foolish to be dissatisfied. We might be labeled a dreamer, a whiner, a perfectionist, presumptuous, not a team player, or any number of other negative terms. Sometimes dissatisfaction is suppressed in order to maintain harmony.

Our reasons for dissatisfaction may be inconceivable to others. Can you conceptualize what beautiful equations look like? Most mathematicians can; there is even a term, "poetry math," that some mathematicians use. But it is understandable that non-mathematicians might find dissatisfaction with an equation's ugliness an uninteresting luxury rather than a crucial driver of progress.

We can have difficulty justifying dissatisfaction to ourselves. We may not be able to point to any specific issue with the story as a problem or deficiency. Sometimes we can put our finger on what is bothering us, but often we just feel uneasy or frustrated. Dissatisfaction frequently grows over time rather than arriving in a specific moment, making it difficult to identify and difficult to decide that now is the time to act upon it. Acknowledging our own dissatisfaction as worthy of time and effort to fix may be the primary challenge to leveraging this cue.

To help stiffen your resolve to take your dissatisfaction seriously, we note that dissatisfaction was the most commonly mentioned cue among the most eminent creators we interviewed. The inability to be satisfied with stories that worked well enough differentiated those who were renowned for their creative work from those whose work was at the amateur level. It likely takes strong self-concepts for all of us to acknowledge our dissatisfaction as a basis for turning the stoplight red and going into the void, especially as others are clamoring for us to keep advancing our stories.

Our first task in using dissatisfaction effectively, then, is to treat the feeling with respect. We need to grant that our dissatisfaction has value. We should at least take it as a signal that our story deserves more careful consideration. Respect tends to increase compliance with challenging mandates[31] and deepen processing of others' requests,[32] hence we surmise that we can use it on ourselves as well. We need to take our feelings seriously as information about what we are recognizing in the environment even if the source of those feelings is hard to identify or verbalize. In the end, those feelings might turn out to be misattributed or less important than they at first felt. But they are often worth our attention, as they indicate we are recognizing that something is off.

What we are doing by taking our dissatisfaction seriously is taking our self-concepts seriously. We need to have some confidence, based on the legitimacy of our self-concepts and the values we hold as a result, to uphold our perspectives. Confidence is sometimes mistaken for the brashness of youth or ego, but it can also stem from a kind of authority that occurs when people uphold high standards for the sake of the work. People's beliefs and commitment to how stories *should* be told often distinguished novices from seasoned professionals. The professionals have been around long enough to learn to trust their own instincts, and this often is what leads them to make inconceivable improvements when others think the status quo is fine.

Interestingly, among the people we interviewed, those who were the most skilled in their craft seemed also to be the most open to the dissatisfaction of others. We consistently heard from our interviewees that the best (that is, most skilled) creators were the easiest to work with. They were the most open to addressing and remedying dissatisfaction coming from others. They were not threatened by others' dissatisfaction; they used it as a cue to explore.

People can, of course, go too far with dissatisfaction. Perfectionism can slow productive work. For example, Burt Miller, an inventor of the Pungo wine preserver, was discussing his practice of making components that are flawless, and bemoaning the time and effort it took. We asked him, "If you know that the returns have diminished, why do you keep doing it?" "Well," he said with a laugh, "that's the sickness." We certainly relate—we believe it was the Argentine writer Borges who wrote, "One publishes in order to stop editing." So dissatisfaction has its limits. But as dissatisfaction can provide a productive impulse, it can be cultivated appropriately.

Dedication to and care for one's domain, activity, or profession, through intrinsic motivation or identification with the domain or purpose, can promote the kind of concern that could lead to productive dissatisfaction. It takes a point of view, a set of values, an aesthetic, to be dissatisfied. Thus it is not just care and high aspirations, but also a refined sense of specific criteria or style.

SURPRISE

The third cue to change our perspectives is **surprise**. Surprise is our reaction when the situation does not fit what we expected on the basis of our story. Surprise is thus not simply a failure when we apply our actions or some unfortunate event that pops up. We can understand and even expect failures as well as normal, chance variations. Surprise is an alteration to the situation that we cannot explain—something that we thought could not happen, even though we see that it did. It is our inability to assimilate what we perceive using our perspective that makes a situation surprising. Surprises can motivate us to try to change our perspective because they signal something is wrong with our understanding of what is happening in the story. Surprises emerge when we perceive a situation that does not fit with our story, and then we fail to be able to add to our perspective to account for what we perceived. Something about our current perspective is wrong or missing.

Surprises have multiple sources. We might have used an action on a part and the outcome was not what we expected. Or something in the situation happened, and now we are unable to make sense of how it happened or what it means: "John quit his job? I thought he loved his job!" Magic tricks and jokes often rest on setting up expectations that will then be violated, generating surprise. Surprises are usually experienced as surprising not because of anything inherent to what happened, but rather because our stories had made that happening inconceivable. We know that many people quit their jobs. Our friend quitting is only surprising because of our assumptions about our friend and his relation to his job. If we knew that our friend hated his job, the news would not have been a surprise.

Next to impasse, surprise is probably the most familiar cue to creativity. There are entire books on products resulting from surprises.[33] Great scientific enlightenments have come from surprises. For example, Alexander Fleming was surprised that bacteria were not growing as he expected them to, thus paving the way for knowledge about antibiotics. An "Aha!" moment is a surprise. So too is a, "Hmmm, that's funny" moment. If we failed to expect something, then the surprise indicates that there is something for us to pay attention to. Surprise increases arousal and amplifies our emotional experience.[34] Surprises can be happy or unpleasant. Surprises can resolve quickly or leave us in confusion. In all cases though, surprises tell us there is something to be learned. It is why surprises are the most likely to lead to an enlightenment. If we are unable to explain something, it means our knowledge on that topic needs development.

We are not often surprised. Perspectives are based on experience. This means that our perspectives usually lead us to expect what actually happens. And when it doesn't, we can usually figure out why it didn't. Our perspectives provide sufficient flexibility that, even though many things can happen in the world, we can explain most of them. In our offices, much goes on, and much is mundane and typical. Sometimes things are atypical, but these rarities are still easily explained. Much of what we experience is sufficiently ordinary that we can use our perspectives to fit the story to what happened. When an experience is not, we can usually add to our perspectives and accommodate it that way.

Our perspectives also reduce our likelihood of experiencing surprises because they focus our attention in any situation. Our perspectives indicate what is important and what is not. Perspectives keep us from noticing activities and events that do not conform to what we think is important in our story. We experience fewer surprises than we might because we do not form expectations about and do not notice many of the happenings around us. For example, the psychologist Dan Simons, in a long series of research, has shown that people fail to notice all manner of changes and unusual items because they were attending elsewhere.[35] In one study, a student asked someone for directions, and in the middle of the response, two people walked through the conversation carrying a door. When they walked by, the student who had asked for directions switched places with one of the people carrying the door. The question was, once the door was no longer in the way, what would the person giving directions do? In the majority of instances, those giving directions simply continued, failing to notice that they were now giving directions to a different person.[36] Our experience does not provide us with many instances of people switching places, and so we fail to notice and are not surprised. Experience trains us to ignore variations that have not mattered in the past.[37] Accordingly, a major reason we are not surprised is because we do not perceive the information in situations that our perspectives lead us away from noticing. We have no idea how many biologists before Alexander Fleming could have made the same observation but were not surprised by what they were seeing.

Even if we are surprised, this is not a guarantee of changing our perspective. Our perspective will provide ample ways to explain away surprises, just as we do for impasses. For example, Thao-Chi Vo was a student studying neuroscience. She was examining the effect of high potassium concentrations outside neurons, which she expected would increase the concentration of potassium inside neurons. The surprise in this case was that the increase in potassium outside neurons *decreased* the level of potassium inside them. What she knew about potassium, osmosis, and neurons told her that this was not supposed to happen. Her first thought was not, "I have discovered something" but rather, "I made a mistake in the procedure." She re-ran the experiment a number of times and with a number of tissue samples and got the same result. She tested what happened when the concentration of potassium outside neurons was low, and found that the concentration inside neurons was higher.

The original finding was not an error, it was a signal that there was something to learn.[38] But the first impulse upon experiencing the surprise was to try to use perspective to explain it away as a simple mistake. Her perspective did not just make the mistake story possible, it made it easy—she was an inexperienced student, so she probably messed something up. We often dismiss surprises because we find a reason with which to explain them away.[39]

Sometimes we ignore surprises altogether. When we encounter something surprising, we can acknowledge surprise but think no further about it. This is especially easy if the surprise is not central to our story. After all, the surprise could be a chance event or part of some other aspect in the story that we don't really care about. And because it will take more effort to find out if it is something worth our attention, surprises may turn into shrugs and then be forgotten.

However, following up on the surprise can yield great discoveries, as shown by two researchers at Bell Labs in Holmdel, New Jersey, Arno Penzias and Robert Wilson. They were doing experiments on radio waves using a very sensitive listening device called "The Holmdel Horn." The radio waves they were detecting were extremely weak, so they needed to get rid of all possible interference noise. As they were working with the technology, they were surprised to find that they could not get rid of a noise. They started to trace the source of the noise and guessed that it was from a pigeon nest inside one of their devices. They took multiple new actions to remove the pigeons. But the noise remained. Rather than dismissing the surprising noise, they continued trying to generate an explanation for it, which led them to discover evidence for a theory by the astrophysicists Dicke, Peebles, and Wilkinson, who had proposed that there should be residual noise in the universe if the universe was not in a steady state but expanding. It turned out that the noise Penzias and Wilson discovered was an exact fit to the noise that these researchers had theorized. In the end, the surprising noise was not pigeons but some of the first evidence for the Big Bang theory of the universe. Many surprises turn out to be something as uninteresting as pigeons nesting, but then again, some of them turn out to be major enlightenments about the nature of the universe.

Finally, we can fail to be surprised because we fail to generate expectations in the first place. For example, Pavlov was a scientist studying digestion. He used dogs in his research. Pavlov would come into the room with the dogs and provide them with food. One day, he was surprised to find that the dogs were salivating *before* they got the food. Had Pavlov not been focused on salivation, had he not had a theory of salivation that predicted that salivation came after tasting food, he might not have been surprised by dogs salivating before receiving food. But he was surprised, and that surprise led him to try to understand why a dog might salivate before tasting food. Pavlov ended up not only making large contributions to the science of digestion (winning a Nobel Prize in physiology) but also generating a new science of learning, and is often considered one of the most influential twentieth-century scientists as a result.

All of these illustrations show ways in which we can miss surprises. They are also illustrations of the value of surprise as a cue to change our perspectives. The question then becomes what we can do to help ourselves be surprised and consider the possibility of changing our perspectives when we experience surprise. One way to facilitate exploiting surprise is slack resources.[40] If we are working every minute with every dollar just to advance our stories, then we do not have any time to think. Surprises are a distraction, a signal of error, and unlikely to be tolerated. In contrast, spare time and extra dollars allow us an opportunity to stop using our perspectives and so change them.

In addition to resource slack, there is also a social version of slack that can help us to address rather than dismiss surprises. It is common for social situations to encourage conformity. Surprises represent deviation, and so are not often well received. As a result, having a basis of credibility or respect can make others tolerant of surprising deviations and therefore open to considering their worth.[41] It is an old but still useful idea.

A further reason to attend to surprises is a concern for the story. A lack of curiosity[42] or a lack of desire to reopen seemingly settled issues[43] can reduce our willingness to pursue explanations for surprises. In contrast, a desire to understand and its accompanying interest in solving mysteries support leveraging a surprise to change our perspectives. A desire to understand would lead us to try to explain what is going on around us, and so form expectations. If our desire to understand situations is general, then it might expand the range of happenings in situations to which we try to attend.[44] These tendencies, in turn, would increase the likelihood of experiencing and pursuing surprises.

In addition to widespread curiosity, a habit of forming guesses can also help us make use of surprise as a cue to creativity. We can try to predict what will occur. We can form a hypothesis and generate a test, conducting an experiment to check our intuitions. We can also make a habit of trying different variations. For example, Grammy-winning producer Bob Dawson explained that he would sometimes make a rough demo of a song he wanted to produce, and then tell the studio musicians, "Let's go run it down some." Bob encourages everyone to avoid having a firm view of the song and coaxes musicians to "just try it." We can court surprise, in other words, by generating situations in which we are not sure what will happen and we are monitoring the outcome. The world need not always come to us. We can generate situations that have the potential to provide us with something unexpected. Because we often overestimate how much we understand in a situation or how well we can predict what will happen, generating surprise might be easier than we imagine.[45]

Finally, we need to have enough openness that we do not simply ignore the implications of the surprise.[46] For example, apparently popsicles came from a boy leaving flavored water with a stirring stick in it outside in the cold over-night.[47] Apparently chocolate chip cookies came from the erroneous use of semi-sweet chocolate instead of baker's chocolate.[48] Someone had to be open and curious enough to examine these surprising outcomes rather than just throwing away their mistakes.

CROSSTALK

The fourth cue is **crosstalk**. We experience crosstalk when we feel that something in one story connects to a different story. When we first encounter a situation, we perceive it and recognize aspects of the situation as instances of knowledge we have learned from experience. As we draw from the same knowledge base to form perspectives on many stories, it is often possible for one story to remind us of another story because they draw on similar knowledge. Consequently, even if the overall perspectives for two stories differ considerably, if there are strong, focused similarities we may notice the connection. This connection can then serve as a basis for changing our perspectives.

For example, engineering professor Brian Mark was working on what is called "cognitive radio," a way for broadcasters to sense, in real time, unused radio frequencies so that it would be possible to use radio bandwidth efficiently. Brian was also involved in another project on speech recognition. He realized in a meeting about speech recognition that the mathematical approach he was using for speech recognition would help in recognizing unused radio frequencies, and that provided a breakthrough on the cognitive radio project.

Whereas the other cues tend to be about noticing issues with respect to the currently active story, crosstalk happens across stories. What we wind up seeing is a correspondence in some portion of the PAGES. This means that the crosstalk cue typically provides not only a prompt to change our perspectives but also a specific starting point for how to do so. The surprise cue indicates there is something to explain but may not provide any clue about how to do so. The crosstalk cue not only indicates that there might be a connection but also usually indicates an initial link as a starting point for consideration. This means that the crosstalk cue is not just a potential suggestion to change our perspectives, but also usually provides a discovery about what the change might be.

What the link is between stories can vary considerably, and only some kinds of links are likely to be of any use. The most common crosstalk is the most mundane and least likely to promote changes to our perspectives. We may notice correspondence between stories because the two stories are nearly identical. For example, if we hear a story about calling a box office for tickets to a play, it might well remind us of a time when we called another box office for tickets to another play.[49] This kind of crosstalk reinforces our current perspective. We simply call that "experience."

A second kind of correspondence between stories is also mundane but even less helpful. These are instances in which one story is like another story because they share some distinctive parts or actions. For example, one story about an armadillo might remind us of another story about an armadillo for the simple reason that we do not know many stories about armadillos. However, this does not mean the connection between the two stories is of any use for fruitfully changing our perspective. The two stories might otherwise have nothing to do with one another. This form of crosstalk we might call surface.

A similarly unhelpful form of crosstalk arises from stories that are close together in time or situation. Perhaps we just read something in the newspaper on the way to work and then when we arrive at work we see a similarity. Or, perhaps we hear a story while walking the dog and talking to a friend on the phone, and this reminds us of another story we heard while walking the dog and talking to another friend. The link between stories may arise just because of accidental juxtaposition in time or context. The two stories might otherwise have little to do with one another. This is also a form of surface crosstalk.

These common forms of crosstalk that are unhelpful for changing our perspectives are one reason that the experience of crosstalk itself need not be taken seriously. That one story reminds us of another or seems connected to another need not indicate anything much. Thus it is easy to dismiss the cue as unhelpful. Crosstalk can seem to be a distraction, a tangent, an oddity that stops us from advancing one story and provides us no benefit to another story.

Where crosstalk is actually beneficial as a basis for changing our perspectives is when the patterns among concepts indicate that the goals or events bear a non-obvious similarity. While we often link stories on the basis of an obvious part or action similarity, we often do not link stories if they do not have obvious part or action similarities. A story about car salespeople failing to move cars off the lot is taken to be different from a story about accountants, and these two stories are taken to be different from a story about a theater opening. But the particular parts involved in a story are not the reason for linking two stories. If the story about car salespeople concerns their being unmotivated, and the theater story is about why people are motivated to buy tickets to see a play, then perhaps there is something to be learned from crosstalk between the two stories. Both are about customer motivation and sales. If the story is about car dealerships and the depreciation of the cars' value the longer they sit on the lot, then perhaps the accounting story would provide useful crosstalk to the car dealer owners. The reason crosstalk will be useful has little to do with obvious surface similarities; it has much more to do with the pattern of the PAGES. It is not important that we are talking about accounting, theater, or car dealerships. What is important are the larger patterns about how the concepts that are playing roles in the perspective fit together, and the similarity between the patterns across stories. It is that pattern similarity from which we can learn how to change our perspectives.[50] That is the form of crosstalk that is most likely to be useful.

Our tendency to focus on mundane part and action similarities across stories rather than pattern similarities across stories is why useful crosstalk is rare. The mundane forms of crosstalk distract us, and the failure to experience useful crosstalk is widespread and well documented. For example, a study of mid-career consultants learning to be better negotiators presented the consultants with two negotiation stories.[51] One was about two brothers selling their farm, the other was about a buyer and a seller arranging the shipment of some goods. The consultants read one story right after the other. In both stories, the parties faced exactly the same kind of challenge and resolved it using exactly the same kind of contract. The similarities between the stories were important: one group of consultants was asked explicitly if the two stories were similar, and about 70 percent described how they faced the same kind of challenge and resolved it using the same kind of contract. However, another group of consultants was not told anything about comparing the two stories. They just read the stories one after another. For this group, only about 15 percent even mentioned the first story when analyzing the solution in the second story immediately afterward. There was nothing wrong with these consultants! Rather, it simply does not tend to occur to us to make comparisons of PAGES across stories when they do not have obvious part and action similarities. It does not naturally occur to us that it will be helpful. We think that we are on to a different story.

The primary challenge of crosstalk is noticing a connection between a new story and a prior story that will result in a changed perspective to one of the stories. More often we connect two stories but fail to draw out anything new to change either perspective from the connection. The car sales story might remind us of selling tickets for the play, but we might stop there and leave it at that. Both are stories about selling things. That, in itself, is not useful because it indicates no changes to our assumptions. One story has to involve something that is not evident in the other. Perhaps in the car sales story, incentive-based pay for car salespeople is common, but we never thought to provide incentive-based pay for theater box office staff.

Thus successful crosstalk is difficult because it requires a number of conditions to be true. First, we have to see beyond the surface parts and actions to the patterns among PAGES in both situations. Second, we have to notice a correspondence between the patterns of PAGES in the perspectives for the two stories. Third, we have to notice that there is an aspect of one perspective that contrasts with or fills an unrecognized gap in the other perspective. We have to realize, for instance, that the car dealership and the theater are alike in some fundamental ways, but that, say, the theater has a more effective perspective on some aspects of PAGES and that the car dealership could actually apply a similar approach as well. Useful crosstalk is not all that common because so much has to line up.

A further reason that crosstalk can be limited is because we can be motivated to keep our stories separate. Anyone who has tried to give advice to a teenager can appreciate how one person can see their story as "different" and the other's experience as "irrelevant." This is actually a natural consequence of enriching our perspectives over time. As general concepts become instantiated in specific situations, we can come to focus on the particulars. We can be consumed by the details. As such concepts become embedded in particular relationships, they seem, as a structure, more distinctive. The advantage of developing a detailed perspective and story is that we can form more accurate expectations about what is happening. The disadvantage is that stories become distinct thought worlds, making it more difficult for crosstalk to spread useful knowledge.

Useful crosstalk is rare, but there are several ways to make it more likely to occur. A common prescription, but one we are skeptical about, is engaging in play. Certainly being playful can make people less concerned about staying consistent with their perspectives. This might allow us to stumble into links between stories, provided that we notice that we have made a notable connection. Yet it is neither efficient nor deep.

A more strongly supported way to increase effective crosstalk is to think about simple versions of our stories. The richer and more detailed our stories are, the more the particular parts and actions will influence the connections we make. By focusing on portions of our stories and simplifying our stories down to their essential patterns, it is more likely that later, when we are thinking about another story, we will be able to connect it with the first one.[52]

Another way to increase crosstalk is to, well, talk. Crosstalk requires putting one story aside and thinking about a different story. Thus crosstalk requires stopping working on our current story. Leaving a story open and unresolved makes it more likely it will keep buzzing about in the backs of our minds, and so be more likely to connect with new stories.[53] We can then switch to work on another story, or, far easier, we can talk to people about their stories. When we talk with other people, they tend to emphasize the gist, the essential patterns, rather than every last detail. As a result, it is easier to connect our stories to their stories.[54] In addition, by talking with different kinds of people, we will tend to hear different kinds of stories and we will tend to think about our stories in different ways, and as a result have more and more diverse opportunities for crosstalk.[55]

The hardest but most reliable way to increase crosstalk is to develop greater expertise.[56] When our stories are about topics we know well, we are more likely to find connections when we are hearing new stories. This is because expertise tends to make clearer what is an irrelevant part or action and what is an essential pattern organizing our perspectives and stories. Further, when we hear new stories, we are less likely to focus on the surface details and more likely to focus on the essential patterns. Consequently, if the most useful crosstalk is crosstalk based on essential patterns, it is helpful to develop deeper understandings and think about deeper concerns rather than surface details when we hear new stories. Part of the craft of creativity is developing the habit of clarifying the patterns in our perspectives that drive our stories so that we can cultivate the likelihood of fruitful crosstalk.[57]

CUES AS CLUES

The four cues, impasse, dissatisfaction, surprise, and crosstalk, are the most common prompts we have found for people to stop using their perspectives and the most common clues about how to start changing them. The cues have a variety of similarities and differences. In a way, impasse and dissatisfaction both indicate that there is a problem with our current perspective, and surprise and crosstalk both indicate that there is an opportunity to develop our perspective. Surprise and crosstalk typically provide crucial information about how to change our perspective, whereas impasse and dissatisfaction rarely do. Impasse and dissatisfaction can come on slowly but surprise and crosstalk, while resting on existing perspectives, happen quickly. All four cues have an emotional side to the experience of them, indicating that we should attend to our emotions for signals about opportunities to change our perspectives. Although this chapter has discussed the four cues one at a time, they have similarities and they can be experienced not just in isolation but also in combination.

For example, roughly around 1840, Charles Goodyear thought that rubber had the potential to be far more useful than it was at the time. Rubber in its raw state is sensitive to temperature and quite sticky. It would melt in the summer and crack in the winter. Thus, even though many products were made using rubber, Goodyear was dissatisfied. That dissatisfaction prodded Goodyear to experiment with ways to stabilize rubber. He started combining rubber with different chemicals and in different ways. At some point while he was working at Eagle India Rubber company, he mixed rubber and sulfur and then heated it. This led to a surprise: rather than soften when heated, the rubber hardened. The two cues, dissatisfaction and surprise, were critical to the invention of vulcanized rubber, which in turn changed manufacturing and such common products as car tires and rubber-soled shoes. The involvement of more than one cue is common in inventions. Stories can be long and take many twists and turns to reach the end. Cues are our first clue that we could be turning. Becoming more sensitive to cues is part of the craft of creativity.

PRACTICE

Vocabulary

1. **Cue**: A belief you sense during the telling of a story that alerts you to the potential utility of trying to change your perspective

2. **Impasse**: The sense that you are stuck and have no useful responses available

3. **Dissatisfaction**: The sense of being unhappy with some aspect of the story's progression

4. **Surprise**: An unexpected change to the conditions in the situation that you cannot explain using the current perspective or your current domain knowledge

5. **Crosstalk**: Noticing that some structure of PAGES from one event or story may have corresponding functions in another event or story

Exercises

Name the cues in each of the following situations.

1. George Crum kept getting the fried potatoes he served back from an unsatisfied customer who wanted them sliced thinner and fried crispier. In exasperation Crum sliced the potatoes paper thin and fried them till they were hard. The customer really liked them, and the potato chip was born.

2. Rogaine was originally a heart medicine, but the manufacturers noticed that a side effect was hair growth.

3. Bubble wrap was originally created as a textured wallpaper by Al Fielding and Marc Chavannes. (Un)fortunately this was a bit of a fad, and so the inventors tried to sell it as an insulator for greenhouses. That did not work, but when IBM announced their new 1401 variable-word-length computer, the inventors pitched bubble wrap as a packaging material for the fragile new technology. It worked.[58]

4. The standard bar code was developed in 1974, and it tended to max out at about twenty characters of data because it held data in only one direction. As more and more products came into the world and tracking became more sophisticated, more characters were needed. At first the developers stacked the bar codes on top of each other, but this had its limits and was prone to error. Eventually they developed two-directional bar codes (like the QR codes we are all familiar with).

5. The painter looked up from the canvas. "I just can't get this flower to work in this painting!"

6. "Well I don't know what to tell you. You want me to shave another $10K off this budget? I just don't see how that is going to happen."

7. "This problem seems familiar. Have I seen it before? I haven't . . . but still . . ."

8. "Hey, why haven't Cronin and Loewenstein talked about Steve Jobs? I can't figure it out!"

Answers

1. Surprise—Crum was surprised at the customer's reaction (even if he was dissatisfied with the customer).

2. Crosstalk from heart to hair.

3. Impasse (What are we gonna do with all this stuff?!?!)

4. Dissatisfaction (Stacking was an imperfect solution.)

5. Either impasse or dissatisfaction depending on what you assume about how bad the flower is and if the artist can actually fix it.

6. Impasse.

7. The beginnings of crosstalk (a faint hint).

8. Surprise!

THINKING TOOLS

There is no longer any browsing along the beaten paths; and into the primeval
forest only those may venture who are equipped with the sharpest tools.
—Heinrich Burkhardt

If a cue calls us to question our perspectives, then we are launched into the
process of changing our perspectives. We have to identify knowledge outside of
our perspectives. This means going into the void.

When we go into the void, we do not have clear guidance in our thinking as
we try to navigate the change process. Articulating PAGES can make this easier.
Yet even so, our current perspective, the very thing we are seeking to change,
exerts a pull toward consistency. That pull gets stronger the more strongly committed we are to our assumptions. In addition, our current perspective shapes
how we evaluate any possibilities we identify and provides an inclination to
discredit inconsistent interpretations—the very thing we are seeking. Thus our
task is to identify a way to restructure our perspectives, typically by identifying
alternative concepts in long-term memory.

Help in navigating the void is critical because the challenge is, at the root,
cognitive. We can be motivated to change our perspectives, maintain an openness to alternative perspectives, and utilize resources and social support for
finding and using new perspectives. Yet these are all supports to accomplishing
the cognitive work of identifying an alternative pattern of concepts. To do the
cognitive work, we need cognitive tools to guide our trip into the void so that
we return with possibilities for changing our perspectives.

Cognitive tools act on the concepts we are currently thinking about and
bring other related concepts to mind. It is a little like searching the Internet. We
can type what we want into a search box, but once we submit a search, what

comes back is governed by the search system, not us. To emphasize that the search is beyond our control is to ignore the opportunity of learning to craft better search entries. We could also use a fishing metaphor. The ocean is vast, but we can learn to better bait our hooks and cast our lines. So it is with the cognitive tools. We can learn to use the cognitive tools to probe our long-term memories more effectively and in different ways so that we are more likely to bring to mind something that could be helpful. But the tools are not wholly under our deliberate control. This is a good thing. If they were under our control, we would limit them to work within our perspectives. The cognitive tools are helpful in large part because they are not bound by our current perspectives. They can lead us to think about different and potentially inconsistent knowledge. Cognitive tools are also helpful because they are focused. They lead us to retrieve a limited amount of knowledge, meaning they do not overwhelm working memory. Learning to wield cognitive tools to navigate the void and return with concepts outside our current perspective is part of the craft of creativity.

We emphasize four cognitive tools: **activation**, **analogy**, **combination**, and **recategorization**. These are distinct, widely studied, fundamental mechanisms for processing information. Some discussions of creativity make it seem as if there is a single means to generating creative ideas—that it is all about making distant associations,[1] or it is all about making unusual combinations,[2] or it is all about allowing unconscious thought processes to have their way.[3] Our view is that each proposal captures an important aspect of how people change their perspectives, but none fully replaces the others. Other discussions emphasize that there are 1,001 ways to be creative.[4] For example, we have read long lists of games, seen piles of flash cards, heard about types of roles, and all manner of other heuristics that might prod people to think differently. Our view is that the heuristics are nearly all reducible to stimulating one or more of the four cognitive tools or simply hoping to trigger random chance. We are doubtful about relying on chance because, as with most lotteries, the odds are strongly unfavorable. We will focus instead on developing skill with the cognitive tools.

ACTIVATION

Perceiving a situation brings concepts to mind. An inference that we generate by using our perspective to advance our story can bring concepts to mind. Another influence on what comes to mind is **activation**, the cognitive mechanism that brings concepts into working memory that are associated with the concepts that are already in working memory. Experience teaches us that some concepts go together. Reading the word *bread* likely makes us think about *butter* or *jam* because these often appear together. We do not think about *lamp* or *pen* because these do not often appear with bread. Psychologists talk about activation spreading from one concept to another, making the next concept more likely to come into awareness.[5] In fact, it is probably the common use of the term *spreading* that made us think about bread and butter as an example when we talk about activation. And that is how activation works. We have one concept in mind, such as *activation*, and that brings another to mind that is commonly used with it, such as *spreading*, and that in turn makes other concepts that are also related more likely to come to mind, such as *butter* and *bread*. Of course, butter and bread do not have anything to do with the topic of activation and cognitive mechanisms. Yet because the concept of spreading is relevant both to activation and cognitive mechanisms and also to bread and butter, our thinking can progress from one to the other. And this is why activation is key for the creative process. It can lead us out beyond our current perspective. Activation spreads to any concept that has been historically related, even if it is not relevant. Activation can take us into the void.

Activation is a pervasive, automatic influence on what we think next. We think about one concept, and activation spreads to related concepts, with the most strongly related concepts in our prior experience being most likely to come to mind, all else being equal. Activation starts when we direct our attention to a particular concept. When we think of bread and butter, we are directing a lot of activation toward those concepts. Activation then spreads from every concept we are thinking about to concepts historically related to them. Consequently, if we are thinking about not just *bread* but also *butter*, then activation is most likely to bring to mind concepts that are historically related to both of these concepts, such as *knife*, *jam*, or *spreading*. As a result, activation makes it easy for us to think about familiar situations.

In a familiar situation, we perceive items that bring a few concepts to mind as interpretations of them. Activation spreading from those concepts readies us for what else we might expect to find in the situation. If we see a table, a pitcher, a small plate, a knife, and some bread, then activation is likely to lead us to think about butter. As an episode goes on, we activate concepts that come into focus at any moment. While at our favorite restaurant, spreading butter on bread, we might simply move on to thinking about drinking water from a glass and talking to a friend. We are then activating concepts such as drinking, water, glass, friend, and so forth. It is easy to bring *bread* back to mind because it is still relevant in the situation, but also because we have already activated it. And each time we do circle back around to thinking about *bread*, maybe because it is a part that we see or the recipient of an action (for example, bite), then activation from that concept will make every linked concept in long-term (semantic) memory more likely to come to mind. Though we may not consciously think about it, concepts such as baking, money, sandwich, sliced, and so on become more activated by what spreads from bread.

If this is a familiar situation for us—perhaps this is a favorite restaurant or our kitchen table at home—then activation also leverages a functional history. Such concepts are cast into familiar parts, actions, and goals, within an event and with a particular self-concept; these guide our thinking. A familiar perspective brings to mind the ideas that commonly advance our stories, with activation stimulating us to think about what normally follows, what is normally present, and what normally is related. In this way, activation usually supports craft.

What allows activation to support creativity as well as craft is that activation is not restricted by perspective.[6] We use the same concepts for one story that we use for other stories. Thus concepts in our perspective can activate historically related concepts, even those that are inconsistent with our momentary perspective. That is how we can be eating at our favorite restaurant, thinking about spreading butter on bread, and start thinking about bakeries, our salary, sandwiches, and more. These tangents as our minds wander down pathways in semantic memory, rather than our current situation, perspective, and story, can result in useless, temporary distractions. But they can also be useful.

Activation is often discussed in connection to the "Aha!" experience.[7] For example, if we reconsider the priest riddle that we discussed in an earlier chapter, we can imagine how activation might play a role. The concepts *married, divorced, woman, man,* and maybe even *polygamist* are all linked to *weddings* and also, crucially, to *priest* or *officiate*. As we think of the initial concepts, activation accumulates in related concepts. If we are not racing ahead to think about other concepts, but continually thinking about these concepts, then sufficient activation can accumulate to bring *priest* to mind.[8] The concept *priest* was not directly raised by the riddle. But because it is historically related in our experience, and therefore in semantic memory, to several concepts that were directly raised by the riddle, it can still come to mind. Activation spreads across the links in the network, and when enough accumulates in the target concept, it pops into awareness.[9] We might then discover that integrating the new concept, *priest*, into our perspective would help.

Activation is one way to guide the inquiry process to bring concepts from the void into our perspective. To use it, there has to be some basis for identifying concepts not in our perspective that nonetheless might be relevant. Normally, activation brings to mind concepts that are part of our perspectives but not what we were just thinking about, concepts that are consistent with and build on our existing perspective, or concepts that are not helpful for our perspective. Activation tends to bring to mind whatever concepts prior experience indicates are most related. We typically latch onto a strongly related concept and proceed directly to the next activated concept. Yet we could intervene in the process and so use activation deliberately in an effort to go into the void to identify concepts we might use to change our perspectives.

Activation spreads from the concepts we have in mind, and so we can deliberately turn our attention to particular concepts and stick with them.[10] For example, we can bring particular PAGES into working memory, not to advance our stories but just to consider them. In doing so, we allow activation to build from these concepts without moving on to the most strongly associated concepts. This can allow less strongly associated concepts to come to mind. Stopping our use of our perspectives to advance our stories and instead turning our attention to some aspect of our perspective can give us an opportunity to consider associated concepts that are not included in our perspective already. To get beyond our current perspective with activation, we have to avoid our tendency to use our perspectives.

While activation is an automatic process, there is evidence that the amount of activation available to spread depends on how engaged working memory is. If we are busy applying actions on parts, even in a different story, it can make it take longer to find an insight. Even a simple working memory task like tracing a picture made it take longer for people to get insights in riddles like the priest riddle in Chapter 2.[11] The theory is that the amount of activation one has to use in a moment is fixed, and when it is used by craft processes it leaves little more to spread. Even if that craft is related to our story, it expends the activation on the concepts that are already in working memory. It is why in the egg challenge task described in Chapter 1, restricting someone on a team from being able to use actions on parts left them with more residual activation to spread and helped the teams generate more insights and better inventions.[12] What the teams lost in craft production capacity they made up for in creative idea production.

The general principle is that to use activation effectively, beyond picking good starting concepts, we need to do less deliberate thinking. When we are using our perspectives to advance our stories, activation rarely accumulates anywhere for long. We move on and the residual activation fades. In contrast, when we stop advancing our stories and stop deliberately thinking from one set of concepts to the next and then right on to the next, we are in a different position. Activation can accumulate sufficiently to bring weaker associations that are not already part of our perspective, but could be, to mind. This would explain why people often have insights when they go jogging, take a shower, or stroll through the park. All of these were common events mentioned when we asked people about insights they had, and they resonate with many famous stories of insights. Walking or jogging in the woods or in a park—looking at or moving through nature—seems particularly likely to be helpful.[13] These activities require very little of working memory, leaving more activation to spread.

Activation can spread with one story as we begin thinking about another. We can have unfinished stories, unmet goals, and unresolved events buzzing in the backs of our minds, activating related concepts.[14] A little mindless activity can provide an opportunity for activation to generate possibilities even when we are not directly thinking about a particular story.[15] When we are thinking deliberately to advance our stories, activation is not able to spread far.[16] We can reduce our demands on working memory and give activation an opportunity to spread more widely.

Activation is the cognitive mechanism underlying a variety of discussions around how to foster creativity. Allowing activation to spread to connected concepts by holding off from deliberate thinking is effectively synonymous with discussions of wandering minds and engaging in associative thinking.[17] Activation helps to clarify the limits of gathering unusual concepts, stray ideas, chance encounters, and the like as means to promote creativity. These experiences encourage us to think about concepts that are not linked to the ones we were thinking about, and then activation spreads from those concepts as well as from our perspectives, and perhaps something useful lies at the intersection. The hope is that the distant or unusual concepts these experiences bring to mind can link back to our own story and integrate into our perspective. That hope needs to be tempered by an acknowledgment of the low likelihood of success. In the insight experiment described earlier, tracing pictures of the wrong answer (for example, a picture of a man with a harem for the priest problem) made people get the insight more quickly than tracing an unrelated picture (a city skyline). The wrong answer is closer (conceptually) than the unrelated one, and so there was a shorter path for activation to spread.

Possibly the biggest challenge to using activation effectively is that we have to slow progress on our stories. Musing on the problem is not going to feel productive. It will seem as if we are wasting our time. If we are clear about activation as a tool to change our perspectives and clear that a change in perspective would be appropriate, then we can give ourselves the space to wait for a modestly associated concept to bubble up into consideration. It does not require doing absolutely nothing. We might engage in easy, related tasks. People who are trying to find insights are more likely than those just working to complete a task to seize upon environmental cues to discover their needed insight.[18] For example, in the mutilated checkerboard problem discussed in the previous chapter, if the experimenter "accidentally" said "maybe it's impossible," it led participants not only to realize it was impossible, but to discover why. Or, in the experiment using the priest riddle, participants who earlier had looked at pictures of people dressed in different uniforms (although no priests) were more likely to come up with the answer to the riddle.[19] The participants were not aware of a connection though. When asked how they arrived at the solution to the riddle, only one person mentioned the pictures. Others just said it popped into their minds. The activation generated as a result of seeing the pictures of people in uniform likely made them think of concepts of other professionals, which in combination with the wedding context of the riddle led them to the associated concept *priest*. Thus, given an opportunity, activation can foster going into the void and returning with possibilities for changing our perspectives.

CEO, game designer, and professor at Carnegie Mellon's Entertainment Technology Center Jesse Schell described managing activation as a sort of personal assistant. "You have to give him tasks, and he goes away and comes back with the answer. You have to keep giving him tasks so that he doesn't get lazy, but you can't be looking over his shoulder all the time. Otherwise he is like 'Go away!' You also have to listen to his ideas when he comes back."

ANALOGY

Experience teaches us that some stories are familiar. Sometimes we go through nearly the same episode. Sometimes the likeness is less evident, and we might wonder if we have ever heard of a similar story. For example, most of us have never run a restaurant. So we might wonder how to think about it. We might think about a restaurant we have been to, and think about how our restaurant might be like it. Or we might look farther afield. Chef Ferran Adria, one of the greatest chefs of his generation, ran one of the most famous restaurants in the world, El Bulli. Describing Adria this way might lead us to make an analogy between the restaurant and an artist's studio, emphasizing the famous chef's efforts at producing a kind of artwork. Yet a different analogy comes if we think about the actual running of the restaurant; we might think about a restaurant as being like a manufacturing plant, engaging in carefully developed processes on raw supplies, with substantial process controls, to produce value-added end products for customers. A restaurant and a manufacturing plant do not look alike on the surface, and there are many differences. But they share some underlying patterns. The cognitive mechanism of identifying similarities in underlying patterns of concepts, rather than perceptual surface features, is *analogy*.[20]

Adria thought about that analogy between a manufacturing plant and a restaurant and drew an inference. He realized that many manufacturers have research and development laboratories, with a staff separate from the manufacturing plant. He further realized that those laboratories are often located at a distance from the manufacturing plant, giving the research and development team greater flexibility and fostering a longer-term view to invent entirely new products. Accordingly, Adria developed a kitchen laboratory two hours away from his restaurant, with distinct staff, purely for the purposes of inventing new kinds of dishes that he could later serve at his restaurant. The analogy between a restaurant and a manufacturing plant provided a way to think about the processes at the restaurant and led to generating a guess about the possibility of a separate laboratory kitchen and staff. Analogies allow us to draw on existing knowledge from another story—knowledge that might be inconsistent with our current perspective—and consider whether our current story could be made to incorporate such knowledge. This is why analogy is a primary tool for the creative process. Analogy can identify knowledge outside of our current perspective, off in the void, which could elaborate what is in our perspective in an unpredicted way.

There are three broad phases to drawing analogies to change our perspectives. The first phase is to identify an event from another story that might be like an event in our current story. The second phase is to draw specific correspondences between the prior story and the current story. The third phase is to make guesses about the current story based on aspects in the prior story.[21] The first phase, identifying a similar event, is the hardest to do. But as the first phase is only useful if it leads to the next two phases, it is helpful to understand the next two phases in a bit more detail to understand what makes a good analogy. That will help provide an understanding of why the first phase, finding a similar event, is hard and of what we might do to improve our chances of identifying a similar event that could help us change our perspectives.

Thinking through the analogy between a restaurant and a manufacturing plant, we can notice that they have a lot in common. The kitchen is like a factory floor. The line cooks, dishwashers, and other kitchen staff are like the machine operators, maintenance staff, and other factory workers. The vegetables, spices, grains, and other ingredients that will be turned into dinners are like the raw materials—metals, plastics, paints, and so forth—that are the inputs into the manufacturing process. The carefully designed and monitored processes for transforming ingredients into dishes—this kind of cleaning, cutting, combining, heating, and so forth—are like the carefully designed and monitored processes—stamping, printing, painting, filling—for transforming raw materials into end products. There are many more likenesses. But the key is to notice not only that there are many similarities, but also that the correspondences fit together into a larger pattern. They relate to one another. The processes for transforming ingredients into dishes is done by the kitchen staff with pots, pans, stoves, and ovens and the ingredients entering the kitchen, all of which in turn is done to generate consistent, high-quality dishes for diners. This is just like the processes for transforming raw materials into products being done by factory workers with machines and raw materials to generate consistent, high-quality products for customers.

Analogies are productive the more you can draw correspondence between multiple PAGES in the structure. It is not that a restaurant might be in an old warehouse like a manufacturing plant, or that a kitchen employee might wear an apron with pockets just like the people in manufacturing plants. These are idiosyncratic similarities that, even if they match, are isolated rather than being critical to the larger pattern the two have in common. Good analogies have large patterns of concepts that correspond with the current event. That way, when we notice elements in one event that are not in the other, like a research and development facility that benefits a manufacturing plant, we have a basis for considering whether and how introducing corresponding elements in our current stories could be done—maybe a restaurant could benefit from a laboratory kitchen.

As a second example, *Grand Theft Auto*, a popular and profitable video game series, took inspiration from an analogy with the earlier arcade game *Pac-Man*.[22] In *Pac-Man*, a creature is moving through a maze while being chased by ghosts, and in *Grand Theft Auto*, cars drive through a city while being chased by police. The *Pac-Man* creature ate dots while moving through the maze, which led the *Grand Theft Auto* game designers to consider what could play a corresponding role in their video game, an activity for the people to do in their cars as they drove around the city. The fact that the ghosts could be made vulnerable in *Pac-Man* led *Grand Theft Auto* designers to think about whether the police cars could be made vulnerable. *Pac-Man* had a weakness of becoming boring over time, as the only change was the speed at which the ghosts moved. This served as a warning to the *Grand Theft Auto* designers to not adopt the analogy entirely but have some contrasting elements. To stave off boredom, they generated variety in the game by, for example, changing the street map over time. The foundation of an analogy is matching patterns between two stories. The pattern from a known story provides a way to think about a new story if we still do not have much of a perspective. The pattern from the known story also provides a basis for elaborating on the new story. This might be *Grand Theft Auto* built from *Pac-Man*, or *West Side Story* built from *Romeo and Juliet*, built from prior tragic love stories back to Pyramus and Thisbe and earlier still. Analogies work by aligning and mapping between the patterns of concepts in two stories. In contrast to activation, which is concerned with tracing links between concepts to identify perhaps one concept that might stimulate a focused change to our perspectives, analogies are concerned with larger patterns of concepts and therefore often make large changes to our perspectives.

Analogy makes changes to our perspectives by leveraging pattern similarities. The correspondences between the PAGES in one story and the PAGES in another story are not driven by specific part similarities. It is not that the car in *Grand Theft Auto* was made to look like the *Pac-Man* figure in the old video game. It is not that police are in any obvious surface way like ghosts. Rather, the similarities are about the roles that *Pac-Man* and ghosts play in the pattern in that game being like the roles the cars and the police play in the pattern in *Grand Theft Auto*. Likewise, it is not that sheets of metal and machine oil coming into manufacturing plants are obviously like leaves of lettuce and dish soap coming into a restaurant kitchen. The important similarities are not at the level of the items themselves. The similarities are at the level of how these concepts work together in the pattern constituting PAGES.

Similarities in patterns of concepts are hard to find, much harder than similarities between parts. This is why the first phase of analogy, identifying another story that has a pattern similar to the current one, is the most challenging phase of the process of drawing an analogy. It is much easier to notice that one event is about a car chase around a city, just like another event is about a car chase around a city. It is easy to notice that one restaurant is like another restaurant. These nearly identical episodes allow us to recognize that we are once more going to tell a car chase story or a restaurant story. As so much of our lives consist of telling slight variations of previously told stories in nearly identical episodes, this allows us to draw on our experience quite efficiently. What is much harder is noticing that a restaurant is like a manufacturing plant, that one story has a pattern similar to another, without them sharing obvious similarities such as the same parts. The reason it is harder is that when we are thinking about our current story, we are likely to be reminded of nearly similar prior stories.[23] When students are asked what video game inspired *Grand Theft Auto*, it is almost always another driving game that they suggest. Our minds are trying to bring the most relevant information into awareness, as that is most likely to be useful.

When we retrieve another story from memory, we bring to mind stories that are the most similar to the current story that we know. That means that stories with highly similar PAGES will tend to come to mind. If we are aiming for an analogy, though, all the similarities due to this part being like that part, this action being like that action, will not be particularly helpful. The more we focus on the specific parts and actions in our stories, the less likely we are to recall an analogy. We are more likely to recall another story with similar parts and actions. Making a salad is like making a salad. Filling out a report is like filling out a report.

For analogies to be helpful in changing our perspectives, they must be specific not vague. There must be patterns of concepts. But when we think about specificities, we often fall into thinking about the contextual details of specific parts and actions, which nudges us toward nearly identical prior stories. If we think very broadly, our self-concepts can bring stories to mind that do not involve similar parts and actions. For example, being a tourist in Vienna might remind us of being a tourist in Montreal. The challenge with thinking this broadly is that there is not much of a pattern to it to provide the correspondences needed for a useful analogy. Thinking about goals and events is usually more helpful. That would get us thinking about what a tourist wants to do and what tourist events might be, at which point there could be useful correspondences.

Given the difficulties of the first phase of analogy, identifying another story with a similar pattern of concepts that is not nearly identical, to develop our skill at using analogy it is useful to focus here on ways to find analogies. The second two steps are less often the source of difficulty. Following are recommendations based on analogy research.[24] The first is a long-term strategy, rather than a specific action we can take in a moment when we are stuck. It is to learn and develop our understandings of our stories. Analogies are concerned with finding stories with similar patterns of concepts. They require understanding what is really going on in our stories so we have a pattern of concepts capturing what matters. To draw an analogy between a restaurant and a manufacturing plant, we have to know something about what happens in a restaurant and something about what happens in a manufacturing plant. If our stories and our perspectives are not well developed, then we will not be able to generate interesting analogies between them: "Um, people work in both restaurants and manufacturing plants?" We want to understand what causes what, how things work, what matters. That way we have a basis for drawing analogies. Consequently, making a habit of enriching our understanding of stories rather than only having shallow understandings will provide us with the basis for drawing analogies later.

To develop a habit of forming deep as opposed to shallow understandings, it helps to develop an awareness of how fully we understand something. We often have the illusion that we understand what is happening in our stories.[25] For example, we feel we know how our hearts work, or how bicycles work, or how lights work. But those understandings tend to be far from complete, even laughably so. Try drawing a bicycle from memory, and then look at a real bicycle, and you will quickly notice that what you drew is probably not something you could actually ride.[26] Or try explaining how our hearts work, and then look at a medical illustration. To find the limits of our knowledge and test the quality of our understandings, it is not enough to feel that we know what the story is. We have to try to explain why things happened in the story either to ourselves or to someone else. The old saying in training is "watch one, do one, teach one." That "teach one" part forces us to articulate our explanation to see if there are gaps or if we really do understand what is happening.

To develop our understanding further, if we somehow have not gotten a complete understanding, it helps to start with a simple similarity. It is hard to find analogies, as we noted, but it is not hard to think about two stories that are clearly similar. The Italian restaurant down the block is like the Chinese restaurant around the corner. But then do not stop there. We rarely think through all the ways in which these obviously similar items are alike. Pushing ourselves to think through the correspondences is useful.[27] Even boring analogies, such as, "The professor is a goldmine," do not have to be simplistic.[28] Sure, we could just think, "The professor has valuable things to say." That would be a shallow understanding. But we could push the analogy. With a goldmine, you have to work to dig beneath the surface, find something that may not look promising initially, and then clean it up before it is valuable. Perhaps the professor is unassuming, what she says at first is not immediately recognizable as valuable, but if we think more about it we might realize its worth. More generally, things that are obviously alike are usually not only alike in simple ways, but also alike in richer ways. Stopping to think through all those richer ways can help us develop more complete understandings of the pattern of concepts they have in common that can then, later, provide us with the ability to generate analogies.

Developing better understandings so that we can later form analogies is all well and good, but if we have a story now and we are trying to think of an analogy to help ourselves change our perspectives now, then it is not particularly helpful advice. Fortunately, there are a few other things we can try. All of them rest on the idea that if finding an analogy means allowing a prior story to be like our current story, then it would help to think about our current story in ways that emphasize what is important about the story rather than the idiosyncratic surface details that would not matter to an analogy. When we are drawing an analogy between a restaurant and a manufacturing plant, whether the restaurant serves pizza or barbecue is probably irrelevant. So anything we can do to deemphasize the idiosyncratic information in our stories and emphasize the larger pattern is likely to foster identifying an analogy, because it will decrease the likelihood of finding uninteresting similarities and increase the likelihood of finding useful similarities.

For example, we can talk to others about our stories. As noted during the crosstalk cue discussion, speaking to someone about our stories encourages us to emphasize the gist. We build up a sense of the story as a whole, and we forget some of the specific details. That means our stories are closer to just the portions we would want to emphasize in an analogy, which then makes it easier to identify analogies.[29]

We can also work to simplify our stories, even if we are not talking with anyone else. If we think about how a pizza restaurant and a barbecue restaurant are alike, that is likely to encourage us to deemphasize idiosyncrasies and emphasize the common aspects. Those common aspects are likely what we need to match with an analogy. As a result, doing so helps in identifying analogies.[30]

As a final means for how we can promote the identification of analogies, we can be thoughtful about the particular words and concepts we are using to think about our stories. We could describe what comes into a restaurant as lettuce, parsley, and flour, or we could talk about them as supplies. We could describe what leaves the kitchen as salads and apple tarts, or as products. Using the abstract terms that emphasize the roles the items are playing in the larger pattern rather than the specific characteristics of the items themselves can foster the identifying of analogies.[31]

Once we have identified a possible analogy, whether by using abstract concepts, simplifying our stories, or talking to others, we can draw correspondences and generate guesses. These are possibilities for changing our perspective. As analogies can be compelling, it is worth noting that they are offering possible interpretations. The changes to our perspectives may or may not turn out to be useful, and the guesses we generate as a result of drawing analogies could turn out to be wrong. This is the case for any change to our perspectives. Analogies just often seem convincing, so we note the warning here against overconfidence.

Analogy is commonly linked to creativity,[32] so the emphasis on this tool is probably not a surprise. Some writers emphasize metaphor as opposed to analogy,[33] but they usually mean comparing two patterns of concepts, so the same points hold. The aim is to identify an event or story like the one we are currently considering so that we can reinterpret our current story. The new story might provide us with a solution to a problem we are facing currently. Or, the new story might be an opportunity to apply the lessons from our current story, and so we advance another story.[34] In either case, analogy provides us with a way of using one story to help us understand another.

By bridging two stories, analogy is one basis for crosstalk. With crosstalk, we are exploring a connection we have already noticed between two stories. That connection might turn out to be a useful analogy, or it might be something else. The discussion of analogy here has focused on what we can do when we have one story and are taking a particular approach to going into the void: trying to find a matching story. It has outlined ways to build up our skill at identifying another story in memory that has a pattern of concepts corresponding to the one in our current story. Finding analogies does not have to be accidental, it can be intentional.

COMBINATION

The third cognitive tool for identifying concepts to use to change our perspectives is combination. Combination is the joining together of two concepts.[35] Usually one concept is already part of our perspective, and we combine it with another concept from outside the perspective. For example, combining "video rental" and "mail order" led to a new business model for movie rentals, as Netflix demonstrated in the 2000s. The "mail order video rental" combination led to such novelties as a list of desired movies, a national market, a massive database of related movies, and positive incentives to return a movie (back when you had to return them). Netflix then turned to streaming movies, another combination, which also yielded emergent properties, including being able to watch movies on something other than a television, being able to start a movie immediately upon deciding, and being able to watch a movie in any location. Combinations can be a source of creativity, whether during a story, at the beginning of a story, and even to prompt a new story.[36]

Combinations are usually mundane. We do not think it special to generate, say, the combination "blue bus." The concept *blue* combines with the concept *bus* in a typical way. A bus is a kind of thing that can have a color, and blue is a kind of color. These sorts of mundane combinations indicate that we are used to thinking about how one concept can be integrated with another concept. The combinations that change our perspectives are those that combine concepts that are at first inconceivable to bring together or that have unexpected emergent properties.[37]

To form a useful combination, there are two challenges we have to address. We have to identify concepts to combine, and we have to work out what the combination means. The first challenge probably seems obvious, and it certainly does pose difficulties. But the second challenge may not seem apparent. It might seem that the meaning of the combination would be obvious. Yet there are often several possible interpretations. For example, "community design" might mean the design of a community or a design generated by a community. Thus combinations can be ambiguous and can require interpretation.

Interpreting a combination can itself require changing our perspectives. Our perspectives are likely to lead us to adopt interpretations of a combination that are compatible with how we have been thinking. For example, we might think about earrings, necklaces, and pins, and therefore think about "zipper jewelry" as jewelry that attaches to a zipper pull. With that perspective, we are unlikely to consider the combination to have the potential to mean jewelry made out of zippers.[38] That is a different way of interpreting both zippers and jewelry. More generally, producing the interpretation of a combination can in itself involve a change in perspective.

When we are unable to form an initial interpretation of a combination it can spur us to make a change in our perspectives. For example, in the 1950s, when radios were furniture, Sony set out to make a "pocketable radio." At the time, this combination was a dramatic change in perspective. It indicated a change in size so large that it meant using entirely different technology, much like a "briefcase car" might strike us today. Thus, the "pocketable radio" combination represented a change in perspective and a challenge to undertake.

What the challenge in interpreting combinations demonstrates is that putting together two concepts typically involves far more than just those two concepts themselves. The assumptions we are making about what they mean and how they relate to one another indicate that we are engaging additional knowledge. That knowledge is often revealed in the form of emergent properties. In the case of a pocketable radio, that included entirely new uses and opportunities for listening to the radio. The combination indicated a change in perspective about what radios could do and where they could be used. In looking for an interpretation of a combination, we are enabling the generation of emergent properties that follow from the interpretation. Effective combinations involve both a comparison process to figure out how the two concepts might relate to one another and then a construction process to work through the implications of that interpretation.[39]

Unfortunately, we do not yet know as much as we might like about combinations. We do not know enough about how people choose to interpret the combination of two concepts and about how the construction process works. Worse, as most research on combinations is about the kinds of interpretations people form of given combinations, we have even less information on how people spontaneously identify concepts to combine.

We can make a few guesses, though, on how to generate potentially useful combinations. If the aim of combining concepts is to change our perspectives, then we should seek out not bizarre combinations of simply unrelated words but combinations with one concept that seems incompatible with or negates an assumption in the other. Consider, for example, two words at random: "cabbage hostage." Here we get something fairly unhelpful, because the two concepts have little to do with one another. They do not relate to the commitments of the other, and together little seems to emerge. In contrast, "pocketable radio" used one term, *pocketable*, to break an assumption about the other, that radios are large. Likewise, "mail order" broke a commitment about video rentals at the time, which was that we had to go get the video, rather than the video coming to us. The two concepts as a whole need not be opposites, although paradoxes can certainly be fruitful.[40] One concept just needs to negate assumptions made by the other concept, such as tiny houses or virtual reality, to yield a fruitful combination.

There are many discussions of combination as a tool for producing creative products. Whether they are described as hybrids, mashups, blends, or some other term, the notion is consistent with this discussion of fusing two concepts to arrive at a third. There are also broader discussions of combination that apply the term not just to fusions of concepts but also to generating new patterns of concepts that constitute a new perspective.[41] There is something helpful about recognizing that forming a distinctive, new pattern of concepts—a changed perspective—involves combining concepts in new ways. However, we separate out our discussion of a tool for generating new concepts by fusing existing ones from our discussion of a broader collection of processes for changing perspectives. We do so because the fusions that are formed with combination tend to remain combined. People hardly notice that "paper towel," "corporate governance," "coffee shop" and countless other concepts are the result of prior combinations. These become new additions to the knowledge base that people use in countless stories. In contrast, the particular pattern of concepts constituting a particular perspective is a larger, more complex, and more readily decomposable collection of knowledge that is more variably applied across episodes. Thus combination is a tool for forming new, hybrid concepts that can then be integrated into perspectives, providing new responses and leading to distinct products.

RECATEGORIZATION

The fourth and final cognitive tool commonly responsible for changing our perspectives is recategorization. Recategorization involves swapping out one concept to interpret an item in place of another concept. The large cardboard shipping box that arrived at our home becomes a storage container for camping gear over the winter, an imaginary boat for the preschooler in the spring, and a drop cloth for repainting some bookshelves in the summer. The manager's behaviors indicate being "involved" or "controlling," "confident" or "arrogant," "rational" or "cold," depending on one's view. With recategorization, we are focusing on some aspect of the situation and applying a different concept to make sense of it. As a result, different properties become prominent and some formerly prominent properties fade to the background. That change in one concept might then influence how it fits with other concepts and might bring additional concepts to mind to include in our perspectives. Thus recategorization guides our journey into the void by focusing us on alternative interpretations of an aspect of the episode.

Swapping out one concept for another can be mundane. We frequently consider alternative concepts for the same item as a matter of course. It is a cat and it is a pet (and it is trouble!). A recategorization need not be inconsistent with our existing perspectives. Often, recategorizations just add to our perspectives. Of course, we would not be discussing recategorization as a tool for creativity if it were not also possible for the swap in concepts to yield a substantive change to our perspectives. The key for recategorization to do so is not that the concept be unrelated. Incorporating unrelated concepts need not require any changes to our perspectives, but can usually just be added. Recategorization changes our perspectives when the swapped concept brings a release from assumptions implied by the old concept and an imposition of new assumptions from the new concept. For example, Rogaine was initially created as a medicine for a heart condition. But attending to its side effects led to a recategorization from "heart medication" to "hair replacement medicine." That took the story in a different direction.

The primary challenge to recategorizing is that we are often fairly attached to the concepts we are using to represent aspects in the episode. Some concepts are so compelling or so taken for granted that they are treated as defining the aspects themselves. For example, if we have a pet cat, we probably think of it as a cat by default, and that it would be, for now and all time, a cat. That categorization is so fundamental that even if we could also think about it as an animal, as a pet, or as living in Philadelphia, it is still also, in our minds, a cat. Perhaps oddly, we have similarly strong beliefs about all kinds of other items. Doritos are a kind of food that we eat, not something we use as tinder to light fires. Computers are technological devices, not consumer products. Planetary orbits are perfectly circular. When we take a particular concept not just as applying to an item but as defining the essence of that item,[42] then we not only make assumptions about the item but commit strongly to those assumptions. That makes recategorization difficult.

When we categorize something, when we select a particular concept to apply to an aspect of the episode, we are perceiving the properties of the aspect, using the level of detail at which we are thinking, and considering the context of the other concepts already in our perspectives.[43] For instance, at the point of a computer's manufacture, conceptualizing it as an electronic device is likely to be most salient; at the point of purchase, conceptualizing it as a consumer product is likely to be most salient; and when at home, conceptualizing it as a communication device is likely to be most salient. Each concept highlights different properties, an appropriate level of detail, and which other concepts are relevant and important for the particular context. Consequently, to recategorize, we need to shift our focus to different properties, shift the level of detail we consider relevant, or shift what other concepts are providing the context for our thinking.

As there are several influences on categorization choices, there are many ways people can prompt themselves to recategorize. For example, as the properties of some aspect of an episode are part of people's decision to use a particular category, and as a particular category is going to make some properties salient and others less so, one way to prompt recategorization is to perceive the aspect anew and consider its properties. It can be challenging just to think about the aspect, as people's thinking is so strongly shaped by the concepts they are using. Perceiving those aspects anew often makes the task easier.[44] For example, we have seen UPS and Federal Express trucks, packages, and advertisements for decades. But it was only a few years ago that someone pointed out to us the "FedEx arrow." We had no idea what they were talking about. Further, it continued not to make any sense to us until we looked up an image of the company's logo. We had never noticed it before. Thus one way to foster recategorizations is to take another look at the situation.

Another way to foster recategorization is to consider variations and oppositions. This is often discussed under the heading "counterfactual thinking."[45] If only it was cheap instead of expensive! What if we were late instead of on time? Counterfactuals such as these encourage us to imagine that some aspect of the episode is not represented by the concept we are currently using, but instead a contrasting concept. Then we can think about how that recategorization might lead to further changes to our perspective, and whether they are productive. There are all manner of counterfactuals, such as changes in valence (from good to bad or vice versa), changes in agency (from something we control to something out of our control or vice versa), and changes in inclusion (from something included to something excluded or vice versa). The main point to emphasize though is that we are relaxing our assumptions about which concepts apply and allowing ourselves to consider inconsistent alternatives.

An additional way to recategorize is to change the level of detail we are using to interpret an episode. We can zoom in and zoom out as we consider parts, actions, goals, events, or self-concepts. For example, many concepts are part of a classification taxonomy or can be considered at different levels of abstraction. An IBM 5150 is a personal computer, which is a kind of computer, which is a kind of electronic device, which is a kind of product. We can zoom in to look more closely at something, and this can lead us to think about features we had been skipping over. As a result, we can then bring to mind a more specific category to use to think about the item. For example, she was not just a manager she was a vice president. We can also zoom out. She was not just a manager she was a member of the organization. Zooming in and zooming out lead to recategorizations, which in turn can lead to thinking about properties that were not salient before and about other concepts that could be related that we had previously ignored. Thinking about a computer as a product leads to concerns over, perhaps, where and how it is sold. Thinking about a manager as a vice president leads to concerns over, perhaps, authority and tenure with the company. Recategorization can arise through changes in abstraction.

At the same level of abstraction, we can also recategorize by considering a neighboring concept. For example, rather than chairs as a form of seating, we might recategorize to couches. Chairs and couches, like other neighboring categories, have many properties in common but also some differences. This recategorization from chairs to couches has led to different approaches to, for example, airline seating and movie theater seating. We do not need to look in remote places for a recategorization. They can be right nearby.

One final point to emphasize regarding recategorizing as a tool for changing our perspectives is that making one change in our concepts can yield changes to further concepts if we make the effort to consider them. For example, if we recategorize from chair to couch, that is likely to make us think about people sitting with others they know. That, in turn, can make us recategorize actions (buying pairs or groups of tickets), recategorize events (family packages), and so forth. Earlier we noted that making changes to our self-concepts and events tends to cause the largest changes to our perspectives, whereas part and action changes tend to have more localized effects on our perspectives and so our stories. Consequently, as long as we are deliberately attempting to recategorize items in our stories, we might well consider items from each of the PAGES, and in particular consider the concepts we are using for the event and for our self-concept. Recategorization of those concepts often results in large changes to our perspectives.

Recategorization can happen in many ways, and many discussions of creativity rely on recategorization. We have already mentioned counterfactual reasoning. There are also discussions indicating that we should consider a different point of view or imagine we are in a different role in the same situation;[46] these are recategorizations of our self-concepts. Discussions of mindfulness and creativity often emphasize the importance of drawing distinctions, or the boundaries between concepts.[47] Thus recategorization is key here as well. Finally, the ability to use an example in a novel way based on overlooked properties is one of the oldest tests of creativity.[48] It is instantiated in such ideas as flexibility[49] and the capacity to break perceptual set.[50] We see these as recategorization at work, as people reexamine items and attend to different properties such that they notice a fit to alternative concepts.

TOOLS OF THE TRADE

Learning to use the four cognitive tools for changing our perspectives—activation, analogy, combination, and recategorization—is central to the craft of creativity. A challenging aspect of the creative process is being confronted by the void. Our knowledge is vast. Not knowing what tiny portion of that knowledge to bring to bear to change our perspective can stall our progress and paralyze our thinking. The value of every one of these tools comes from focusing on just a portion of our perspective and using that as a starting point for connecting to knowledge beyond the current story and perspective. By understanding what the tools are, how they can help us to change our perspective, and how we can learn to wield them more capably, we are seeking to advance our craft of creativity.

To further advance that craft of creativity, it is useful to emphasize that we are not bound to using the tools once and then shifting back to craft. When we make a change to our perspectives, we have a new starting point from which to think. This has mostly been discussed as an opportunity to use our (now changed) perspectives to advance our stories in new kinds of ways. But the change in our perspectives is also a new starting point from which to apply the tools so that we can make still further changes to our perspectives. Consequently, whether we have identified a new concept through association, are considering a second story as an analogy, have combined two concepts, or have recategorized an aspect using a new concept, having done so we open up new opportunities for applying a different tool using the new concepts as a new beginning. There is no rule that says we can only make one creative change and then we have to switch back to craft.

There is also no rule that we can only try one tool to change our perspectives. If we are unable to make a change to our perspectives with one tool, we can switch to try a different one. The different tools work through different mechanisms, and there are different reasons why we are prompted to use each of them. If one tool is not working—we have taken a walk to let our minds wander, but association did not reward us with anything in particular today—then we can try deliberately recategorizing. If we have no luck identifying useful analogies, we can try combining one of the core concepts in PAGES with something that contradicts one of its key assumptions. By having specific alternative tools to try, we are in a better position to avoid getting stuck. We can deliberately seek useful changes to our perspectives.

We do not have to seek changes to our perspectives alone. Earlier, we noted that the crosstalk cue can prompt us to change our perspectives through information that arises while talking with other people. That is, we can be cued to be creative by interacting with other people. We can also go through the process of changing our perspectives with other people. Our thoughts are in our minds, and the four tools operate in our minds, but we can talk about what we are thinking and we can share the results of using the tools with others and they with us. What is particularly helpful about working together with other people to apply the tools is that someone else might easily identify knowledge that might be difficult for us to access. We all have different knowledge. For example, earlier we discussed an engineering challenge requiring teams to transport an egg over a wall and down to a target using cardboard boxes, string, tape, and other odds and ends. In one team, one person's activation led from string to rope. Another person's activation led from rope to cable. They ended up forming a cable car to transport their egg. The change in perspective from string to cable was critical. The team arrived at that change through combining the activation patterns from two people to generate a change that neither alone might have made. Our changes in perspective can be collective rather than individual.

There is also no reason that our group is limited to one of the four thinking tools. The activation that leads one of us to a concept can in turn trigger a recategorization for someone else, and then an analogy for a third person. Teams introduce challenges to creativity.[51] But teams can also provide opportunities to expand our ability to generate creative products, and the tools provide clear reasons why.[52] Other people activate concepts we are not thinking about, they make different analogies, they have different categorizations, and they might combine concepts in ways we would not.

As a result, we might be more deliberate in how we interact with others and even how to design our jobs so that we are more likely to be able to use the four tools with others. Cross-training so that we can perform multiple roles involved in the same task, for instance, can be a way to deepen our knowledge about how others conceptualize situations, increasing our capacity to understand them. This might be done by rotating people through different areas of a company. It might be done by holding team problem-solving sessions. It might be any number of things. Complexity in our jobs and the opportunity to talk substantively with different people about our tasks[53] can provide an environment in which the four tools can be stimulated in the course of practice.

Being thoughtful about the knowledge diversity in our social situations is also important for thinking about how to use these tools. If we set up our work groups so that the people with whom we are working bring diverse knowledge to our conversations,[54] then we might use the four tools to facilitate communication across knowledge boundaries. It is well established that if we are located in a social network position in which we talk to people with different knowledge who do not talk to each other,[55] or talk to a wider array of people infrequently,[56] then we have the capacity to have nonredundant information. Here again, the tools can be used to develop the unfamiliar ideas. Such ideas could be deliberately identified as input for associations, combinations, analogies, and recategorizations, and not merely objects to judge. Using the tools with the other people, they become more than just tools for navigating the void, they become tools for communicating.

Finally, we can also take steps to be with people who know different information and who tend to rely on assumptions different from ours. We could travel or live in a different community.[57] Whether that is a different community nearby or on the other side of the world, engaging with people from different cultures often encourages us to confront assumptions we did not notice we were making and reconsider our perspectives given that others seem to have different ones. The patterns of activation they experience, the categorizations they make, the analogies they use, and the combinations they form that are ordinary for them but new to us can be instructive, even enlightening. More generally, engaging with people from other cultures is a strong reminder of the fact that we form perspectives and act on the basis of those perspectives, and there are many options that never cross our minds because we have forgotten or never noticed all the assumptions to which we had committed ourselves.

We do not have to go it alone. We can change our perspectives by talking to different kinds of people about our stories. They might have different perspectives from what we have and so they can lead us to change our own perspective. They might change their perspective in ways we would have been less likely to try. They might simply force us to rethink because we are talking to someone who is different from the kinds of people we normally talk to, so they can influence us without even opening their mouths. But this is not an easy process. If it is hard for one person to find and accept their own perspective-inconsistent ideas, we should not assume that it will be easier to accept those ideas coming from others. Most often it is harder because we prioritize our own beliefs over others' statements.

The exception that we heard to the tendency to dismiss others, and we heard it often, is that when discrepant ideas came from those whom our interviewees respected, it encouraged them to think more deeply about those ideas. Even if the ideas were mentioned off-handedly, like a suggestion to study cellphones in poor, rural Africa or to stop doing industrial design and learn how to make Italian suits, the ideas prompted more thought and more use of the tools to change perspectives. The first idea was said to anthropology student Emily Mann by her advisor while she was doing fieldwork in Africa, and it turned into an honors thesis. The second idea was said to Joe Genuardi by his father, and Genuardi is now a master tailor at Martin Greenberg, one of the world's best suit makers.

These examples illustrate the last thing we need to address when talking about perspective change. It can be confusing and anxiety-provoking just as much as exciting and eye-opening. Indeed, the entire process of creativity involves difficulties and joys. Thus far, we have purposefully avoided talking about how the creative process *feels*. The cognitive process of turning the inconceivable into the thinkable and then the actual presents ample complexity and opportunity for improvement. Yet it is not an emotionally neutral process. We have hinted at the motivational and emotional aspects of initiating the creative process and going into the void. We have indicated the challenge involved in a long, drawn-out creative process. We have noted that the longer people have been using their perspectives, the more committed they are to their assumptions, and so the more challenging it will be to go through the creative process. Thus, while part of the craft of creativity is learning how to start and how to advance through the process of identifying and modifying PAGES, people also need to learn how to identify and manage their feelings, as the creative process can be a long and challenging road.

PRACTICE

Vocabulary

1. **Activation**: A process by which concepts we are considering automatically stimulate associated concepts within and outside our current perspective, making them easier to bring into working memory

2. **Analogy**: The process of drawing comparisons between patterns of concepts in one event or story with those in another event or story

3. **Combination**: The process of integrating two concepts to form a new hybrid concept

4. **Recategorization**: The process of selecting an alternative concept to use to interpret some aspect of the situation

Exercises

1. Jane, the head of her company's IT support group, has been tasked with reorganizing her department so that they can be more effective and efficient in responding to the needs of the IT users in the company. Jane is stuck. She is pretty sure she has squeezed out all the efficiency and responsiveness she can. Consider which of the following activities might help Jane's association processes work most effectively (and why) if she does them.

   a. Read a fantasy novel (Jane gets engrossed in fantasy stories)

   b. Have a meeting with the IT folks to brainstorm about solutions

   c. Go for a run (Jane likes to jog)

   d. Read a magazine article on how small hospitals manage community health problems when the need exceeds their capacity

   e. Read a magazine article on IT at Microsoft

    f.   Work on a different problem, like next month's budget

    g. Go talk to some users

2. Jane realizes that maybe she is not thinking the right way about what "efficient" and "effective" are supposed to mean in this situation. A broader category for these words is "adds value." Jane wonders what her department does that adds value. She decides to recategorize what value might mean to different people. Help Jane by first thinking about value from the perspective of an IT user (which most of us are). Then think about what value means in different categories. Here are some ideas; you can think of others too.

    a. Specific situation—When your computer is crashing. When your computer needs to update. When you are connecting remotely.

    b. Zoom in—What adds value in using the IT support group on a day-to-day basis?

    c. Zoom out—If you reflect on months or years, what makes you happy versus disgruntled with the IT support group?

    d. Neighboring categories—What is it that IT helps you do? Could the support group help with that? What can't you do with IT but would like to?

    e. Different context—There are other arms of support in an organization; what makes these useful?

    f. Contradict properties—What if IT support did not need to care about the user and only building their own department, what would you fear most? What if they cut the department altogether, what would you miss?

3. Jane finds out that people really want to get their work done, and they just want IT to help and not hinder them. Jane realizes that there might be new features that she could add to her IT support tool belt if she could conceive of some new tools. At the same time she has her own concerns, such as security and robustness of data, which these users just don't see. So she thinks about making some combinations that can do both. She makes a table with concepts that matter to the IT infrastructure in the columns but those that matter to the users in the rows (Table 6.1). Help Jane by looking at the intersections in the table and see if there are empty cells that are seeming opposites, such

TABLE 6.1. Combination Grid.

	Robust	Secure	Up to Date	Scalable	Always Running
Forgiving					
Unobtrusive					
Learnable					
Intuitive					
Responsive					

as "forgiving security" or "unobtrusive updates." These will require breaking commitments in at least one of the concepts, but it might spur the making of new concepts and commitments.

4. Jane realizes that, in a way, what her group is doing is much like occupational safety in organizations. Because the company is so big and IT is given so little, it is like trying to maintain safety in a very resource-constrained environment.[58] Jane reads up on the problem to see past the surface features and to understand the role structures. She then tries to draw an analogy between those committed to safety in such environments and her own situation. You can help by thinking about the following:

a. There are psychosocial costs paid by the workers in safety environments; what are they for those in the IT department? How might these further erode the relationships with other stakeholders?

b. The goals of the safety workers can be in conflict with some of the goals of the individuals they serve. Other goals may be more aligned. Is that true in Jane's IT department? What goal structures might you think about to find out?

c. What kinds of actions do safety workers perform for those they serve? Some of these are promotion-focused and others are prevention-focused. How do they gain compliance? What are the analogous practices in IT?

d. Are there support structures, educational opportunities, and standards of practice in health care that have analogues in IT?

e. Try to take a very different situation, one with which you are very familiar, and draw analogical correspondence between it and Jane's problem.

Answers

1. Only question 1 has objective or verifiable answers; the rest should be platforms for your exploration.

    a. Read a fantasy novel (Jane gets engrossed in fantasy stories)— probably not good; the concepts are unlikely to connect to Jane's situation and may distract her deliberate processes too much (she might get engrossed in the story).

    b. Have a meeting with the IT folks to brainstorm about solutions— not good; these people will reinforce activation to the same concepts already in use.

    c. Go for a run (Jane likes to jog)—good; this is low-conscious demand and something Jane enjoys (increasing categorical inclusiveness), allowing activation to spread liberally.

    d. Read a magazine article on how small hospitals manage community health problems when the need exceeds their capacity—probably very good if she can sense the deep structural features (in fact this inspired question 4).

    e. Read a magazine article on IT at Microsoft—probably not good; the fit between concepts is mostly surface.

    f. Work on a different problem, like next month's budget—probably not good; there are few conceptual correspondences, and this can take a lot of deliberate demand to solve.

    g. Go talk to some users—very good; it is easy to do this, and the concepts they highlight are the most likely to be outside Jane's mental network.

THE VALUE OF PERSISTENCE

I would like to beg you, dear Sir, as well as I can, to have patience
with everything unresolved in your heart and to try to love the questions
themselves.
—Rainer Maria Rilke

One view of the craft of creativity is that it is about addressing the challenges of the creative process. Part of the challenge of the creative process is getting started, which is why we discussed cues. Part of the challenge of the creative process is identifying concepts that people might use to change their perspectives, which is why we discussed tools. The third major challenge in the creative process—and if there is a villain in our stories, this is it—is uncertainty. Uncertainty pushes people out of the creative process. Uncertainty even keeps them away from the creative process in the first place. To advance the craft of creativity then, it helps to understand why uncertainty arises and how it might be addressed.

For example, if we have been helpful to two young entrepreneurs, Asad Ali and Sammy Kassim, then it is mainly by helping them handle uncertainty. Their story began with dissatisfaction. Actually, being good children, they began with their parents' dissatisfaction. They noticed that their immigrant parents wanted to watch movies from their home countries. Yet finding "foreign films" was difficult. The best option was to go to a local ethnic shop and rent one of the few films it had available. Ali and Kassim had an insight based on an analogy to RedBox, the video rental vending machine company. They called their idea Globox, a video rental vending machine specifically for foreign films. With the increasingly diverse populations in cities around the United States, they envisioned an invention that they could commercialize to yield a successful business. It would make their parents happy two times over, once for the movies, and twice for their children's success.

Ali and Kassim ran the numbers on what it would cost to generate prototype machines to test their idea and realized that they would need $150,000 just
to get started. They were in their mid-twenties, so could not conceive of how
to raise that kind of money. The uncertainty about a way forward meant they
were at an impasse. The uncertainty also meant they were feeling a bit overwhelmed by their story.

We have described the creative process as concerned with changing perspectives to advance stories. What we have not emphasized thus far is that
people live through their stories. They get excited by their insights and dis-
mayed by impasses. They are proud of their inventions and jolted by surprises. They are driven to form enlightenments and frustrated when their
stories drag. These are all typical and noteworthy aspects of the creative process. The process raises and is influenced by all manner of emotions and motivations.[1] Without denying the importance of the multitude of emotions and
motivations that arise in the creative process, we think the place to start is
with uncertainty.

Uncertainty is unavoidable and pervasive in the creative process. Changing our perspectives means that we are confronting the inconceivable, and
that generates uncertainty. We have to think about what had previously not
seemed thinkable, and that generates uncertainty. Uncertainty is often the
cause of other emotional reactions, such as feeling stumped, frustrated, and
even annoyed by a simple riddle. But in a larger story, when important goals,
important events, and even our self-concepts are on the line, the uncertainty
generated by the inconceivable can be paralyzing. Uncertainty often manifests
as confusion, doubt, fear, and even hopelessness. Our goal in developing our
craft of creativity is to learn to handle the uncertainty that the creative process
generates, if not turn the uncertainty into excitement and hope.

When Matt spoke with Ali and Kassim at a moment when they were confronted by the uncertainty of not knowing how to proceed with their story, he
tried to encourage them. He knew it must be possible to raise the money, as
others had similarly done so. After a few months of talking to friends, family,
and other contacts, the two raised $200,000, allowing them to purchase ten
prototype machines. They were thrilled.

The next part of their story was getting actual machines into the world.
They had to get machines made and delivered. They had to get the machines
to work. They had to form contracts with stores to host the machines. There
was more creativity, endless craft, and plenty of sleepless nights in all of this

work on advancing their story. They got the machines up and running, and people started using them. They came back to Matt and said, "We need to leave town."

They had started just outside Washington, D.C., a city that does not have a particularly strong community of venture capitalists providing funding for starting up new businesses. They realized after the machines were installed that $200,000 was enough to get them started, but not enough to maintain or grow the enterprise. The story had developed into being about the growth potential of the area, not funding for proof of concept. This led Ali and Kassim to be dissatisfied with where their story was headed. They generated a great many arguments as to why D.C. was a dead end. The arguments were, in some ways, sensible. Washington, D.C., is not Palo Alto, and there was no way for them raise another half a million dollars from friends and family. They could not conceive of a way to stay in Washington and also raise the capital they needed. The uncertain future for their story led them to conclude, "This can't work here." Rather than encourage them to tear down what they had done and begin anew in another region, Matt encouraged them to maintain that as one option but to keep exploring the void.

The insight that brought them out of the void was realizing that they had not spoken with the local stores where the prototype machines, the Globoxes, were placed. Many of these stores stepped up as investors. Ali and Kassim raised the half a million dollars they needed to continue. Once more they had found a way to persist despite uncertainty, navigate the void, change their perspective, and continue their story.

Not long after, Ali and Kassim came back to Matt dejected. "We are done," they said. The company they had hired to produce the Globox machines was in chaos and could not make the machines. The team from the company that actually made their machines left to start their own company, but the team had a noncompete agreement that prevented them from making Ali and Kassim the machines they needed. Ali and Kassim did not have the time and money needed to start over making machines with a different small manufacturer. They did not have the funds to use RedBox's manufacturer, who would not talk to them unless they wanted to order a thousand Globox machines. So Ali and Kassim despaired once more, uncertain about their future. The story seemed to have been wrested from their control.

Matt sat and listened to Ali and Kassim tell us how it was "game over." He said, "Once more into the void." He drew out the nine dot problem on a scrap of paper and went through the same kind of demonstration that was shown in Chapter 3. He talked about how each time people have an insight and generate a solution, they think that now they know all there is to know. Yet there are inevitably more insights and more solutions than people can currently imagine. They just have to keep changing their perspective. "You have already made the inconceivable happen several times!" he raved, "Now you just need to do it again." He was hopeful. They were annoyed.

In retelling this story to our current students, Ali describes that day in this way: "We were talking about how our company was ruined, and this guy starts drawing dots and giving us puzzles. We thought 'What the **** is this?'" Riding out their annoyance with Matt and the situation, they persisted. And persisting in the face of uncertainty resulted in them generating yet another new way forward for their story. They would ask to form a partnership with the team who left their former machine manufacturer. Through the application of craft and creativity, the team agreed to absorb Globox, to take Ali and Kassim on as directors, and to let them bring with them all the investors that had been part of Globox. The creativity involved here was substantial. Their goals, the event, and their self-concepts all changed. This was the end of the Globox invention, because of the team's noncompete agreement. But from those ashes rose Ali and Kassim as the funding and development arm of this new company that did automated retail for anything from salad to medical marijuana. Once more they had found a way to overcome the uncertainty and generate a new perspective of their story.

There were more twists and turns still to come in Ali and Kassim's story. But even this much indicates how uncertainty in the creative process threatens our stories. Confronting uncertainty when at an impasse and not seeing any way to advance our stories can lead us to despair. Confronting uncertainty when going into the void to identify new concepts to change our perspectives is often unpleasant. Confronting uncertainty about where a change in perspective will take us and what it will mean can be disorienting. Most of the time, we do not race toward uncertainty but away from it. We do not seek to increase it but decrease it. Uncertainty makes us feel as if there is no point, as if we are being inefficient, as if we are doing something risky, as if we are disrupting our ability to be understood by and coordinate with others, and worse. Who wants more of that in their lives? Consequently, part of the craft of creativity is managing our emotions and maintaining our motivation to continue our stories in the face of uncertainty.

THAT VILLAIN UNCERTAINTY

Typically, we seek to avoid uncertainty. We can see this tendency in many areas of life, if we think broadly about uncertainty. Finance scholars try to estimate how much more people pay to avoid taking on more uncertainty and risk.[2] Scholars who study national cultures find that cultures vary as to how strongly they lead people to avoid uncertainty.[3] Communication scholars describe a primary motivation driving social interaction and conversation as the reduction of uncertainty.[4] There are many more discussions, but these indicate the general tenor of conclusions about uncertainty across a wide array of contexts: people tend to want to reduce, not increase, uncertainty.

As a simple example, consider the following situation. We are at work and we have two stacks of equally important tasks to get done. We have to go through a set of straightforward questions and requests to provide answers. And we have to address several thorny problems with no clear answer. Do we start with the first or second stack? Most people start answering the straightforward questions and put off the problems with no clear answer. When we can be fairly certain that our efforts will result in satisfactory resolutions, we are more motivated to start working than if we are uncertain about the outcome of our efforts.[5] This has clear implications for creativity. If we have a general tendency to avoid engaging in work when we are uncertain that we will make progress, and the creative process inherently raises uncertainties about whether we will make progress, then we have a general tendency to avoid the creative process.

To step away from craft and into the creative process is to introduce uncertainty about our progress. For example, in one of the classic studies on insight, students were given either algebra problems or puzzles and riddles.[6] They were asked every so often about whether they were making progress toward a resolution. With the algebra problems, students reported fairly steady progress over time. With the puzzles and riddles, students reported no progress at all up until they identified a resolution. Students also predicted they would have greater success with the algebra problems than with the puzzles and riddles. Is it any wonder then that the tendency in many organizations is for employees to work on straightforward tasks and avoid uncertain tasks? The uncertainty means we could be wasting our time, as we do not know how to proceed toward a resolution. The uncertainty means that while we are working on these tasks we will not know if we are making any progress. This can make it difficult to justify to ourselves and to others the time, effort, money, and other resources we are expending on these tasks. Engaging in the creative process is to a significant extent a choice. The uncertainty inherent to the creative process often steers us to choose craft and to reject creativity.

If we do step into the creative process, then we confront another source of uncertainty, which is the void. As indicated by the students solving puzzles and riddles, they did not have any sense of progress. They were going into the void. The process of trying to identify concepts beyond those already in our perspective is daunting because we could think of anything. It is disorienting not to know what to think about. Not only that, we might be changing our goals and the event in which we are involved. This means that the very criteria we are using for evaluating whether we are doing well or poorly might change. This means that we have no way to know whether we are making any progress. To make progress, we have to have a yardstick against which we are measuring our efforts. Creativity can change the yardstick, and so we have no way to measure our efforts. Until we find something and discover a means to integrate it in our perspective we are not able to generate a sense of progress, because only then will we have the yardstick of an event and goals against which to gauge progress. The uncertainties generated by going into the void are usually experienced as frustrating and bewildering, if not overwhelming.

For example, many years ago Jeff spent a very long day in art school, in a painting studio, flailing badly. At around seven in the evening, the painting instructor walked in and was surprised to see Jeff still there. "How's it going?" he asked. "Awful! I've got nothing, I have no idea what I'm doing!" came the frustrated reply. To which the painting instructor said, enthusiastically and earnestly, "That's great!" Jeff would have liked to be able to say that he was happy, appreciative, or pleasantly surprised by this response. Instead, he was angry.

As noted, venturing into the void can make us feel lost. We can lose track of what we are trying to do and what a good outcome would be, precisely because our goals, the event, and our self-concept might all change. Because creativity involves our self-concepts, feeling uncertain about whether we are making any progress and whether we have a way to understand what we are doing is readily interpretable as a signal of failure. We often do not know what we are doing. We are incompetent. So "That's great!" would not at first seem the earnest comment it truly was.

Fortunately, the painting instructor continued, "You are getting somewhere new." The painting instructor knew from experience that sometimes creativity involves going into the void for extended periods of time. The uncertainty is painful. But it means that we are in the process of formulating a new perspective. As a new perspective can lead to inventions and enlightenments, it can be worth the pain. If we vividly experience the challenge of venturing into the void and successfully navigate it, the thrill and excitement of our accomplishment can work against the negative feelings. But we spend a lot more time searching the void than we do finding new perspectives. So we need to get comfortable with the uncertainty of going into the void.

If we return from the void with an insight, there is usually still more uncertainty ahead. In the case of most riddles and puzzles, insights often lead directly to resolutions. Yet our stories are typically much larger efforts. Consequently, after generating an insight, we might have a different perspective but not know where this changed perspective will take our stories. As the saying goes, predictions are hard, especially about the future.

For example, one summer day with a young child, Jeff had both a trip to the doctor's office and an evening picnic. There was crying over getting a shot at the doctor's office, whereas there was just a little scratching upon finding mosquito bites that must have happened during the picnic. In both cases, blood was drawn, but in only one case was there crying. What is it about a mosquito that enables it to draw blood with minimal pain? This was not a question that could be taken very far. Whether it involved a useful insight or a foolish one was not clear. Was it worth investing time and effort in pursuing it? Jeff had limited craft knowledge about the biology and the engineering involved. But it turns out that the same question has led bioengineers to study mosquitos and to explore fabricating what are called microneedles.[7] At the point of drawing the analogy between needles and mosquitos though, it was not clear whether there was an interesting way forward for that story. There is uncertainty over whether a change in perspective is worth exploring. Maybe it will be fruitful, but maybe it will be a waste of time or even a failure.

It is not just people's own judgment about taking on the uncertainty of creativity that matters. There is also uncertainty about how others will receive the creativity that is undertaken.[8] Allowing creativity to flourish with others is partly about developing supportive social and organizational contexts.[9] A student of Matt's once described his place of employment as "where ideas go to die" and this is, unfortunately, common.

For example, we heard a devastating story from musical director DG. DG was hired to be the musical director on a ship for a major cruise company.[10] The musical director coordinates all the entertainment that happens on the ship. The passengers had high expectations, and the company wanted to commit its resources to impressing them. DG was delighted and generated many ideas that would draw on all of DG's considerable talent. Getting to be the musical director on this cruise seemed as if it would be a highlight of DG's career. Then the call came.

Senior decision makers at the company called DG and said that they had conducted focus groups to decide what kind of skits and entertainment worked best with audiences. DG was no longer musical director, but a project administrator. DG's first administrative duty was to inform all the musicians on the cruise, many of whom were trained at the finest conservatories in the world, that they would be pretending to play their instruments alongside prerecorded tracks in predetermined shows.

We can understand how in the minds of the corporate office this decision would reduce uncertainty about whether the average passenger would enjoy the shows. Yet clearly this decision cut off the creative process DG and the musicians had planned to engage in before that process could even begin. The capacity to have something superlative emerge was now impossible. They were left to settle for what George Mason's dean for the College of Visual and Performing Arts, Rick Davis, called the "pleasant mediocrity" that comes from such excessive need for predictability. It also is not something most professionals who take pride in their craft appreciate. In fact, DG was so incensed that his inflammatory response led the corporate office to issue an edict to confine DG to the brig of the ship for the remainder of the cruise.

It does not have to be this way.[11] There are many ways to be more tolerant of creativity in teams and organizations.[12] More important, creativity is not some frivolous extravagance that organizations with serious objectives can't afford. One of the most inspiring examples that we heard came from a person we interviewed who described his organization's "principle of on-scene initiative." Those who are executing tasks should "be given latitude to act quickly and decisively [within their task responsibility], without waiting for direction from higher levels [in the organization] . . . initiative *and creative thinking* [emphasis added] have always been crucial to the success [of our organization]."

We heard this from Admiral Thad Allen. It is the Coast Guard Doctrine.[13] Allen described the doctrine to us when discussing flying helicopters in 60 knot winds on the backside of Hurricane Katrina to rescue people off the tops of buildings in New Orleans. "They deployed the helicopters outside the range of the hurricane, and the minute they had flyable conditions they went right in and started picking people up. Nobody told them to do it." There was considerable uncertainty, but the people were capable (they had sufficient craft), and they knew the principle of on-scene initiative. They knew that even if they lost communications, they could handle the uncertainties because they had clear values and priorities.

Poor reactions to uncertainty provide us with many opportunities to abandon creativity. Uncertainty keeps us from initiating creativity. Attempting to change our perspectives might fail, and there are opportunity costs of having taken that time and having it not yield good outcomes. Uncertainty makes the process of changing our perspectives aversive. Going into the void can be confusing: there is no clear sense of when we will emerge, and we do not know what we will have when we do emerge. Uncertainty about the implications of changing our perspectives can limit our willingness to be creative. Changing our perspectives means we might be letting go of something that was effective for something that might not, at least not yet, be as effective. Uncertainty makes us doubt whether the changes to our perspectives will be useful for advancing our stories. Changing our perspectives means we might end up with outcomes that are not readily understandable or even measurable using the old perspective. Uncertainty makes us doubt whether others will tolerate our creative efforts. Changing perspectives also means disrupting coordination, as now some of us are thinking differently from others. Thus creativity brings with it an array of uncertainties that tend to keep us out of the creative process and instead sticking to craft.

If we develop our craft of creativity, we can address at least some of these uncertainties and learn to cope with the remaining ones. As part of the craft of creativity is managing uncertainty, it is not surprising that researchers find persistent, modest associations[14] between creativity and personality traits around a willingness to take risks, a tolerance for ambiguity, and an openness to experience.[15] Simply being more willing to confront uncertainty tends to be associated with generating more creative products. We speculate that the reason these associations are weak, rather than strong, is that tolerating uncertainty alone does not generate changes to perspectives. There is still a cognitive process of changing perspectives that has to occur. This is why we started our discussion with the cognitive process of changing perspectives, followed by the cues and tools for initiating and navigating the creative process. But our guess is that people are more likely to take those cues and use those tools to change their perspectives if they are willing to tolerate the many uncertainties that arise. Consequently, it is helpful to examine some of the main methods for addressing uncertainty so as to advance the craft of creativity.

COMMIT TO THE TOP PRIORITY

One way to face uncertainty is to commit to what we feel is important and what is outside ourselves. Charles Goodyear spent years working to find a way to toughen rubber so it would not melt in the heat.[16] His losses were so substantial and frequent that he repeatedly ended up in debtor's prison, where he continued conducting his experiments. The author J. K. Rowling said that after having utterly failed with her first career and marriage she "began to direct all my energy into finishing the only work that mattered to me."[17] Stories of persistence are legion in the history of inventions.

The most common way of talking about persistence has been to talk about loving what we do. Loving what we do is wonderful. Everyone we interviewed talked about the importance of loving what they did. Scholars also stress the importance of fascination, of passion, of loving the work.[18] Loving the work is a positive force drawing us in so that we want to pursue it. In addition to love, there is also a value in seeing the work as important.[19] When something is important, suffering the slings and arrows of outrageous fortune is simply the price of our commitment to that priority. The creative process is not all joy and happiness. There are many difficulties. A commitment to the importance of what we are doing matters for handling those difficulties.

The idea that finding a topic intrinsically motivating (because we love it or think it is important) can counteract the dislike of uncertainty is very old news; it is a cornerstone in creativity pioneer Teresa Amabile's work. It is worth repeating here because, as DG's supervisor demonstrated, not everyone has gotten the message. Maybe a lot of people need to hear this, and it is why Dan Pink's reiteration of this point in his TED talk on motivation has been viewed close to twenty million times.[20] But it is important to add an interesting discovery about that which people find to be intrinsically motivating. It seems to be very, very narrow.

Artist Kariann Fuqua was far more strongly motivated by abstract art relating to geospatial relations than by any other kind. Some network engineers we spoke to were really engaged by file structure and thought of security protocol as a necessary bother, while other network engineers were bored by file structure and could happily spend hours thinking about security breaches and defense. Even though Professor Tayur enjoys discrete time queuing models, his real passion is for continuous time queuing models. He described reading about these queuing models as being "like watching a James Bond movie. I do it because it is fun, and not because I am trying to get something useful out of it. That is, this activity is enjoyable *in itself.*" We might speculate a bit as to why such interests seem, to the casual observer, to be so narrow. In adding to and refining concepts about a topic, there is an unbounded space for exploration.

For example, artist Robert Mars has produced over a hundred works of art inspired by the signs used by the roadside motels that were popular in the 1960s. They are held in galleries all over the world. If you ask Mars about why he is so interested in the signs used by roadside motels, he will tell you a complex and fascinating story about what these signs symbolize about American society and the changes to that society from the 1960s through today. Mars connects these signs and their attributes to many aspects of modern life. To him the topic is a lens through which to see a large swath of late twentieth-century American society and on to fundamental aspects of the human condition. Earlier we noted that people's stories can become thought worlds. It helps to find and love your specific thought world. It also helps to commit to your thought world as being an important, fundamental, top priority in your life so that you are willing to overcome the challenges of uncertainty to be creative in advancing it.

DEVELOP EMOTIONAL MATURITY

What is important is larger than any one insight, but it takes experience to develop the emotional maturity to separate the short term from the long term. Or as Drew Davidson, Carnegie Mellon's director of entertainment technology, put it, "Novices treat their ideas like gold." It is normal to be proud of personal achievements. The emotional roller coaster experience of generating insights can also make them seem powerful to us because of what it took from us to generate them and how excited we were to have found them. Yet these are personal experiences for the creator. These experiences do not mean that the creative products themselves are actually momentous either to the creator or to the rest of the world. Without undercutting the value and effort of that experience, it is usually only after repeated experience that we learn to separate the experience of generating insights from the value of our insights for generating inventions and enlightenments.

Repeated experience also bolsters us to the vagaries of going into the void. Novices often want to get out of the void as soon as possible. As was noted, people are uncomfortable with uncertainty. Part of the cure is simply to become more familiar with it. The time to muse without our attention being directed and drawn into something immediate seems increasingly challenging.[21] It means that we are less often in the void, less often experiencing the feeling of not reacting, not knowing what we might think next. Part of handling uncertainty is repeated experience with it. The painting instructor's exhortation that working all day and having nothing to show for it was "great" indicated a wisdom about the value of persisting in the void to generate a changed perspective.

One further result of repeated experience is that it helps us to separate what an invention or enlightenment means to us, the creators, from what it means to others who come to the product as outside evaluators. Many experienced creators spoke of novices who were frustrated and even angry when others did not appreciate their insights. Caring about our creations is understandable. We all get attached to our ideas, especially when they are hard won. But experienced creators seemed to believe that emotional attachments are signs of sentimentality—or even that something is going wrong. Veteran video game producer John Comes talked about how he looks out for the times when he finds himself defending an idea beyond what is warranted. When that happens, he abandons the idea as a matter of principle, as he feels his ability to make decisions has been compromised. He was far from the only professional who had this attitude. Most successful creators that we interviewed showed an emotional maturity about their work. They saw the products of creativity, even the hard won ones, as others might the mundane happenings in a mundane story. They neither clung to their successes nor despaired at their failures. They understood both to be normal parts of the creative process. The experienced creators knew that successes tend to give way to future challenges, and that failures often spur to new successes.

The experienced creators also knew that the products they generated had to fit into a larger world. Other people's evaluations of their products were a concern distinct from their own creative journeys. The experienced creators were unapologetic about their high standards and their desire to go beyond the merely good enough. But they realize that their stories are connecting with the stories of others and that others have their own say. They develop the emotional maturity to recognize that they are not the entire story, but they have a rightful place. Artist Robert Mars put it this way: "When someone buys my art they are going to put it on the wall next to a Warhol or a Hearst. My product *has* to fit there—I make it with that in mind. But it still has my voice and vision in it."

TAKE SHORTCUTS

If uncertainty is aversive, then finding shortcuts in the creative process that diminish uncertainty is helpful. Experienced creators generate a variety of tactics for making it just a little easier. One reason we outlined the cues—impasse, dissatisfaction, surprise, and crosstalk—and the cognitive tools—activation, analogy, combination, and recategorization—for changing our perspectives is so that people can be more deliberate about invoking them. By deliberately seeking ways to prompt the cues, by learning to attend to the cues, we can increase our willingness to take on the uncertainty of the creative process. By deliberately seeking ways to apply the tools to the PAGES of our perspective, we can shorten the time spent in the void.

For example, we can put ourselves into situations in which crosstalk and surprises are likely to occur. We can encounter new people. We can encounter new information. How this works in detail depends on the domain. Artist Jim Sulkowski described one tactic for generating opportunities to be cued: walking his dog. Sulkowski takes his morning and evening dog walks at times when the light is often evocative—what photographers call the "golden hours" of the day. "I walk my dog every morning in the park. I'll see the light hitting a certain way. I'll see a painting." Why wander into the void lost when we can find ways to jump straight to identifying a starting point for changing our perspectives?

We can also generate opportunities to bring our perspectives into focus. Our perspectives are often in the background. We tend to try to advance our stories more than consider our perspectives, which is why the stoplight model is used to emphasize that we stop our stories to change our perspectives. Well, one natural time when we are stopping our stories is when we are talking about our stories to other people. We are not attempting to advance our stories but recount them. Consequently, talking to others can help us be aware of our perspectives and so change our perspectives. If we are talking to someone who is not an expert in the area, we can be forced to think about the big picture, the broad importance of what we are doing, and that can help keep us from getting lost in our stories. But of even more importance, if we are talking to someone who is an expert, we are forced to think through our own perspective more carefully. As mathematician Tim Sauer said, "If I am talking to my grandmother I don't need to get the details right." Experts might tell us something we are not seeing. In addition, there is also simply a benefit of having to describe our story to experts. This can trigger us to generate realizations ourselves about opportunities for changing our perspectives.

As a final point, if uncertainty keeps us from starting the creative process, pushes us out of the creative process, and prevents us from pursuing the products we generate from the creative process, then two of the best actions we can take are as much about craft as they are about creativity. As Grammy-winning producer Bob Dawson told us, "You hone your craft so you can capitalize on your creativity." Expertise can reduce some of the uncertainties about whether the creative process is worth undertaking and whether what we generate is worthwhile. Developing our craft is not antithetical to creativity but complementary. And second, our commitment to our craft as well as to the creative process matters in the simple form of showing up and putting in the work. Author Alan Cheuse told us his strategy for generating creativity, which he learned from another great writer, William Maxwell: "I use an age-old method" he said. "Apply ass to chair."

REVISITING ASSUMPTIONS

The discussion of overcoming uncertainty, cognitive tools for changing perspectives, and cues to initiate the creative process has been aimed at detailing core elements of the craft of creativity. The background assumptions are that it is useful to think about creativity as a process over which people can have some control and at which they can improve. We are not emphasizing creativity as a trait that people possess to a fixed degree, for the simple reason that we do not think that is an accurate or helpful perspective. We are not emphasizing sudden, uncontrollable "Aha!" moments because they represent a tiny (but noticeable) proportion of the forms that creativity takes. We said that it is more useful to talk about what happens before such moments, what people can do to spur such moments, what happens after those moments, and why those moments are neither central nor necessary to the creative process. Insights can arrive slowly, and insights are just one product of the creative process.

Yet a great deal of research has been built up around these "Aha!" moments, and this can give a distorted view about how creativity should happen. These "should" beliefs are assumptions about creativity itself—they are the conceptual structures that guide thought in the creativity domain. And like any structure of commitments, they can be improved, and sometimes that improvement means abandoning long-standing and fundamental beliefs. As a final means of improving the craft of creativity then, we consider some of the assumptions held about creativity, why they might be limiting, and why, if you believe what we have covered so far in this book, you will be better off dispensing with them.

Probably the oldest view of the creative process that is still in use gets us to think about creativity as illumination after we get stuck. The illumination model describes the creative process as a series of stages. They are (1) preparation, (2) impasse, (3) incubation, (4) illumination, and (5) verification.[22] This could be a description of one way to form an insight. We start on a story (preparation), we reach an impasse, we engage in unrelated mindless activity in the hope that activation generates a possibility, it does so suddenly (illumination), and then we discover how to integrate and elaborate on it to form a new perspective (verification). Considering this view of the creative process in more detail reveals some assumptions we do not want to make about creativity.

We will start with preparation. Calling a stage preparation implies an intention to engage in some kind of creative effort. Yet our entrance into the creative process need not be planned or even anticipated. Further, preparation suggests a start when we encounter a problem. Yet the experienced creators that were interviewed described their efforts as relying on an array of knowledge, some of which was gathered decades before it was used. For example, Sridhar Tayur generated an insight about discrete time inventory management in part on the basis of a paper he read in graduate school (about the modeling of waterfalls and dams) and in part on the basis of general domain knowledge learned over many years. His earlier work on scheduling time-sharing with jet aircraft (itself a new idea at the time) later formed the basis of OrganJet, his social enterprise that is saving lives through smart multiple listing for organ transplantation. While the analogy between jet scheduling and organ delivery has been described as "imaginative," "a genius idea," and " disruptive," this was his first foray into organ transplantation. There was no preparation before that particular insight, as that subject was one about which he did not know anything prior to the insight.

We have said that people can improve their readiness to be creative, but preparation as it stands obfuscates what that means. The problem with preparation is the intentionality and focus. We have reinforced that people must build up their craft so that they have knowledge upon which to draw when they seek to change their perspectives, or when they develop the ideas into actual usable inventions or enlightenments. Without knowledge people can do very little with their new perspectives.[23] But the main point is that preparation is not some discrete and focused activity, it is broader learning that may not even relate to the problem or domain for which creativity may eventually be needed.

Abandoning the assumption about preparation as a discrete stage in the creative process allows us to temper our belief that we can foresee all the ways that our knowledge might be relevant. Given our tendencies toward impatience and our all-too-frequent "just tell me what I need to know" attitude, we can form the mistaken impression that all the knowledge we need is already within our perspectives. We think that reading about models of how dams control water only applies to dams and water, not inventory. This assumption limits our ability to imagine that there might be analogies to other events or domains. Worse, if we are not broadly curious, we will not learn about other areas and so not have the knowledge to use to form analogies. This is why "read widely" was a common refrain among experienced creators. They did not believe in a narrow view of preparation.

The second stage is impasse. Chapter 5 outlined four cues that prompt us to be creative, with impasse being one. Consequently, while arriving at an impasse is one reason we might turn to creativity, it is neither necessary nor sufficient for creativity. We might instead be prompted by dissatisfaction, surprise, or crosstalk. And those are just the cues that bring us out of craft. We can also deliberately set out to consider changing our perspectives. We can consider the PAGES of our perspective and apply tools to navigate the void without ever encountering an impasse (or any other cue, for that matter). Assuming impasse is necessary limits creativity's potential.

The third stage is incubation—an unconscious process that happens when we step away from the story. We should realize that impasse is what can allow nondeliberate activation processes or crosstalk the chance to bring ideas to mind. But again, incubation is neither necessary nor sufficient for creativity. There is no need to step away from thinking about how to change our perspectives to be creative. A nondeliberate activation process is not the only basis for generating possibilities for changing our perspectives.[24] More important, as was discussed with the association tool, incubation can be made more or less effective. Stepping away and doing something else is not really incubation as much as it is distraction, but even that is qualified by how related the other task might be. The point here is that a reevaluation of what incubation means and how it operates in regard to association will make its use more effective. But we do not need to condition creativity on it.

The fourth stage is illumination. This is the proverbial "Aha!" moment in which we generate an insight suddenly. The usual discussions around illumination indicate that we generate fully formed insights, like the ancient Greek myth of Athena born as an adult straight from Zeus's head. A fully formed insight is possible, such as when we are making simple changes to our perspectives (for example, insight problems), or linking two well-known domains of knowledge (as did Poincaré). But insights can also arrive slowly. We can identify concepts that might be relevant, and take some time to discover how they might be integrated into our perspective, and then after further effort realize how to elaborate on the change to yield new inferences that indicate a response. This process can itself be quite fuzzy.

Dancer Anna Hulse recalled such a story: "It was raining a lot outside. And I got stuck in the rainstorm and I was soaking wet and I was freezing, but I put my hand on the sidewalk and it was really warm. And this warmth radiated up my arm, and I loved that feeling. Then I went inside and a song came on and I got this sense of rain from the music." And thus started the inspiration for one of her dances. Of course giving form to the feeling so she could even think about what that might look like as a dance took a great deal more. Illumination encourages us to think that all of those steps have to be packed into one moment of thought. This discussion has shown that inquiry, discovery, and restructuring might take multiple cycles. More to the point, abandoning the illumination commitment can get us to have appropriate expectations about the kind of creativity that can come in a moment's flash, and can get us to develop rather than dismiss the fuzzy and half-formed insights.

The fifth and final stage is verification. This is a process of checking to see if an insight works. Thinking about this as a stage is limiting because of what it leads us to expect about what *works* means. The intuitive meaning is "leads to an invention." This is just one way in which an insight can work. Insights can fail but move the story to a new place from which further new insights emerge. They might not work without further insight—engineer Brian Mark's insight to port speech recognition functionality to his cognitive radio project did not become viable without his second insight to change the mathematical formulation to a different kind of model. Alternatively, an insight might indicate that the current story is not worth continuing, which may prevent throwing good money after bad. Insights, because they are ideas, might even be useful for another story. Composer Jesse Guessford says that he has to remind students, "Just because the idea was written for the current piece [of music], it doesn't necessarily belong in *that* piece." It is why many songwriters, such as Steve Turner, have "idea drawers." Actually, many experienced creators who were interviewed had idea drawers. Insights change how we can think, and if that lets us productively continue our story or some other story, then that is plenty good.

The more subtle problem with assuming a verification process is that what works is not fixed over the course of the story. This was the point of the Aramis story. As a large story progresses, its needs change. Even if there was a clear and direct way to determine that the insight led to the satisfaction of a goal, goals can change. This does nothing to diminish the discovered relationship between the insight and the goal, it just says that the insight's value is no longer appropriate in this event. We have said that insights can fail, and so clearly there is a need for the process of seeing if they pan out. We heard many stories of ideas that seemed great when people thought of them but failed immediately when put into action. But such stories are exceptions; more often the utility of any idea or product remains nebulous as the story progresses. The notion of verification has the potential to lead creators to expect more clarity about insights than is feasible.

As this review indicates, if we try to force fit our creative activities to the traditional stage model of the creative process it will be deeply restricted. If we draw on the discussion of the stoplight model; the PAGES approach to understanding perspectives; the distinction between insights, inventions, and enlightenments; the identifying of multiple cues; and the identifying of multiple cognitive tools, then we should see many possibilities beyond the illumination model. We should also have different ways of thinking about the stages identified in the traditional stage model, reasons to believe that these stages need not occur in this order, that these stages are not all necessary, that there are other "stages" possible, and that this is a truncated view of the creative process.

A better way to think of the creative process, but one that still needs development, is the model of creativity as problem solving. This process is described as (1) identifying and analyzing a problem, (2) preparing or gathering information and improving required skills, (3) generating ideas or responses, and (4) alidating or testing solutions.[25] The problem-solving model recognizes that people can cycle between these stages.[26] Yet this model needs to be expanded, and some of those expansions may be incompatible with the original intent.

The model needs expansion because by itself it is not a description of just the creative process. The problem-solving model just as readily applies to pure craft. For example, reordering office supplies involves analyzing the problem ("It appears we are out of paper"), gathering information ("How and from where can I order paper?"), generating ideas ("We can order twenty boxes using the departmental account and standard provider"), and testing the solution ("We used eighteen boxes last month"). There is nothing distinctive to generating creative products in this model. Some have used this correspondence to claim, therefore, that there is no specific creative process.[27] Yet just because the underlying cognitive machinery of craft and creativity is the same, it does not mean the machinery is always used in the same way. This is why we think it is meaningful to talk about a distinct creative process, without any need for there to be cognitive modules distinct to creativity.

Where we elaborate on the problem-solving model is in the nature of the process. The problem-solving model assumes that the difference between craft and creativity is not in the process itself but with what people bring into the process; the inputs. It suggests that if they start with a love for the domain, domain knowledge, certain cognitive styles, and certain personality characteristics, then they are more likely to come out with a creative solution.[28] We see all of these elements as potential facilitators, but if these are all that people have, then creativity is a relatively fixed skill and the capacity to become more creative is much more limited. Intrinsic motivation, skill level, and personality are unlikely to change much on the timescale of resolving a story. But more to the point, we have attempted to provide a more detailed model that demonstrates where people can learn to better apply their thinking skills to develop creative products. With this you can better understand what it means to "generate ideas" or even "identify the problem."[29] It also should motivate you to develop your skill rather than rely only on general, relatively fixed tendencies.

Another way in which people tend to think about the creative process is idea generation and selection. The most commonly used model of this approach, an evolutionary process described as blind variation and selective retention, owes a great debt to sustained and pioneering work by Campbell and by Simonton.[30] Brainstorming sessions are in many ways an embodiment of this approach. We generate a variety of ideas without any attempt to consider whether they will turn out to be worthwhile. There is often an instruction that we should not be limited by the past but should instead feel free to suggest anything, even crazy possibilities. Then, once we have produced a large number of possibilities, we pick the winning ideas.

"Blind variation" is in some ways a helpful way to characterize why producing creative ideas feels different from using craft. As our perspectives are the "eyes" with which we are currently perceiving and assessing situations, to not use our perspectives will in some sense blind us. In this sense, looking to get beyond our perspective means leaving the known and venturing off with no guidance. This has been described earlier as *going into the void*, because when we try to change our perspectives we feel like we are walking in the dark or groping blindly in the seeming emptiness. Yet the feeling of groping in the void is just that, a feeling. The seeming void is filled with unlimited possibilities—our entire base of knowledge. It is just that we feel paralyzed by the unlimited possibilities and seem to think of nothing at all.[31] Thus "blind variation" describes this feeling of entering the void, or engaging in a search that cannot be guided, the destination of which is unknown, and the progress of which cannot be tracked.[32] This description, "blind variation," also fits with what we have been saying about breaking commitments to particular assumptions. It is hard because once people view their perspectives as subject to change, they might replace any assumption with possibly anything else that they know. That is overwhelming.

Yet the idea of blind variation also makes some assumptions that are hindrances. One that seems to continue, despite long-standing efforts to put an end to it,[33] is the belief that creative idea generation is a genuinely random process. This view comes from early evolutionary theorizing about random variation. It also links to research arguing that any idea we generate has an equal probability of being creative, and so whether we happen to get lucky or not with any particular idea is a matter of chance.[34] If this is so, the reasoning goes, the more ideas we can produce, the more likely we are to have produced a creative one among them.

We imagine that the automaticity of the associative process is what contributes to the persistence of "random" as a descriptor of the creative process. Ideas often pop into our heads of their own accord, seemingly from nowhere. Because such ideas may not seem to follow from our current focus, they can also seem random. But they are not random. They are associated with concepts that are or were recently active in working memory, and that have accumulated activation over time. For example, imagine we are driving down the road and we pass a store. If we see a bank it cues different thoughts than if we see a grocery store, even if our thinking quickly moves on. Perhaps we keep driving and we pass a picnic, a restaurant, and a baseball field. If an idea was to pop into our heads, it is more likely to be, "I wonder if we should have a cookout this weekend" than, "I wonder what the time is in Amsterdam right now?" If we generated ideas randomly, each of these ideas would be equally likely to occur. That is what "random" implies, but it is not an accurate characterization of our thinking. If the intent is to get better at being creative, then even if there is a random element, it makes improvement impossible aside from the capacity to produce more ideas. This characterization is in opposition to how professionals describe experienced creators. Everyone from music producers to engineers said the same thing—the experts don't need to run through a thousand ideas to get to five good ones; they start with five good ones.

Blind variation describes how part of generating creative ideas can feel, and corroborates that going into the void is not the same as using our perspectives in the service of craft. But even if we try to reinterpret "blind" as "shortsighted,"[35] we are still unnecessarily limited by this model. First, because this model talks about generating and selecting ideas but does not distinguish between insights, inventions, and enlightenments, it is almost certainly too crude. This matters because the primary suggestion to improve creativity from this model is to generate as many "ideas" as possible.[36] A further difficulty is that the evolutionary model suggests that ideas emerge fully formed and ready to be selected and used. Yet there is often a great distance between insights and the other two products, inventions and enlightenments. This distance makes a sharp separation between generating ideas and selecting ideas untenable. In addition, it overestimates how good our selection criteria will be.

A final problem with random variation is that it suggests that any idea can be as useful as any other as we make random combinations. This is often instantiated in a widely held view that creativity comes from bringing together different, previously unrelated ideas.[37] We call this the mix approach. The basic claim is that the more original the mix of concepts people bring together, the more creative the result.[38] There are many examples that can be viewed in this way. For example, much earlier we discussed the redesign of the Japanese Shinkansen train using what we could describe as a mix of a train entering a tunnel and a kingfisher diving into a pond. The mix approach proposes a specific means for generating creative outcomes: make a compound of concepts that somehow fit together and result in something new.

The mix approach is helpful because it represents a solution to a key paradox about creativity. The paradox is that in order to think of something new, the only choice we have is to use existing knowledge, yet how can existing knowledge lead us to something new? The mix approach's answer is that what we know provides building blocks that we can assemble in countless new ways, and it is the combinations that are new. This is an important point about the creative process: the creative process is not simply about breaking commitments to assumptions, it is about building new assumptions as well.[39] The mix approach, by emphasizing that we are putting together concepts in new ways, concisely captures this core point.

The mix approach does, however, gloss over patterns structuring concepts and how hard it is to determine how unconnected concepts might fit together. Thus it makes overly optimistic assumptions that can lead us to imagine creativity to be easier than it is. The first assumption has to do with how ideas go together. The mix approach treats ideas like coins in different baskets. When we put coins from different baskets together, we are being creative. But this view ignores the fact that we have assumptions about concepts and about how concepts can combine. Fitting ideas together is, not coincidentally, like putting words together into sentences. It is easy to randomly generate a list of five words to toss in a basket. However, it is an entirely different matter to form interpretable five-word sentences. We do not just throw two ideas together, we have to figure out how they fit together. And the pattern we are most likely to use to fit them together is one that is consistent with our current perspective.

Thus the mix approach is too optimistic about whether novel combinations will lead to changing our perspectives. For example, a "penguin train" might mean many things, such as a train for penguins, a train that looks like a penguin, a train that runs in the Antarctic, or a line of penguins marching forward. All of these interpretations of "penguin train" were mundane, even though we suspect that penguin and train were previously unrelated ideas. They were mundane because, as was discussed in Chapter 2, we put concepts together in structures that seem to fit best with our common experience. Just mixing concepts together does not automatically channel us into an insight.[40] If we are unable to fit the concepts together into a sensible pattern, then we are most likely to conclude they do not fit together rather than change our assumptions to find a way to fit them together.

The final overly optimistic assumption that the mix model makes is that we can identify good mixes when we see them. But discovery and restructuring are not trivial. Even when we know how ideas can go together, we can still reject the combination as being without merit or ill-suited to our goals. For example, many people find mixing Coke with rum to be a successful combination. If we were to ask what other liquids can be combined with Coke to produce a novel mix, the ideas that come to mind are likely to be based on our concept of Coke, and this will limit what we consider. We might think about lemonade, or even milk (especially if you remember the old TV show *Laverne and Shirley*, where Laverne liked to drink milk and Pepsi), but we probably will not think about chocolate syrup, olive oil, or orange juice. These do not seem to fit, given how we think about the attributes of each concept. Not only do we imagine these to be bad, when we actually make them we are likely to perceive them as unappealing. If you mix diet coke and orange juice, for example, it looks disgusting. It actually tastes good to many people though (try 2/3 coke, 1/3 OJ).[41] We struggle to make inferences about the utility of the mix because we are often using our old perspectives to draw the inferences.

In a way, the mix approach seems to be an overly optimistic version of the combination tool. It confuses the act of linking unrelated concepts with the act of building previously inconceivable new patterns of concepts out of them. These are not the same processes. The nature of concepts is that they are meant to be flexible in how they can be put together. Few of us have ever thought of making sandwiches for actuaries in Katmandu, for example, but that mix of previously unrelated ideas is surely mundane, not creative. We are almost certainly using those concepts in typical ways, in ways that we assume, because of our semantic knowledge, that they can be used. Building insights through combination is hard because it requires us to put together concepts in ways that we initially assume *cannot* go together. This is why we replace the "mix" model as a complete model of the creative process with the "combination" tool as one means for changing our perspectives. Creativity is not as simple as using a random word generator.[42]

The reason to consider the complexities of the creative process, and to consider the assumptions underlying commonly used models of this process, is to be realistic about what the creative process involves. The way we think about creativity and its constituent processes affects how we engage with the process. We all have stories about creativity itself, and many of these stories start out as being helpful but then become constraining. It is time to change our perspective about the creative process. Accordingly, this discussion has reexamined some of the common perspectives on creativity to identify their helpful and unhelpful assumptions. It also has sought to build new knowledge so that we can rely on the helpful assumptions and set aside the unhelpful ones to the extent possible. Part of the craft of creativity is changing some assumptions and learning some new assumptions about creativity itself.

Our view of creativity is necessarily more complicated than the others we have reviewed. Following Einstein, we wanted to make our understanding as simple as possible but no simpler. Telling a creator that creativity is just about making novel idea combinations until a useful one arrives is too simple, and so is saying that creativity is just going through a problem-solving process when one really loves the problem. When people learn what a perspective is and what it means to change one, they are more open to learning the craft of creativity, and better equipped to endure the uncertainties that arise in the creative process.

PRACTICE

Exercises

In this chapter we talked about the kinds of things that cause people to increase or decrease their motivation to be creative. There was less about specific techniques and more about having appropriate expectations. We reinforce some of the concepts here.

1. Top priorities

    a. Name some activities you love. These would be activities that you would devote money and time to even if you got no tangible return (don't include activities from which the benefits are social, such as spending time with friends, seeing your kids, and so on. These are important but will muddy your understanding of the concept).

    b. Name some activities that you find important. These would be tasks or causes that you feel must be maintained in the world. They would be activities that exist outside of your own personal world, and would also be things that you would devote money and time to if others could not do them. They may also not be enjoyable, but you could see them as in some way sacred (again, don't include the social or personal).

    c. In contrast to the first two, name activities that you are extrinsically motivated by—you do these not for the activity's sake but rather for some reward you get from them. These would be activities that you would cease doing if the reward stopped.

2. It is possible to think about intrinsically *un*motivating activities. These would be activities you would seek to avoid if at all possible. Much of human invention (for example, escalators, washing machines, microwave ovens) actually comes from a desire to avoid undertakings that could be found to be tedious or unpleasant, even though such undertakings might not be tedious to all. Think about tasks that you really dislike doing or you find to be utterly useless wastes of time, those that you wish you could automate or outsource;

these are examples of avoidance-based motivation that might still cause creativity.

3. Emotional maturity takes practice, and that practice seems to come with failure and criticism (that was a consistent theme across our interviewees). Nonetheless, people are often sensitive about what they create.

   a. What are some strategies you can use to not be wounded when people react negatively to your work?

   b. What are some situations that you should avoid because ultimately they are not helpful or productive?

4. Shortcuts tend to be personal and idiosyncratic, but everyone has their own preferences and processes. Some of our colleagues like to write in busy coffee shops, others could not do this. One of us (Matt) has a particular chair he writes in, and the other chairs in that same room are not conducive (despite being equally comfortable). Think about your own facilitators and inhibitors of your process.

   a. What personal things help you to strike out in a new direction? To not get fatigued as you traverse the void? To stimulate other thought? Try to make these as personal and specific as possible.

   b. What personal things distract and disorient you? How will you try to control and limit these things?

5. The time between insights and inventions, as well as the time it takes to see "obvious" mixes and extensions to ideas, is often wildly distorted. Here are some examples to give you perspective (ha ha).[43]

   a. The pocket calculator was invented before email. How long (in years)?

   b. It turns out that the concept of hydrogen-based engines, as was recently explored, given environmental concerns, was an old idea. Guess when the first hydrogen internal combustion engine vehicle was invented?

   c. Which mathematical concept was invented first: algebra, zero, or the decimal system?

   d. How much longer did it take to adopt the + and – signs in mathematics after algebra, zero, or the decimal system were adopted?

e. The first lever was invented by our friend Archimedes around 250 BC. When did John Wyatt invent the compound lever (using one lever to magnify the force of another)?

Answers to the Invention Questions

a. One year; email was first invented in 1972.

b. 1807.

c. Algebra and the decimal system preceded zero by about a century.

d. About 889 years. It took another 142 years before the multiplication sign "x" was adopted.

e. 1743—almost two thousand years later.

DEVELOPING THE CRAFT OF CREATIVITY

The world as we have created it is a process of our thinking.
It cannot be changed without changing our thinking.
—Albert Einstein

Creativity is a skill. There is a process for generating creative products, and we can improve our skill at entering, navigating, and making use of the products which come from that process. It might at first seem as if creativity would be quite different across accounting, painting, plumbing, software design and so forth. However, it is the craft of these domains that is different, not the creativity. The knowledge and practices of each domain differ considerably. Creativity is consistently concerned with changing our perspectives, regardless of what those perspectives are about. Consequently, the preceding chapters have attempted to provide a general guide to the process of changing our perspectives and then, given that process, how it is that we can improve our ability to go through that process—our craft of creativity.

The focus has been on the creator's own thinking process. We have not focused on special creators. While there are certain creators who have achieved wide renown, we have not started our analysis with them or sought to identify a trait they possessed that made them special. Instead, when we considered individuals, we sought to identify whether there was anything we might learn about the creative process from their travails. Our emphasis on the process of changing perspectives also takes the focus away from creative products. Once more though, while there are certain products that have achieved wide renown, we have not sought to identify a quality they possess that makes them special. Instead, when we considered products, we sought to identify what might be learned regarding the creative process from which they emerged. Thus what it means to focus on the creative process is to understand what creators themselves are thinking and how creators have changed their own perspectives. That is the route to identifying how people can learn to be more adept at generating creative products than they are currently.

To improve our skill at generating creative products, we have two main tasks. First, as the creative process builds on and redirects our craft, we need to develop our craft. Whether it is our craft of accounting, painting, plumbing, software design, or anything else, we need to develop our craft for creativity to be possible. Second, we need to develop our skill with the creative process itself, our craft of creativity.

CRAFT FOR CREATIVITY

We need craft in order to be creative. Fortunately, there are many valuable sources for helping us understand how we develop our craft.[1] Thus we do not need to examine here how we can develop our craft. Instead, we need to clarify why developing our craft fosters our creative efforts. After all, a common assumption is that it is novices who have the most creative potential. And universal novices—young children—are often perceived to be creative.[2]

Three main intuitions support the assumption that novices and children are particularly creative, which would imply that craft undermines rather than supports creativity. The first intuition is that novices feel creative because they experience changes to their perspectives fairly often. For example, when we asked honors student Lela Ross what part of an anti-bullying workshop she had developed was creative, she said, "Pretty much every aspect of it. . . . It was [all] creativity because I had never done anything like this before." This is in contrast to experts who experience perspective changes far less often. For example, composer Jesse Guessford told us that, in comparison to the start of his career, "I feel like I am less creative because I have fewer ideas." What is creativity to the novice will become craft as the enlightenments become expert knowledge about that domain. Why then do we say that craft is needed for creativity if tomorrow's craft can be a product of today's creativity? Simply that today's creativity was a product of yesterday's craft. To form an enlightenment about how to use vibrato when singing, one has to know something about vibrato in the first place. It is difficult to make a creative contribution to the study of discrete time queuing models if one does not even know what they are. Craft enables creativity, which in turn builds the capacity for future craft.

The second intuition that supports the assumption that novices and children are particularly creative—meaning craft undermines rather than supports creativity—is that children and novices sometimes generate kinds of products that experts have overlooked. For example, adults, even professional artists, sometimes find the drawings of kindergarten children more creative than those of adults. Products formed by relatively inexperienced adults are also sometimes deemed creative. For example, professor Linda Seligmann told us a story from the start of her career as an anthropologist. She was working in the Andes. She would ride between cities in giant trucks and became interested in the women who rode with her. These women rode the trucks into the city center to work in the urban markets. Professor Seligmann ended up writing a study of the women that broke many assumptions about what most anthropologists at the time considered important and legitimate. Seligmann had never made those assumptions because she was new to the field. She wound up making an enlightenment that was important not only to her but also to others in anthropology by unwittingly disregarding assumptions in the field. In both cases, the kindergartners' drawings and Seligmann's anthropology study, it is critical to separate the creators' own thinking processes from the thinking processes of others evaluating their work. This kind of example is interesting not because of the thinking of the creators in isolation but because of the thinking of those evaluating the work. Those evaluators interpret the work relative to their own craft knowledge. Seligmann commented on the luck involved in her study, as she did not at the time have the craft knowledge to know whether and why the field of anthropology would view her study to be creative. Novices rarely get lucky enough to make products that experts find creative. That novices ever get lucky in this way is not an indication that craft is unimportant for creativity. Instead, the conclusion is that perceptions of creativity are relative to the person doing the perceiving.

The third intuition that supports the assumption that novices and children are particularly creative is that children and novices tend not to be deeply committed to their existing assumptions. They know they have much to learn and are often willing to consider new possibilities. In contrast, experts are often quite committed to their assumptions. The cynical conclusion is perhaps best captured by a quote from the great physicist Max Planck, who wrote, "A new scientific truth does not triumph by convincing its opponents and making them see the light, but rather because its opponents eventually die, and a new generation grows up that is familiar with it." We have said all along that changing perspectives can be difficult, with strong commitments to our assumptions making it particularly challenging. Experts are likely to be most committed to their assumptions due to repeated reliance on their assumptions over extended periods of time. Novices are likely to be least committed to their assumptions. This third intuition about novices being less committed to their assumptions is useful in terms of the potential for craft to limit creativity. We must recognize that it is not craft per se but rather our commitment to prior craft that limits creativity. In practice these often go together.

The limits on our creativity imposed by commitments to our craft are a small price to pay given the extraordinary gains to creativity from developing our craft. To the specific point about committing to our assumptions, note that while these commitments can lead creators to deny or ignore possibilities, these commitments can also spur new creativity. For example, the prompt, "The boss is upset, . . . " could lead to many stories, and logically more stories than the prompt, "The boss is upset with Jim, who just asked for a larger raise even though his performance is lacking. Jane, Jim's manager, is even more annoyed and goes to talk to the boss. . . . " However, the second prompt provides a much richer starting point for stories. Developed perspectives are more useful than undeveloped perspectives for advancing our stories. Craft provides us with developed perspectives. Put another way, our assumptions both enable and constrain our stories. As there is no way to know in advance whether the assumptions will prove more constraining than enabling, it is not clear whether we can assign a price to committing to our assumptions in advance. Clearly experts have committed to assumptions for far too long that later turned out to be widely recognized as faulty. But experts have also dismissed useful assumptions too readily, only to recommit to them later. Thus even the one real concern with craft limiting creativity is not a universal negative.

There are universal positives of craft that support creativity. This is why we reject the intuition that creativity and craft are opposed. The more developed a person's craft, the greater his or her potential creativity. All accomplished creators are expert craftspeople; all accomplished creators recognized this fact in the interviews. Whether it is the craft of accounting, painting, plumbing, software design, or anything else, absent technical knowledge and skilled practice, we will have nothing from which to build, no skills to do the building, and no skills to use what we have made. Absent the concepts to think about a domain, it is not possible to think creatively about the domain. Novices have less ability than experts to discriminate the useful from the useless, and so they are more likely to think they have hit upon something valuable only to find out later it was fools' gold. Of course experts can be wrong, and famously so. Yet the examples that become famous are the relatively rare exceptions when experts are wrong rather than the vast majority of times when they are right. And who can make the most of an insight, realizing its potential for enlightenments and inventions? Once more, the odds strongly favor the experts. Craft is necessary for creativity, and the benefits of craft far outweigh its liabilities.

The experienced creators we interviewed repeatedly extolled the benefits of their craft for their creativity. They talked about how they learned to "hear better," to "become bolder," to "know their own process," and to make sure their voice is "needed, expected, and respected."[3] They developed authority. Some people had novice creativity stories, but everyone had "my craft helped my creativity" stories. No one pined for the days of not having advanced craft knowledge. People need craft for creativity, and so it benefits their creativity to develop their craft.

THE CRAFT OF CREATIVITY

Part of the craft of creativity is appreciating creativity's scope. Creativity is not limited to the arts or any other domain. And because we can adopt a perspective about anything, creativity is possible in anything we do. Creativity is not a property of situations or episodes. The simplicity or complexity, clarity or ambiguity of an episode is relative to the perspective we adopt. We always adopt a perspective to guide our thinking, so every episode allows us a chance to change our perspective and so think creatively. Therefore creativity can be part of small activities as trivial changes in how we do ordinary thinking.[4] Creativity can also be part of major achievements. We think and act in episodes at every scale. We can form perspectives and stories about anything, encompassing a few moments of thinking to a lifetime of thinking.

For example, A. G. Lafley, longtime CEO of Proctor and Gamble (P&G), noted that "historically, P&G and I think a lot of companies have defined innovation narrowly as technology or product and technology. That's just the beginning for us [now]."[5] He continued on to say that innovation could be in the brand, the business model, the way to bring a product to market, the supply chain, and more. We see similar statements from other leaders of innovative companies, such as Eric Schmidt, the former CEO of Google, who said, "We're looking for somebody who gets up in the morning and just can't wait to solve some new, interesting, and hard problem, whether it's in sales, whether it's in policy, whether it's in legal, whether it's in management, and so forth."[6] Creativity can occur anywhere, and being open to that possibility is part of the craft of creativity.

To detail what the craft of creativity involves, we developed a set of concepts for interpreting the creative process. We separated the stories people are developing over time regarding their thinking and behavior in episodes from the particular perspectives they have adopted to interpret it all. We described craft as using and adding to perspectives to advance stories, and we described creativity as changing perspectives (detailed in the stoplight model) and then developing what follows from the change. Perspectives are patterns of concepts, with the concepts filling five roles: parts, actions, goals, event, and self-concept (PAGES). Thus to change perspectives means to change the concepts playing the roles, the roles played by the concepts, or the concepts' locations in the pattern of concepts. The main cues to change perspectives are being stuck at an impasse, being dissatisfied with a story, being surprised, and experiencing crosstalk that connects one story to another. Having been cued to stop a story and change a perspective, the main cognitive tools creators have for making that change and so producing an insight are to allow activation to identify associated concepts, to draw an analogy to another pattern of concepts, to form a combination between concepts, and to recategorize some aspect using an alternative concept. Forming an insight means the creator has changed his or her perspective and so can now take their stories in formerly inconceivable directions. An insight plus further craft—and usually additional insights—can enable people to develop formerly inconceivable resolutions to their stories (inventions) as well as formerly inconceivable new knowledge (enlightenments). Thus, to summarize, we defined creativity as a process of following cues to generate insights that change perspectives, which with craft can be used to develop inventions and enlightenments.

We always adopt a perspective to guide our stories, so at every moment in every episode it is possible to change our perspective and so think creatively. Uncertainty is very often a reason we do not change our perspectives. We continue using and adding to our perspectives because we think it will allow us to advance our stories adequately. We tend not to stop to change our perspectives because we are uncertain it is necessary, we are uncertain we can generate an alternative, we are uncertain it will be fruitful even if we do so, and we are uncertain that any products we generate will be worthwhile. Consequently, the craft of creativity rests on pushing back against our confidence in our own perspectives and our concerns about the many forms of uncertainty involved in changing our perspectives in order to launch an attempt to do so. A willingness to consider alternatives to our current perspective is part of the craft of creativity.

That willingness to change our perspective can arrive at the outset of a story. We might be dissatisfied with the ordinary approaches to stories like the one we believe we are starting. We might be surprised and begin a story to follow where the surprise leads us. A blank page impasse might mean we are not sure which perspective to adopt for the episode and so encourage us to build new knowledge. Or we might deliberately set out to consider alternative perspectives before advancing our stories as part of our craft of creativity.

Our willingness to change our perspective can arrive in the middle of a story. We might be at a dead end impasse and not know how to continue. We might be dissatisfied with how our story is developing or with its prospects going forward. We might be surprised by something in the episode we did not expect. Or we might deliberately take a break to reconsider our perspective as a result of a previously developed enlightenment about the craft of creativity.

Our willingness to change our perspective can arrive at the end of a story. We might be dissatisfied with how our story ended. We might be surprised by something that happened or how it resolved. Or we might deliberately stop to reflect on our perspective as a result of a previously developed enlightenment about the craft of creativity.

Our willingness to change our perspective can also arrive outside of the story for which the perspective is relevant. We might be working on another story when crosstalk indicates something relevant to a story we were not at that moment trying to advance. Or we might deliberately engage with people or in episodes likely to provide information that might be useful to our perspective as a result of a previously developed enlightenment about the craft of creativity.

When it comes to stopping the use of our perspectives and considering changing our perspectives, we can learn to make more use of the cues. We can see a slowing in our progress as regrettable, or we can treat it as a sign of an impasse. We can minimize imperfections and appreciate being at an appropriate location on a cost-benefit curve, or we can treat it as dissatisfaction. We can numbly perceive what the world throws at us, or we can actively consider and predict possibilities and thus increase our experience of surprise. We can keep pushing on what we are doing, or we can intersperse these efforts with engagements in related concerns, observing and listening with care and the mental slack to recognize crosstalk. The cues are only cues if we experience them. Becoming more sensitive to cues that signal alternatives to continuing with our current perspective is part of the craft of creativity.

Venturing more effectively into the void to identify concepts for changing our perspectives is also part of the craft of creativity. We can deliberately think through or write out the PAGES constituting our perspectives. This can help us surface assumptions that we had been making about our own role (self-concept), the type of episode in which we think we are participating (event), our motivations for participating (goals), what we might do (actions), and what is involved (parts). We can shift our focus, bit by bit, to different aspects of our perspectives, and so give ourselves a chance to try different starting points for activation, different opportunities for recategorization and combination, and different prompts for finding analogies. We can also put ourselves in different contexts and engage with others who are different to help us bring different knowledge to mind. We can manage uncertainty by appreciating that our task is not to run out of the void as quickly as possible and not to avoid going back in. Appreciating the potential that changing our perspectives offers is part of the craft of creativity.

Managing the joint development of our stories and of our perspectives is a further aspect of the craft of creativity. Our efforts to develop insights, inventions, and enlightenments are not separate but typically overlap. These overlapping efforts themselves overlap with our efforts to advance our stories in ordinary ways. We do not build complete PAGES and then begin our stories. Instead, we pull together enough PAGES to get going and add more later. We do not need to change PAGES all at once and only then resume our stories. Instead, we usually make provisional changes and see where they take us. We advance our stories as rapidly as we do in large part because we ignore uncertainties, take our assumptions for granted, and try to press on. This is practical because we can make progress, and it is practical because creativity might mean making further changes. Creativity might mean changing the kind of story we think we are telling. Creativity might mean changing our knowledge. Creativity might lead us to build new knowledge. Part of the craft of creativity is managing the simultaneous uncertainties in our story and our perspective, and persisting nonetheless.

The gains from changing our perspective provide reasons for developing our craft of creativity. It is also going to make us more appreciative of craft. Good outcomes are good even if they are developed through craft, not creativity. Creativity need not feel special, and craft need not feel boring. Craft is how we make use of creativity, and creativity is how we extend craft. Appreciating the links between learning and creativity is part of the craft of creativity. And part of the craft of creativity is appreciating that craft is entwined with creativity.

EVALUATING CREATIVE PRODUCTS

If we advance our craft of creativity, we will generate creative products. These creative products raise new uncertainty challenges, as the creativity scholar Jennifer Mueller has emphasized and documented.[7] Creative products represent change. Change can be good or bad or just different. Change usually brings disruption. Some aspects of our craft are left behind. There may be more to learn and do as a result of the change. As noted previously, predictions about the future are difficult. Consequently, creativity brings with it costs in the form of the disruption and uncertainty raised by creative products. Of course, creativity also generates potential for gains that we would not readily have been able to attain otherwise. There are elements of uncertainty that we cannot avoid. Yet there are some sources of uncertainty that we can mitigate if we examine some common assumptions about creative products using our discussion of the process of generating creative products.

The dominant approach to thinking about creative products comes from the widely used definition of creativity as *the production of novel and useful ideas*.[8] The primary assumption underlying this definition is that generating a novel product that turns out to be useful is what it means to generate creativity. This is why many discussions about how to be creative focus on how to help people maximize novelty. There are recommendations to draw ideas from distant places or form unlikely combinations.[9] There are even computer programs that randomly generate words as a means to spur creativity.[10] Yet as we noted earlier when discussing why the "mix" approach to the creative process was unhelpful, maximizing the novelty of mixes is not a means of maximizing their creativity. The key issue in our view is not the novelty of what people end up generating, but rather the change to the perspective that they had formed.

The real problem, we think, comes from believing that "if we have used a creative process then we will have a novel and useful idea" implies "if we have a novel and useful idea then we will have used a creative process." Yet this is a simple logical error akin to claiming that "if it is snowing then I will be cold" means "if I am cold then it is snowing." Novelty is a descriptor we can apply to creative products, not an account of the process for generating one.

Worse, while creative products can be viewed as novel, this does not mean that all novel products are creative. Rarity and bizarreness are forms of novelty, but neither need imply creativity. For example, perhaps we ask a group of people to "give us a number." A response of "7" is just the sort of response we expect, and so not novel, rare, bizarre, or creative. The response "7134" would undoubtedly be rare, despite being perfectly appropriate or useful. But is it creative? Perhaps it is mildly creative because it is not a small integer, but it does not strike us as particularly creative. The response "Novocain" is likely to be perceived as bizarre and not creative. That is, unless we generated the perspective change that "number" could be perceived as "numb-er," as in something that numbs, in which case Novocain is not a bizarre response but a creative response.

While novelty is judged relative to our knowledge, there is nothing in the "novel and useful" approach to defining creative products that distinguishes between the "bizarre" interpretation and the "perspective changing" interpretation of the Novocain response. Perhaps the answer lies in the "usefulness" aspect of the definition. The "perspective changing" interpretation allows the Novocain response to be seen as appropriate and therefore useful, whereas the "bizarre" interpretation does not (unless we are fans of absurdist humor, we suppose). But then why is 7134, which is also a novel and useful response, not as creative as the Novocain response? Novocain is bizarre as a "number," but Novocain is every bit as obvious a "numb-er" as 7 is a "number." We are not able to answer the question of why Novocain the "numb-er" is a creative response (and 7 and 7134 are not) without resorting to changes in perspective.

This is not an isolated example. We could imagine finding $100 on the street—novel and useful, but not creative. We could imagine solving a riddle by using an alternative bit of ordinary knowledge (the man is not the groom but a priest!)—creative, but not novel. Obscure technical artifacts are generally experienced as novel and useful, but not as creative. These are just simple demonstrations to illustrate the inadequacy of the "novel and useful" definition of creative products. Consequently, the conclusion we draw is that it would be helpful to discard the assumptions that "producing novelty" is the key way to think about generating creativity and that evaluating products for "novelty and usefulness" requires a sharpening of what we mean by "novelty" and by "usefulness" when it comes to assessing creativity.

To assess products for creativity, it may be useful to interpret the task as being driven by two factors, whether evaluators experience a change in perspective and whether evaluators perceive external signals that the product is creative. First and foremost, it is useful to examine whether the evaluators experience a change in their perspectives upon perceiving and making sense of the product. Perhaps we read the Novocain response, thought it was bizarre, recognized the change in perspective from "number" to "numb-er," and then reinterpreted the Novocain response not as being bizarre but as having followed from a change in perspective. In this case, we as evaluators interpreted the response following a change in perspective. Most conceptual art works in a similar fashion. For example, Jeff once looked at a reproduction of Magritte's famous painting of a pipe with one of his daughters. Underneath the image of a pipe, Magritte painted the words, "This is not a pipe." Jeff's daughter thought it was bizarre. After she changed her perspective to recognize that the artist was emphasizing the distance between perception and reality, she found it creative, a bit funny, and even a bit profound.

Evaluators need not go through the same perspective change(s) as the creators. In fact, the creators need not go through any change in perspective at all to change the perspective of an evaluator. Outcomes ordinary to creators can be experienced as creative by evaluators if evaluators go through a perspective change. This is why what is experienced as craft by the expert can be experienced as creativity by the novice. And of course, the reverse is possible too: the result of a substantial change in perspective by the creator may be perceived as ordinary by evaluators because they perceive it as fitting their existing perspectives or, worse, failing by the criteria of their existing perspectives. The economist George Akerlof's paper, "The Market for 'Lemons'," changed the field once evaluators recognized the change in perspective it indicated—that information asymmetry had large implications for how markets function.[11] Initially though, the paper was rejected as "trivial."

If this proposal is correct, that evaluators judge products to be creative in part because they experience a change in perspective themselves upon perceiving the products, then we can estimate when products are likely to be perceived as more and less creative. The larger the change to their perspective, the more creative evaluators should perceive the product to be, where "larger" is a function of the amount of change to the pattern of concepts constituting the perspective. In addition, the more fruitful or generative the change in perspective, the more it spurs new inferences and responses, the more creative it should be perceived to be. Our guess is that fruitfulness is probably more important than the size of the change in perspective, because it is turning the inconceivable into the thinkable that matters most when it comes to changes in perspective.

We indicated that when evaluators assess a product for its creativity, there are two influences on their judgments. The first influence is whether evaluators perceive the product and undergo a change in their own perspectives. The second influence is whether the product bears signals that evaluators consider relevant to or associated with creativity.

For example, all else being equal, we would imagine a bias to consider paintings to be creative simply because they are artistic products and art is usually considered a creative product. All else being equal, we tend to consider products creative if they were made by or pitched by someone who looks stereotypically creative.[12] We tend to consider products creative if they are made by a talented person as opposed to one who worked hard, even if we in fact heard the same concert performance and even if we are expert musicians.[13] We often get caught up in the romantic vision of the superlative genius, the isolated artist, and the rule-breaking entrepreneur, even if research yields little support for these stereotypes.[14] More generally, part of why we perceive a product to be creative is because it has the signals that, in our prior experience, have accompanied products we associate with creativity.[15] This can vary dramatically by culture. For example, while in the United States many people seem to believe that inventions aimed for a mass market *are not* likely to be creative, in China many people seem to believe that inventions aimed for a mass market *are* likely to be creative.

In relying on signals of creativity, rather than a change in perspective, we run the risks of stereotyping. We can succumb to assessing creativity on the basis of signals that, upon reflection, might well be irrelevancies.[16] Put more positively, evaluators' judgments of creativity are in part influenced by their cultural histories and their social contexts.[17]

The larger implication of this discussion is that defining creative products when in the role of creator is not the same as defining creative products when in the role of evaluator. Taking the creator role, we defined three creative products: insights (changes to perspective in this moment), inventions (resolutions to stories), and enlightenments (changes to knowledge). Taking the evaluator role, it is possible to assess any of these three products for their creativity, but people are most often in the position of evaluating inventions, followed by enlightenments, and only more rarely do they consider the creativity of someone else's insights. Our proposal was that evaluators judge the creativity of others' products using two forms of information: whether the evaluators themselves change their perspectives when perceiving and interpreting the product, and whether the evaluators perceive signals of creativity in and surrounding the product.

With this new set of assumptions about the task of evaluating products for creativity, we have an opportunity to improve our craft of creativity by improving the quality and reliability of our evaluations. When we are evaluators, we have two tasks. The first task is to work to separate the creative product from the context surrounding its presentation. This is a bit like separating our appraisal of a consumer product from the advertising and packaging of that consumer product. It is challenging, but we can make some headway. The second task is to consider whether the product spurs changes to our perspectives and whether those changes reflect positively on the product. For inventions, the question is usually whether the invention resolves a story or kind of story that we care about in a previously inconceivable way. For insights and enlightenments, the question is usually whether they are sensible and generative.

This effort at evaluating products for creativity will not tell us whether those products will be successful. A product's success is a matter of how the future plays out.[18] For example, one study put people into online discussion groups to listen to and evaluate songs.[19] Songs that tended to be in the top half of the ratings in one online community showed a tendency to be in the top half of the ratings in another online community. Thus there was some consistency in the evaluation of these songs. But the songs that were considered best in any particular community appeared to be a random draw from within the better songs. Why a product of the creative process succeeds in the world, where competitors, media, and many other complexities play crucial roles, is a complex process. There are many forms of success, such as fame or financial success. But at least the effort to understand the product can encourage an understanding of whether and why the product could be of interest. That understanding in itself is of merit, as part of the value of creative products is what we learn from perceiving them.

COMMUNICATING ABOUT CREATIVE PRODUCTS

Once people have generated a creative product, they often want others to use it or at least appreciate it. What we just argued is that evaluators are likely to perceive the product as creative if they change their own perspectives upon perceiving it. Yet evaluators do not need to see the product as creative. Creators often find it sufficient for evaluators to like the product and find it valuable. An even more urgent reason to encourage evaluators to change their perspectives upon perceiving products then, apart from so they appreciate the creativity involved, is so they appreciate the worth of those products.

Creative products initially are inconceivable to their creators, raising uncertainties about the value of those products. A major concern is that the product will be inconceivable to or misunderstood by evaluators. Creators and evaluators often have relatively similar knowledge due to similar education, training, work experience, membership in the same cultural communities, and so forth.[20] If so, then when creators have been creative, they are decreasing the similarity of their knowledge relative to others. They are opening up gaps between what they think and what others think.[21] The other alternative, when creators and evaluators start with different knowledge, simply raises the likelihood that creators' products will be inconceivable to or misunderstood by evaluators. Thus creativity generates challenges for mutual understanding and coordination.

To address this challenge, creators can develop, as part of their craft of creativity, their skills at communicating about their products so that evaluators understand and appreciate them. It is costly to creators to create only to fail at enabling others to appreciate their products. The typical outcome of poor communication is probably evaluators ignoring the creators' products. Evaluators might fail to perceive the product as something new, discounting creators' efforts at overcoming uncertainties, navigating the void, and advancing their stories. Worse, creators' products could be met with derision, and even personal derision toward the creator. This can be mortifying to creators and can lead them to exit an activity altogether, or worse.[22] The more personal the derision, and the more trusted the evaluator, the more damaging this can be.

Even if the outcome is just rejection it can be costly. For example, game designer John Comes told us about one of his company's games. An aspect of his team's craft of creativity is that when they make games, they "find the fun first." Thus they typically use only crude and limited graphics while they work on the actual game mechanics that make it fun. For example, if we think about the classic game *Tetris*, what makes it fun are the mechanics of fitting blocks together. The graphics are not particularly critical. With one of their games, Comes and his team made a crude-looking game with great mechanics. The problem came when they communicated about the game. They showed the game to Microsoft, which passed. Then Comes's team improved the graphics, went back to Microsoft, showed the reviewers the same game, and they loved it.

The point is not that graphics are important. The point is that what was obvious to Comes and his team, the game's mechanics, was not obvious to the team at Microsoft because they had not spent months developing and thinking about the mechanics. Comes and his team were suffering from the curse of knowledge.[23] They were viewing their game through their own perspective. They were failing to appreciate the perspective of the evaluators. The improved graphics were critical to enabling the evaluators to envision the full product. Communication is critical for enabling evaluators to appreciate creative products.

Creators have an opportunity with their communications to lead evaluators to undergo a change in their perspectives. Evaluators do what we all do by default: they interpret what they perceive using their own prior knowledge. Seeing our friend Bill explode at a meeting could be stunning or mundane, depending on what our experience with Bill is. To interpret a product in some other way requires guidance. A story's ending will only reliably surprise its audience if the story sets up the surprise. Our task then as creators is to start a story that our evaluators can understand, lead them to a cue to change their perspectives, help support their change in perspective, and then help guide them toward the winning resolution.[24]

The first step of setting up the story at a point our evaluators can understand is the most overlooked. As creators, we tend to be focused on the product and are eager to talk about it. And as just noted, as creators, we tend to be focused on our own perspectives, not the evaluators' perspectives. Consequently, it feels as if we are stepping backward to start our stories well before the changes in perspective, let alone the resolutions, that yielded the creative product about which we are trying to communicate. Yet creators might need to teach evaluators, to help evaluators build some knowledge, before the product makes sense. For example, most people agree that Nobel Prize–winning ideas are creative, but how many people can pick such an idea out of a lineup? Here is such a lineup: orb photography, quasicrystals, Fraunhofer lines, chromium reification. Most people can only guess, not having the knowledge of these areas of science.[25] Starting with a simple, concrete example is useful for drawing in evaluators and enabling them to understand the story that follows.[26]

Just understanding the story, and so the product, is usually not enough. Absent communicating about products in such a way as to help evaluators appreciate why they matter, communicating to evaluators is at best a statement of facts. Evaluators may not appreciate why those facts matter or what follows from those facts. Evaluators may not evaluate those facts positively. As actor Hayes Gordon discussed, there is a challenge in distinguishing between what is well regarded by evaluators and what is personally satisfying to creators.[27] For example, chef Kevin McGowan talked to us about making omelets. There is a standard for making omelets in the French tradition. They are fluffy and light, they do not get brown, and they are folded in thirds. You do not need to make an omelet that way to enjoy eating it. You can put eggs in a pan, fold it in half and so have an omelet that is browned on one side. Yet in the domain of cooking, that is frowned upon. McGowan noted, "Making that will get you fired from any good restaurant." Or, as a second example, Matt was once in a band with a drummer whose meter wavered throughout a song. When told, "You are speeding up and slowing down throughout the song," the drummer replied, "Yeah, I like it like that." There is no commandment in music saying that a song should maintain a fixed tempo. Maybe such variation can allow a song to "breathe." Yet in most music, inconsistent tempo is not positively regarded but seen as incompetence. More generally, a product that a creator finds personally satisfying may not be well regarded by evaluators if the product does not conform to existing standards. Yet part of creativity may be dropping a commitment to particular standards. In this case, creators need to do more that allows evaluators to understand their products; they also need to communicate new standards of evaluation and establish their merit. The challenges of communication for understanding and appreciation place a burden on creators. Our recommendation is that creators make use of the cues for prompting perspective change and tools for changing perspectives in the course of communicating with evaluators.

We as creators can lead evaluators to experience impasses, dissatisfaction, or surprises so that the evaluators see a reason to consider changing their perspectives. We as creators can guide evaluators to notice particular associations or form certain analogies, combinations, or recategorizations to do the work of changing their perspectives. The cues we use and the tools we set up need not be the ones that led us as creators to the product we are communicating about to evaluators. The evaluators do not have to relive our stories. The evaluators may not start with the same knowledge we did. And our stories changed as we went along, so the products and the importance of those products may have little to do with where we started anyway. Evaluators do not need to know anything about the engineering, design, manufacturing, funding, management, or marketing to rent a movie at a Globox. Evaluators do not have to know Rob Mars's story to enjoy one of his paintings. Yet there is often value in developing not just an understanding of a product but an appreciation of it, and guiding evaluators into and through a change in perspective is a means for enabling them to develop that appreciation.

The typical context of discussing communication and creative products is communication about inventions to funders or consumers. There are other important contexts though. When we are creators communicating about inventions, we typically are trying to obtain resources from evaluators—please approve, fund, honor, or otherwise support our products. When we are communicating about enlightenments, we may be trying to obtain support, but we may often be in the role of a teacher or mentor. In this case, we are not looking for support but providing it. This does not require a radically different communication process than what was just outlined. Instead, there is just an even larger burden placed on supporting the evaluator through each step in the process.

We might also be communicating about inventions and enlightenments with other creators. Our stories link with others' stories. So our creative products become craft not just for ourselves but also for others. Often producers are professionals working in the field: professional artists seeing each other's work; professional accountants giving talks to each other at company or industry events; professional repairmen swapping stories.[28] Yet expert evaluators might also be communities of users and hobbyists.[29] Perhaps with a good enough story developing toward an innovation, they might quit their jobs and become entrepreneurs, thereby joining the professional ranks. But they might just continue engaging in other ways. The point is that effective communication allows for the development of domain craft, not just personal craft. That can change the world.

For example, in 1833, Michael Faraday found that it is possible to increase the electrical conductance in silver sulfide crystals by increasing the temperature. After another 41 years, Ferdinand Braun figured out that current flows freely in only one direction at the contact between a metal point and a galena crystal. After another 52 years, Julius Lilienfeld patented the concept for a field effect device. Some 14 years later, Russell Ohl discovered the p-n junction and photovoltaic effects in silicon. From all of this, in 1945, some 115 years later, William Shockley conceptualized and in 1948 produced the first transistor. The transistor, in turn, is one of the most fruitful inventions in history, having been used in countless ways. Each invention and enlightenment was both a terminal outcome and an intermediate outcome in a larger creative process. We are receivers of others' stories and others' craft and creativity. Communicating effectively about creative products is a key part of the craft of creativity not only for our own benefits, but also so our products can yield collective benefits.

SUPPORTING CREATIVITY

As the creativity scholar Teresa Amabile has so convincingly established, creativity occurs in a social context and so merits social support.[30] Thus people can help creativity to flourish by developing supportive social and organizational contexts.[31] There is much written on this elsewhere, so we will just draw out a few points of contact here.

A commonly raised issue is that our teams and organizations have goals of their own. Brooks Branham, the CFO of Carrolton Technology Partners, put it bluntly. He said, "I never think in terms of creativity—I think in terms of results." Thinking about long-term results as well as short-term results, though, provides a justification for providing resources so that people have the slack to engage in the creative process. It is difficult to stop using our perspectives to advance our stories and instead switch to the uncertain process of changing our perspectives absent that kind of slack. When we spoke with Branham, for example, he had just written a creative compensation formula not on his whiteboard but on his window. That way he could "look through the numbers"[32] for a while and continue to reflect on this invention and whether he could further improve on it. Some degree of slack allows for the experimentation and dead ends in the creative process.

Related to providing slack, a tolerance for failure is also helpful for supporting creativity. For example, we have found companies with a culture of taking a positive attitude toward failure, and this can spur creative behavior and increase their bottom lines.[33] Employees at these companies are likely to feel less fearful or anxious about coming back from the void empty handed. They go in and fail, they learn it is not so bad, and they are emboldened to try, try again until they succeed. This links to our observation that many of the seasoned creators we interviewed said that they got bolder over time. Thus it appears that people can support creativity by viewing failure as a necessary outcome of a process that makes them confront the inconceivable.

As a further example, social validation for the importance of stories and their worthiness of love and fascination supports individuals' efforts to persist with the creative process in the face of uncertainty. We acknowledge the challenges teams and organizations face, though. Teams and organizations rely on cooperation and coordination among members.[34] Creativity disrupts coordination and is benefitted by a tolerance of conflict.[35] Consequently, people can be encouraged to focus on advancing their stories above all else, providing space, rules, and a culture that minimizes the likelihood of social conflict. They also can be matched to tasks that fit their own views about importance and their own loves.

If there is an overarching message about supporting creativity from this discussion of the creative process, it is to promote efforts to grapple with the uncertainty generated in the creative process. We have to work to be open to ideas and products that do not at first make sense to us, and that might even perturb us. Our normal tendency to use our perspectives can fail us when it comes to evaluating creative products because our snap judgment is often to categorize the product as irrelevant or a failure. This is the judgment of our existing perspective, though. Consequently, we have to work to redirect, or at least quell, our default reactions. We can encourage effective communication. Just as important, we can encourage the development of our skill at listening to others. We can appreciate that people might not yet be able to articulate what they are thinking and might not look as if they are being productive. They might still be in the void and not yet able to see a way out. We can appreciate the length of time needed to build new approaches. We can foster respect for one another, for each other's craft, and for the craft of creativity.

CREATIVE POTENTIAL

Confucius apparently said, "Only the wisest and stupidest of people never change." All the rest of us can change our perspectives. It is a necessary, but often long and difficult process. We can wander in the void for a long time. We can struggle to build new knowledge on the basis of new assumptions. We can make one attempt after another to make use of insights and new knowledge as we learn where they might take our stories. To do something beyond what we can imagine right now, to think the inconceivable and then do the hard work to bring it into existence, we need to change our perspectives.

A willingness to change our perspectives and follow where those changes lead requires us to confront uncertainty and see the potential it provides. The potential in a creative product is unbounded, if we are willing to continue allowing it to change our perspectives and yield new inventions and enlightenments.

For example, Herbert Simon, one of the great twentieth-century scholars, who wrote hundreds of papers and several foundational books, and is considered a seminal figure in multiple fields, when reflecting back on his career said, "[A] problem I found in 1935 has lasted me for 52 years. I have never had to find another."[36]

To support people's willingness to engage in creativity and to help them make the most of the potential that creativity provides, we have developed a new formulation of the creative process. We have synthesized research findings and gathered new evidence from a range of creators about the process they go through to generate products. We have expanded our view of the products of creativity, distinguishing among insights, inventions, and enlightenments. We have changed some assumptions about what creativity is and how people produce it. The most important enlightenment along the way is that we as creators can intervene on the creative process. We can initiate creativity more frequently. We can go through the process with a bit less struggle and a bit higher likelihood of success. We can make use of what we find in more and better ways. There is a craft of creativity, and we can improve our craft.

The effects are not just individual. Herbert Simon's efforts were picked up and used by others (including us). Where our efforts will take us we cannot know. For example, in 1976, when newfound concerns arose about the actions of companies and how to provide greater oversight and controls over such large and powerful actors in the world, the political activist Ralph Nader and colleagues wrote a book, *The Taming of the Giant Corporation.*[37] In that book, they developed the combination "corporate governance" to connect the oversight role of political government on society to a need for a new form of governance to oversee companies. That combination, corporate governance, has since further developed and become the overarching term for an elaborate set of practices, institutional arrangements, scholarly analysis, and more, including how firms are audited and how executives are paid. Who knew that such a strong critic of companies would end up providing what is now conventional wisdom about how they are run at the highest of levels? The products of our own creativity are ultimately a collective resource.

Our creative products can change what we collectively view as conceivable. Apparently C. H. Duell, commissioner of the U.S. Office of Patents, said in 1899, "Everything that can be invented has been invented." Our current perspectives are necessary and helpful but are necessarily limited and impose unhelpful biases. Creativity is our tool for changing those limits and biases. That creativity is ongoing means that, even more than being about insights, inventions, and enlightenments, creativity is about increasing our potential. The new perspectives we have, and the new enlightenments and inventions that follow, provide a basis for generating further stories and are the starting point for further creativity. Because creativity rests on and develops knowledge, and because knowledge is shared with others in our cultural communities, we could say that creativity is the primary basis for cultural development.

APPENDIX

Interview Participants

What follows is an alphabetical list of our participants, all of whom we thank heartily. It was in speaking to them all that our understanding emerged and was changed. They made this book possible. We probably got to write in about 2 percent of the interesting and wonderful insights and enlightenments that were passed on to us (if that). Nonetheless, 100 percent of it made us think and develop our story.

Name	Profession
Alan Cheuse	Author, professor
Aldo Iacono	Medical director of the Lung Healing Program at the Shock Trauma Center, UMD[1]
Alexis Lahr	Anthropology undergraduate student focused on nutritional education[2]
Amile Bond	Undergraduate, computer science major
Angela An	Emmy Award–winning news anchor, WBNS-10TV[3]
Anna Hulse	Undergraduate dance student and choreographer
Anthony Pappas	President and executive creative director for DMI
Archie Grefer	Experienced computer programmer and web developer
Asad Ali	Entrepreneur, Globox co-founder
Becky Pedigo	Comic, nonphilanthropist, indie author, and blogger[4]
Bill Foster	CPA and head of Foster and Foley Accountants
Bob Dawson	Grammy-winning music producer and founder of Bias Studios
Brandon Kirk	Recently minted IT network engineer
Brian Mark	Engineer, professor
Brooks Branham	CFO, Carrolton Technology Partners
Burt Miller	Co-inventor of the Pungo, and inventor of quiet blenders, concrete counters, and many, many other things[5]
Carol Cadby	Educator, actor, executive coach, and consultant on arts policy[6]
Constance Dinapoli	Dancer, performer, professor

Dan Boyarski	Typographer, information and interaction designer, professor[7]
Dan Joyce	Dancer, choreographer, professor
Dan Negoianu	Medical director, Inpatient Hemodialysis Unit
Dave Nardolilli	Graphic designer, D.J.
DG	Pianist, cruise ship music director[8]
Drew Davidson	Director of the Entertainment Technology Center at Carnegie Mellon University[9]
Elena Sendolo	GMU honors student studying positive gender images of women in Hungary
Emily Mann	Anthropology student[10]
Gelo Fleisher	Author and game developer, certified public accountant[11]
Hannah King	Dance student and choreographer
Hannah Landsberger	Double major undergraduate student, in theater and management[12]
James Thane Robeson	Bassist, singer, music producer[13]
Jason Core	Graphic and web artist
Jeff Handy	Development lead on various technology projects
Jesse Guessford	Composer, director of music technology, professor
Jesse Schell	CEO of Schell Games, author, TED speaker
James Morris	Dean, professor, entrepreneur[14]
Jim Sulkowski	Classical artist, teacher
Joe Genuardi	Master tailor[15]
John Comes	Design director (video games) at Uber Entertainment
Jonas Wæver	Lead designer on *The Nameless Mod*[16]
Jonathan Biguenet	Developer and programmer
Jordan Garcie	Network engineer
Kariann Fuqua	Fine artist, curator, professor of art, gallery director
Katie De Monsabert	Performer; dancer; puppeteer; singer for Disney, Busch Gardens, and Universal Studios
Kevin McGowan	Chef, educator, former Microsoft programmer
Kyle Herndon	Network architect
Lawrence Laxdal	Producer of *The Nameless Mod*[17]
Lela Ross	Undergraduate student majoring in international studies and conflict analysis and resolution
Leo Badinella	Composer, instrumentalist, arranger, guitarist, producer[18]
Linda Seligmann	Professor of anthropology and a Fulbright Fellow
Luis Rivera	Architect
Mark Cronin	Former head of the criminal law division of the New Jersey Superior Court

Mark Sunshine	Singer, songwriter, artist
Michael D. Weinraub, ESQ	Elder care lawyer
Maureen Walsh	Lobbyist, lawyer
Merv DeMello	Mechanic, racer of diesel trucks, owner of Merv's Auto Repair
Michael Wilkes	Project manager, Daniels Remodeling
Peter Stearns	Former provost of George Mason University[19]
R. Ravi	Operations researcher, professor, guitar player
Ray Mitchell	IT network architect, Carrolton Technology Partners
Rick Davis	Professor of theater; dean, College of Visual and Performing Arts; executive director of the Hylton Performing Arts Center
Robert Mars	Artist, former guitarist in NJ hardcore band Crucial Youth
Sammy Kassim	Entrepreneur, Globox cofounder
Sean Moore	Programmer
Seweta Sedhai	Undergraduate student, premed
Shirley Yee	Graphic designer, professor at the Entertainment Technology Center
Sridhar Tayur	Operations professor, entrepreneur, founder of Organ Jet
Steve Turner	Guitarist, bandleader, teacher
Sushela Mayyappan	Undergraduate bioengineering major
Ted Daniels	CEO, Daniels Design & Remodeling
Thad Allen	Former Coast Guard admiral and twenty-third commandant of the Coast Guard[20]
Thao-Chi Vo	GMU student, studying nerve potentiation in neurons
Tim Sauer	Mathematician, professor
Turley	Magician[21]
Vic Jones	Network architect
Wayne Schnell	Director of IT network development department
Zi Yang	Undergraduate student, history major
Zoltan Munkacsi	Project lead and game mod developer

NOTES

PREFACE AND ACKNOWLEDGMENTS

1. Teresa M. Amabile, "How to Kill Creativity," *Harvard Business Review*, September-October (1998): 76–87; Teresa M. Amabile, Regina Conti, Heather Coon, Jeffrey Lazenby, and Michael Herron, "Assessing the Work Environment for Creativity," *Academy of Management Journal* 39, no. 5 (1996): 1154–1184; Mihaly Csikszentmihalyi and Rustin Wolfe, "New Conceptions and Research Approaches to Creativity: Implications of a Systems Perspective for Creativity in Education," in *The Systems Model of Creativity*, 161–184 (Dordrecht: Springer Netherlands, 2014); Arthur John Cropley, *Creativity in Education & Learning: A Guide for Teachers and Educators* (Abingdon, Oxon, UK: Routledge, 2001); Robert L. DeHaan, "Teaching Creative Science Thinking," *Science* 334, no. 6062 (2011): 1499–1500.

2. Po Bronson and Ashley Merryman, "The Creativity Crisis," *Newsweek*, July 10, 2010; Richard Florida, "America's Looming Creativity Crisis," *Harvard Business Review* 82, no. 10 (2004): 122–136; Kyung Hee Kim, "The Creativity Crisis: The Decrease in Creative Thinking Scores on the Torrance Tests of Creative Thinking," *Creativity Research Journal* 23, no. 4 (2011): 285–295.

3. Mark A. Runco, "Creativity and Education," *New Horizons in Education* 56, no. 1 (2008): n1; "Fact Sheet: The White House Releases New Strategy for American Innovation, Announces Areas of Opportunity from Self-Driving Cars to Smart Cities," White House, October 21, 2015, https://www.whitehouse.gov/the-press-office/2015/10/21/fact-sheet-white-house-releases-new-strategy-american-innovation; National Endowment for the Arts, "Creativity Connects" accessed June 23, 2017, https://www.arts.gov/50th/creativity-connects; "Fact Sheet: Redesigning America's High Schools," U.S. Department of Education, June 7, 2013, http://www.ed.gov/news/press-releases/fact-sheet-redesigning-americas-high-schools.

4. Jennifer S. Mueller, *Creative Change* (New York: Houghton Mifflin Harcourt, 2017).

CHAPTER 1

1. Ravi Mehta, Rui Juliet Zhu, and Amar Cheema, "Is Noise Always Bad? Exploring the Effects of Ambient Noise on Creative Cognition," *Journal of Consumer Research* 39, no. 4 (2012): 784–799.

2. Angela Ka-yee Leung, William W. Maddux, Adam D. Galinsky, and Chi-yue Chiu, "Multicultural Experience Enhances Creativity: The When and How," *American Psychologist* 63, no. 3 (2008): 169–181.

3. Adam M. Grant, Ellen J. Langer, Emily Falk, and Christina Capodilupo, "Mindful Creativity: Drawing to Draw Distinctions," *Creativity Research Journal* 16, no. 2-3 (2004): 261–265.

4. Kimberly D. Elsbach and Andrew B. Hargadon, "Enhancing Creativity Through 'Mindless' Work: A Framework of Workday Design," *Organization Science* 17, no. 4 (2006): 470–483.

5. Teresa M. Amabile, Sigal G. Barsade, Jennifer S. Mueller, and Barry M. Staw, "Affect and Creativity at Work," *Administrative Science Quarterly* 50, no. 3 (2005): 367–403; Alice M. Isen, Kimberly A. Daubman, and Gary P. Nowicki, "Positive Affect Facilitates Creative Problem Solving," *Journal of Personality and Social Psychology* 52, no. 6 (1987): 1122–1131.

6. Carsten K. W. De Dreu, Matthijs Baas, and Bernard A. Nijstad, "Hedonic Tone and Activation Level in the Mood-Creativity Link: Toward a Dual Pathway to Creativity Model," *Journal of Personality and Social Psychology* 94, no. 5 (2008): 739–756; Jennifer M. George and Jing Zhou, "Understanding When Bad Moods Foster Creativity and Good Ones Don't: The Role of Context and Clarity of Feelings," *Journal of Applied Psychology* 87, no. 4 (2002): 687–697.

7. Robert W. Weisberg and Richard Hass, "Commentaries: We Are All Partly Right: Comment on Simonton," *Creativity Research Journal* 19, no. 4 (2007): 345–360.

8. Charalampos Mainemelis and Sarah Ronson, "Ideas Are Born in Fields of Play: Towards a Theory of Play and Creativity in Organizational Settings," *Research in Organizational Behavior* 27 (2006): 81–131; Leigh Thompson, "Improving the Creativity of Organizational Work Groups," *The Academy of Management Executive* 17, no. 1 (2003): 96–109.

9. Richard Florida, *The Rise of the Creative Class* (New York: Basic Books, 2002); Richard Florida, "America's Looming Creativity Crisis," *Harvard Business Review* 82, no. 10 (2004): 136.

10. Teresa M. Amabile, "The Social Psychology of Creativity: A Componential Conceptualization," *Journal of Personality and Social Psychology* 45, no. 2 (1983): 357; Jennifer M. George, "Creativity in Organizations," *The Academy of Management Annals* 1, no. 1 (2007): 439–477. Note that there are related discussions about improvisation (see Colin M. Fisher and Teresa Amabile, "Creativity, Improvisation and Organizations," in *The Routledge Companion to Creativity*, ed. Tudor Rickards, Mark A. Runco, and Susan Moger, 13–24 (Abingdon, Oxon, UK: Routledge, 2009), but we see improvisation as a particular type of creativity, the nuances of which are beyond what we will cover in this book.

11. All quotes in this section are taken from Kazunori Kobayashi, FS Biomimicry Interview Series No. 6: "'Shinkansen Technology Learned from an Owl?' The story of Eiji Nakatsu," *Japan for Sustainability Newsletter* No. 31 (March 2005), http://www.japan fs.org/en/news/archives/news_id027795.html. Available for use under Creative Commons Attribution-NonCommercial-ShareAlike 3.0 License: https://creativecommons .org/licenses/by-nc-sa/3.0.

12. John Seabrook, "The Song Machine: The Hitmakers Behind Rihanna," *The New Yorker*, March 26, 2012, http://www.newyorker.com/magazine/2012/03/26/the-song -machine.

13. Ed Catmull, *Creativity, Inc.: Overcoming the Unseen Forces That Stand in the Way of True Inspiration* (New York: Random House, 2014), 196.

14. Jennifer S. Mueller, *Creative Change* (New York: Houghton Mifflin Harcourt, 2017). Other work has found that novices use stereotypical markers for evaluating creativity with respect to the product; for example, see J. C. Kaufman, J. Baer, D. H. Cropley, R. Reiter-Palmon, and S. Nienhauser, "Furious Activity vs. Understanding: How Much Expertise Is Needed to Evaluate Creative Work? *Psychology of Aesthetics, Creativity, and the Arts* 7, no. 4 (2013): 332.

15. James C. Kaufman and Ronald A. Beghetto, "Beyond Big and Little: The Four C Model of Creativity," *Review of General Psychology* 13, no. 1 (2009): 4. The two sentences that follow are also drawn from this paper. Note also, by the way, that *Cavalcade* has since been released on blu-ray disc.

16. Dean Keith Simonton, "Foresight in Insight? A Darwinian Answer," in *The Nature of Insight*, ed. R. J. Sternberg and J. E. Davidson, 465–494 (Cambridge, MA: MIT Press, 1995).

17. Jeanne M. Brett, *Negotiating Globally: How to Negotiate Deals, Resolve Disputes, and Make Decisions Across Cultural Boundaries*, 2nd ed. (Hoboken, NJ: John Wiley & Sons, 2007), 145.

18. Max H. Bazerman and Ann E. Tenbrunsel, *Blind Spots: Why We Fail to Do What's Right and What to Do About It* (Princeton, NJ: Princeton University Press, 2011.)

19. Michael Lewis, *The Undoing Project: A Friendship That Changed Our Minds* (New York: W.W. Norton, 2017), 230.

20. Neil Anderson, Kristina Potočnik, and Jing Zhou, "Innovation and Creativity in Organizations: A State-of-the-Science Review, Prospective Commentary, and Guiding Framework," *Journal of Management* 40, no. 5 (2014): 1318.

21. Amy C. Edmondson and Stacy E. McManus, "Methodological Fit in Management Field Research," *Academy of Management Review* 32, no. 4 (2007): 1246–1264.

22. We used a grounded interview technique; see Kathleen M. Eisenhardt and Melissa E. Graebner, "Theory Building from Cases: Opportunities and Challenges," *Academy of Management Journal* 50, no. 1 (2007): 25.

23. Of particular inspiration to us was Mihaly Csikszentmihalyi, *Flow and the Psychology of Discovery and Invention* (New York: HarperCollins, 1996).

24. Teresa M. Amabile, *Creativity in Context: Update to "The Social Psychology of Creativity"* (Boulder, CO: Westview Press, 1996).

25. Jack A. Goncalo and Michelle M. Duguid, "Follow the Crowd in a New Direction: When Conformity Pressure Facilitates Group Creativity (and When It Does Not)," *Organizational Behavior and Human Decision Processes* 118, no. 1 (May 2012): 14–23; Ginamarie Scott, Lyle E. Leritz, and Michael D. Mumford, "The Effectiveness of Creativity Training: A Quantitative Review," *Creativity Research Journal* 16, no. 4 (2004): 361–388; Aaron Kozbelt, "Longitudinal Hit Ratios of Classical Composers: Reconciling

'Darwinian' and Expertise Acquisition Perspectives on Lifespan Creativity," *Psychology of Aesthetics, Creativity, and the Arts* 2, no. 4 (2008): 221–235; Christina Shalley and Jill Perry-Smith, "Effects of Social-Psychological Factors on Creative Performance: The Role of Informational and Controlling Expected Evaluation and Modeling Experience," *Organizational Behavior and Human Decision Processes* 84, no. 2001: 1–22.

CHAPTER 2

1. Hayes Gordon, personal communication, June 1993.

2. This point has been made a great many ways in psychology in the course of talking about various subtypes of what psychologists call mental representations, such as problem representations (see Allen Newell and Herbert A. Simon, *Human Problem Solving* (Englewood Cliffs, NJ: Prentice-Hall, 1972); scripts (see Roger C. Schank and Robert P. Abelson, *Scripts, Plans, Goals and Understanding: An Introduction into Human Knowledge Structures* (Hillsdale, NJ: Erlbaum, 1977); schemas (see Susan T. Fiske and Patricia W. Linville, "What Does the Schema Concept Buy Us?" *Personality and Social Psychology Bulletin* 6, no. 4 (1980): 543–557; and mental models (see Dedre Gentner and Albert L. Stevens, Eds., *Mental Models* (Hillsdale, NJ: Erlbaum, 1983)).

3. Herbert A. Simon, "Bounded Rationality and Organizational Learning," *Organization Science* 2, no. 1 (1991): 125–134.

4. Andrew Ward, L. Ross, E. Reed, E. Turiel, and T. Brown, "Naive Realism in Everyday Life: Implications for Social Conflict and Misunderstanding," *Values and Knowledge* 1997: 103–135.

5. Stellan Ohlsson has done a great deal of work advancing this view (Stellan Ohlsson, "Information-Processing Explanations of Insight and Related Phenomena," in *Advances in the Psychology of Thinking*, ed. M. T. Keane and K. J. Gilhooly, 1–44 (London: Harvester-Wheatsheaf, 1992); Stellan Ohlsson, *Deep Learning: How the Mind Overrides Experience* (Cambridge, UK: Cambridge University Press, 2011.) Recently, Jill Perry-Smith has advanced this notion as well, although coming at it from more of a network-structuralist angle (Jill E. Perry-Smith, "Social Network Ties Beyond Non-Redundancy: An Experimental Investigation of the Effect of Knowledge Content and Tie Strength on Creativity," *Journal of Applied Psychology* 99 no. 5 (2014): 831–846.

6. George A. Miller, "The Magical Number Seven, Plus or Minus Two: Some Limits on Our Capacity for Processing Information," *Psychological Review* 63, no. 2 (1956): 81.

7. Gregory Murphy, *The Big Book of Concepts* (Cambridge, MA: MIT Press, 2004).

8. Ibid.

9. Ibid.

10. Michelene T. H. Chi, Paul J. Feltovich, and Robert Glaser, "Categorization and Representation of Physics Problems by Experts and Novices," *Cognitive Science* 5, no. 2 (1981): 121–152.

11. Gary Klein, *Sources of Power: How People Make Decisions* (Cambridge, MA: MIT Press, 1999).

12. Donald T. Campbell, "Blind Variation and Selective Retentions in Creative Thought as in Other Knowledge Processes," *Psychological Review* 67, no. 6 (1960): 380–400.

13. The stoplight model is quite high level for the cognitive science literature and quite detailed for the organizational science literature. That means it runs the risk of seeming naively simplistic to cognitive scientists and overly complex to organizational scientists. We plead guilty. We think this is the optimal level of fuzz for understanding the creative process. See Arthur B. Markman, Jennifer S. Beer, Lisa R. Grimm, Jonathan R. Rein, and W. Todd Maddox, "The Optimal Level of Fuzz: Case Studies in a Methodology for Psychological Research," *Journal of Experimental & Theoretical Artificial Intelligence* 21, no. 3 (2009): 197–215.

14. Herbert A. Simon, *Models of Thought*, Vol. 1 (New Haven, CT: Yale University Press, 1971).

15. Henri Poincaré, "Mathematical Creation," in *The Foundations of Science*, trans. George Bruce Halsted, 383–394 (New York: Science Press, 1913), 388.

16. Dean Keith Simonton, "Scientific Creativity as Constrained Stochastic Behavior: The Integration of Product, Process, and Person Perspectives," *Psychological Bulletin* 129 (2003): 475–494.

17. Usually, the solution is presumed to be concerned with testing how far water rises when the crown is submerged. However, the small difference in displaced water between pure gold and an impure crown would be hard to detect when spread across a surface area large enough to submerge a crown. And Archimedes was cleverer than that. See Chris Rorres, "The Golden Crown," *Archimedes*, accessed June 23, 2017, https://www.math.nyu.edu/~crorres/Archimedes/Crown/CrownIntro.html.

18. Thanks to Jen Mueller for this example.

19. Thanks to Jonathan Cromwell for this riddle.

CHAPTER 3

1. Endel Tulving, "Episodic and Semantic Memory 1," in *Organization of Memory*, ed. Endel Tulving and Wayne Donaldson (London: Academic Press, 1972).

2. Deborah Dougherty used the term *thought world* to describe the universe of possibility that a person sees based on his or her formal training (Deborah Dougherty, "Interpretive Barriers to Successful Product Innovation in Large Firms," *Organization Science* 3, no. 2 (1992): 179–202). We believe the same kind of thing applies easily to stories, it is just that the person's experience in the endeavor, rather than domain training, is what structures the world.

3. Thank you, Cathy Tinsley.

4. Vicks, "Vicks History," accessed June 23, 2017, http://vicks.com/en-us/vicks-history.

5. There are a number of academic studies of the nine dot problem, and we note several in what follows. In addition, there are delightful discussions of the problem in a variety of popular press books, such as *Conceptual Blockbusting* by James Adams. We use it here to connect as well as contrast these prior discussions with the approach developed in this book.

6. Robert W. Weisberg and Joseph W. Alba, "An Examination of the Alleged Role of 'Fixation' in the Solution of Several 'Insight' Problems," *Journal of Experimental Psychology: General* 110, no. 2 (1981): 169–192.

7. Trina C. Kershaw and Stellan Ohlsson. "Multiple Causes of Difficulty in Insight: The Case of the Nine-Dot Problem," *Journal of Experimental Psychology: Learning, Memory, and Cognition* 30, no. 1 (2004): 3–13.

8. The maze metaphor is widely used (for example, see Amabile's "The Social Psychology of Creativity: A Componential Conceptualization," *Journal of Personality and Social Psychology* 45, no. 2 (1983). The metaphor is an apt account of the problem-solving model of creativity that originated with Newell, Shaw, and Simon (Allen Newell, J. Clifford Shaw, and Herbert A. Simon, "The Processes of Creative Thinking," in *Contemporary Approaches to Creative Thinking: A Symposium Held at the University of Colorado*, ed. H. E. Gruber, C. Terrell, and M. Wertheimer, 63–119 (New York: Atherton Press, 1962) and carried through Amabile to many other scholars. Therefore, the discussion of the maze metaphor applies equally to the problem-solving model of creativity.

9. There is a long history of describing the roles that individual pieces of knowledge (such as concepts) play in our interpretations (or mental representations); see Arthur Markman's *Knowledge Representation* (Mahweh, NJ: Psychology Press, 2013). One approach is to consider the functional roles that knowledge can play, which is what we are doing here. We are integrating work from the problem-solving tradition in cognitive science to do so. Specifically, in *Human Problem Solving*, perhaps Newell and Simon's most complete account of problem representations (see Chapter 2, note 1), they discussed goals, actions (they used the word *operators*), and parts (they used the word *elements*). Because they were using well-structured puzzle problems, they did not consider events or self-concepts. Later work demonstrated that the interpretation of the event (problem, in their terms) mattered. See Kenneth Kotovsky, John R. Hayes, and Herbert A. Simon, "Why Are Some Problems Hard? Evidence from Tower of Hanoi," *Cognitive Psychology* 17, no. 2 (1985): 248–294. Further still, James March, in *A Primer on Decision Making: How Decisions Happen* (New York: Simon and Schuster, 1994), noted that we often guide our actions and decisions using a logic of appropriateness: What does a person like me (self-concept) do in a situation like this (event)? Across a range of research on knowledge representation, these five roles recur frequently. Thus with PAGES we are synthesizing into one framework research on the main functional roles that knowledge plays in an interpretation.

10. Thank you, Scott Poole.

11. Jeffrey M. Zacks and Barbara Tversky, "Event Structure in Perception and Conception," *Psychological Bulletin* 127, no. 1 (2001): 3–21.

CHAPTER 4

1. Pungo, accessed June 23, 2017, http://www.pungo.us.

2. Michelene T. H. Chi, Paul J. Feltovich, and Robert Glaser, "Categorization and Representation of Physics Problems by Experts and Novices," *Cognitive Science* 5, no. 2 (1981): 121.

3. Richard Gregory, *The Intelligent Eye* (New York: McGraw-Hill, 1970); Rudolf Arnheim, *Visual Thinking* (Berkeley, CA: University of California Press, 1969).

4. We are working in binary.

5. Lance J. Rips, Sergey Blok, and George Newman, "Tracing the Identity of Objects," *Psychological Review* 113, no. 1 (2006): 1–30.

6. Martin A. Conway and Christopher W. Pleydell-Pearce, "The Construction of Autobiographical Memories in the Self-Memory System," *Psychological Review* 107, no. 2 (2000): 261–288.

7. Susan A. Gelman, *The Essential Child: Origins of Essentialism in Everyday Thought* (New York: Oxford University Press, 2003).

8. Robert L. Goldstone, "Isolated and Interrelated Concepts," *Memory & Cognition* 24, no. 5 (1996): 608–628.

9. John Roach, "'Hot Ice' Planet Discovered, Covered in 'Solid Water,' Experts Say," *National Geographic News*, May 17, 2007, http://news.nationalgeographic.com/news /2007/05/070517-hot-planet.html.

10. A. Van Helden, "Saturn and His Anses," *The Journal of Historical Astronomy* 5, no. 2 (1974): 105; A. Van Helden, "Annulo Singitur: The Solution to the Problem of Saturn," *The Journal of Historical Astronomy* 5, no. 3 (1974): 155.

11. Ibid.

12. Dedre Gentner, Sarah Brem, Ronald W. Ferguson, Arthur B. Markman, Bjorn B. Levidow, Phillip Wolff, and Kenneth D. Forbus, "Analogical Reasoning and Conceptual Change: A Case Study of Johannes Kepler," *The Journal of the Learning Sciences* 6, no. 1 (1997): 3–40.

13. See footnote 7 in Gentner and others, "Analogical Reasoning."

14. This example is from Benjamin Whorf, who, on the basis of his experience as an insurance adjuster reviewing incidents of fire, used it to illustrate how language can shape our thinking. Benjamin Lee Whorf and Stuart Chase, *Language, Thought and Reality: Selected Writings of Benjamin Lee Whorf*, ed. John Bissell Carroll (Cambridge, MA: MIT press, 1956).

15. Clark A. Chinn and William F. Brewer, "The Role of Anomalous Data in Knowledge Acquisition: A Theoretical Framework and Implications for Science Instruction," *Review of Educational Research* 63, no. 1 (1993): 1–49.

16. Bruno Latour, *Aramis, or, The Love of Technology* (Cambridge, MA: Harvard University Press, 1996).

17. Ibid, 108–109.

18. Ibid, 109.

19. Ibid, 280.

20. The classic experiment in this regard showed different people with opposite opinions the identical study; each side took the study as evidence of his or her own position. See Charles G. Lord, Lee Ross, and Mark R. Lepper, "Biased Assimilation and Attitude Polarization: The Effects of Prior Theories on Subsequently Considered Evidence," *Journal of Personality and Social Psychology* 37, no. 11 (1979): 2098.

21. Mary Parker Follett, *Prophet of Management: A Celebration of Writings from the 1920s*, ed. Pauline Graham (Cambridge, MA: Harvard Business School Press, 1995), 75.

22. Certainly the ones we interviewed said this, as well as the painters, engineers, and so on.

23. Latour, *Aramis*, 281.

CHAPTER 5

1. For one example, see Clark's *Using Language*, which is essentially about how we accomplish the task of communicating with others so that we actually understand each other, and illustrates how challenging it is to be in sync. (Herbert H. Clark, *Using Language* (Cambridge, UK: Cambridge University Press, 1996).

2. Dean Keith Simonton, "Foresight in Insight? A Darwinian Answer," in *The Nature of Insight*, ed. R. J. Sternberg and J. E. Davidson, 465–494 (Cambridge, MA: MIT Press, 1995), 465.

3. Daniel Kahneman and Amos Tversky, "Prospect Theory: An Analysis of Decision Under Risk," *Econometrica* 47 no. 2 (1979): 263–291.

4. Ming Hsu, Meghana Bhatt, Ralph Adolphs, Daniel Tranel, and Colin F. Camerer, "Neural Systems Responding to Degrees of Uncertainty in Human Decision-Making," *Science* 310, no. 5754 (2005): 1680–1683.

5. Jennifer S. Mueller, Shimul Melwani, and Jack A. Goncalo, "The Bias Against Creativity: Why People Desire but Reject Creative Ideas," *Psychological Science* 23, no. 1 (2012): 13–17.

6. One of us (Matt) used to have to turn his car around on his narrow street each morning to go to work. After about a year and a half of making nine-point turns, he realized he could turn the car around in one fluid motion if he just backed up instead of going forward. It saved a lot of time and effort and still made him feel like an idiot.

7. This definition is not substantively different from the one offered by more august sources, and it is admirably succinct.

8. Janet Metcalfe and David Wiebe, "Intuition in Insight and Noninsight Problem Solving," *Memory & Cognition* 15, no. 3 (1987): 238–246.

9. This is a long-noticed point, and a good one. William James noted it in his discussion of habit. Arthur Koestler noted it in discussing the trade-off between habit and originality. More recently, it is often discussed under the term *competency trap*. So we do not belabor the point here. See Barbara Levitt and James G. March, "Organizational Learning," *Annual Review of Sociology* (1988): 319–340.

10. In one example, Roger Martin devotes a section of his book *The Design of Business* to our preference for "reliability over validity," or for things that are predictable despite known flaws over things that are more effective but less consistent. See Roger L. Martin, *The Design of Business: Why Design Thinking Is the Next Competitive Advantage* (Boston: Harvard Business Publishing, 2009).

11. Barry M. Staw, "Why No One Really Wants Creativity," *Creative Action in Organizations* (1995): 161–166.

12. James G. March, "Exploration and Exploitation in Organizational Learning," *Organization Science* 2, no. 1 (1991): 71–87; Chris Argyris and Donald A. Schön, *Organizational Learning II: Theory, Method and Practice* (Reading, MA: Addison-Wesley, 1996).

13. Stellan Ohlsson, "Information-Processing Explanations of Insight and Related Phenomena," in *Advances in the Psychology of Thinking*, ed. M. T. Keane and K. J. Gilhooly, 1–44 (London: Harvester-Wheatsheaf, 1992).

14. Craig A. Kaplan and Herbert A. Simon, "In Search of Insight," *Cognitive Psychology* 22, no. 3 (1990): 374–419.

15. Ibid.

16. Here is a hint if you do not feel like spending many minutes sorting out why the problem is impossible with the ordinary setup: What color are the missing squares?

17. Our confidence in our own ability to be creative is called creative self-efficacy. Pamela Tierney and Steven M. Farmer, "Creative Self-Efficacy: Its Potential Antecedents and Relationship to Creative Performance," *Academy of Management Journal* 45, no. 6 (2002): 1137–1148.

18. Research on impasses and creativity goes back at least to Köhler's research on insight in the early twentieth century, including work with apes. There is also a variety of research on learning, including work on double-loop learning and on conceptual change, which emphasizes mid-story challenges that prompt us to restructure our understandings. Wolfgang Köhler, *The Mentality of Apes* (Abingdon, Oxon, UK: Routledge 2013 [1924]); Chris Argyris, "Single-Loop and Double-Loop Models in Research on Decision Making," *Administrative Science Quarterly* (1976): 363–375; George J. Posner, Kenneth A. Strike, Peter W. Hewson, and William A. Gertzog, "Accommodation of a Scientific Conception: Toward a Theory of Conceptual Change," *Science Education* 66, no. 2 (1982): 211–227; Susan Carey, *Conceptual Change in Childhood* (Cambridge, MA: MIT Press, 1987).

19. Barry Schwartz, *The Paradox of Choice: Why More Is Less* (New York: Ecco, 2004); Sheena Iyengar, *The Art of Choosing* (New York: Twelve, 2010).

20. Janet McDonnell, "Impositions of Order: A Comparison Between Design and Fine Art Practices," *Design Studies* 32, no. 6 (2011): 557–572.

21. Mihaly Csikszentmihalyi and Jacob W. Getzels, "Discovery-Oriented Behavior and the Originality of Creative Products: A Study with Artists," *Journal of Personality and Social Psychology* 19, no. 1 (1971): 47–52; Jacob W. Getzels and Mihaly Csikszentmihalyi, *The Creative Vision* (Hoboken, NJ: John Wiley & Sons, 1976).

22. Marwan Sinaceur, William W. Maddux, Dimitri Vasiljevic, Ricardo Perez Nückel, and Adam D. Galinsky, "Good Things Come to Those Who Wait: Late First Offers Facilitate Creative Agreements in Negotiation," *Personality and Social Psychology Bulletin* 39, no. 6 (2013): 814–825.

23. The actual alternative path, for the mathematically minded, was the use of infinitesimal perturbation analysis (IPA) derivatives. It indeed broke the impasse, and has been used to solve the practical inventory problems in global supply chains.

24. For example, James C. Collins and Jerry I. Porras, *Built to Last: Successful Habits of Visionary Companies* (New York: Random House, 2005), known for popularizing the phrase "big hairy audacious goals."

25. Eric Schmidt and Jonathan Rosenberg, *How Google Works* (London: Hachette UK, 2014).

26. This is the conclusion of hundreds of studies on goals, in particular work on goal-setting theory, such as Edwin A. Locke and Gary P. Latham, "Building a Practically Useful Theory of Goal setting and Task Motivation," *American Psychologist* 57, no. 9 (2002): 705–717.

27. Carol S. Dweck, "Motivational Processes Affecting Learning," *American Psychologist* 41, no. 10 (1986): 1040.

28. This is what negotiation scholars discuss as committing to pursue our underlying interests; for example, see Bruce Patton, William Ury, and Roger Fisher, *Getting to Yes* (New York: Simon & Schuster, 1981); Mary P. Follett, "The Psychology of Control," in *Dynamic Administration: The Collected Papers of Mary Parker Follett*, ed. Lyndall F. Urwick and Henry C. Metcalf, 183–209 (Mansfield Centre, CT: Martino, 2013); Richard E. Walton and Robert B. McKersie, *A Behavioral Theory of Labor Negotiations: An Analysis of a Social Interaction System* (Ithaca, NY: Cornell University Press, 1965).

29. Jennifer M. George and Jing Zhou, "Understanding When Bad Moods Foster Creativity and Good Ones Don't: The Role of Context and Clarity of Feelings," *Journal of Applied Psychology* 87, no. 4 (2002): 687.

30. Teresa M. Amabile, "The Social Psychology of Creativity: A Componential Conceptualization," *Journal of Personality and Social Psychology* 45, no. 2 (1983): 357–376.

31. E. Allan Lind and T. R. Tyler, "A Relational Model of Authority in Groups," *Advances in Experimental Social Psychology* 25 (1992): 115–192.

32. Matthew A. Cronin, "The Effect of Respect on Interdependent Work," (doctoral dissertation, Carnegie Mellon University, 2004).

33. For example, Royston M. Roberts, *Serendipity: Accidental Discoveries in Science* (Hoboken, NJ: Wiley-VCH, 1989).

34. Barbara A. Mellers, "Choice and the Relative Pleasure of Consequences," *Psychological Bulletin* 126, no. 6 (2000): 910.

35. Daniel J. Simons and Christopher F. Chabris, "Gorillas in Our Midst: Sustained Inattentional Blindness for Dynamic Events," *Perception* 28, no. 9 (1999): 1059–1074; Christopher Chabris and Daniel Simons, *The Invisible Gorilla: And Other Ways Our Intuitions Deceive Us* (New York: Harmony, 2010).

36. Daniel J. Simons and Daniel T. Levin, "Failure to Detect Changes to People During a Real-World Interaction," *Psychonomic Bulletin and Review* 5 (1998): 644–649.

37. Robert L. Goldstone, "Influences of Categorization on Perceptual Discrimination," *Journal of Experimental Psychology: General* 123, no. 2 (1994): 178.

38. At the time of this writing, she is still trying to figure out why.

39. Clark A. Chinn and William F. Brewer, "The Role of Anomalous Data in Knowledge Acquisition: A Theoretical Framework and Implications for Science Instruction," *Review of Educational Research* 63, no. 1 (1993): 1–49.

40. Nitin Nohria and Ranjay Gulati, "Is Slack Good or Bad for Innovation?" *Academy of Management Journal* 39, no. 5 (1996): 1245–1264.

41. Edwin P. Hollander, "Conformity, Status, and Idiosyncrasy Credit," *Psychological Review* 65, no. 2 (1958): 117–127.

42. Todd B. Kashdan and Paul J. Silvia. "Curiosity and Interest: The Benefits of

Thriving on Novelty and Challenge," *Oxford Handbook of Positive Psychology* 2 (2009): 367–374; Todd B. Kashdan, Paul Rose, and Frank D. Fincham, "Curiosity and Exploration: Facilitating Positive Subjective Experiences and Personal Growth Opportunities," *Journal of Personality Assessment* 82, no. 3 (2004): 291–305.

43. Donna M. Webster and Arie W. Kruglanski, "Cognitive and Social Consequences of the Need for Cognitive Closure," *European Review of Social Psychology* 8, no. 1 (1997): 133–173.

44. Arthur B. Markman, *Smart Thinking: Three Essential Keys to Solve Problems, Innovate, and Get Things Done* (New York: Perigee/Penguin Group, 2013).

45. Leonid Rozenblit and Frank Keil, "The Misunderstood Limits of Folk Science: An Illusion of Explanatory Depth," *Cognitive Science* 26, no. 5 (2002): 521–562.

46. Beth A. Bechky and Gerardo A. Okhuysen, "Expecting the Unexpected? How SWAT Officers and Film Crews Handle Surprises," *Academy of Management Journal* 54, no. 2 (2011): 239–261.

47. Shelby Pope, "How an 11-Year-Old Boy Invented the Popsicle," NPR, July 22, 2015, http://www.npr.org/sections/thesalt/2015/07/22/425294957/how-an-11-year-old -boy-invented-the-popsicle.

48. "Ruth Wakefield: Chocolate Chip Cookie Inventor," *Famous Women Inventors*, accessed June 23, 2017, http://www.women-inventors.com/Ruth-Wakefield.asp.

49. Dedre Gentner, Mary Jo Rattermann, and Kenneth D. Forbus, "The Roles of Similarity in Transfer: Separating Retrievability from Inferential Soundness," *Cognitive Psychology* 25, no. 4 (1993): 524–575.

50. Dedre Gentner, "Structure-Mapping: A Theoretical Framework for Analogy," *Cognitive Science* 7, no. 2 (1983): 155–170.

51. Dedre Gentner, Jeffrey Loewenstein, Leigh Thompson, and Kenneth D. Forbus, "Reviving Inert Knowledge: Analogical Abstraction Supports Relational Retrieval of Past Events," *Cognitive Science* 33, no. 8 (2009): 1343–1382.

52. Ibid.

53. Kurt Lewin, "Untersuchungen zur Handlungs-und Affektpsychologie. III. Zeigarnik, B. Das Behalten erledigter und unerledigter Handlungen [Investigations on the Psychology of Action and Affection. III. The Memory of Completed and Uncompleted Actions]," *Psychologische Forschung* 9 (1927): 1–85.

54. Arthur B. Markman, Eric Taylor, and Dedre Gentner, "Auditory Presentation Leads to Better Analogical Retrieval Than Written Presentation," *Psychonomic Bulletin & Review* 14, no. 6 (2007): 1101–1106.

55. Kevin Dunbar, "How Scientists Really Reason: Scientific Reasoning in Real-World Laboratories," *The Nature of Insight* 18 (1995): 365–395; Kevin Dunbar, "How Scientists Build Models in Vivo Science as a Window on the Scientific Mind," in *Model-Based Reasoning in Scientific Discovery*, ed. Lorenzo Magnani, Nancy J. Nersessian, and Paul Thagard, 85–99 (New York; London: Kluwer Academic/Plenum, 1999); K. Williams and C. O'Reilly, "The Complexity of Diversity: A Review of Forty Years of Research," *Research in Organizational Behavior* 21 (1998): 77–140.

56. Jeffrey Loewenstein, "How One's Hook Is Baited Matters for Catching an Anal-

ogy," *Psychology of Learning and Motivation* 53 (2010): 149–182; Laura R. Novick, "Analogical Transfer, Problem Similarity, and Expertise," *Journal of Experimental Psychology: Learning, Memory, and Cognition* 14, no. 3 (1988): 510.

57. Markman, *Smart Thinking*.

58. Hannah Keyser and Haley Sweetland Edwards, "11 Successful Products Originally Invented for Something Else," *Mental Floss*, October 8, 2015, http://mentalfloss .com/article/57861/11-successful-products-originally-invented-something-else.

CHAPTER 6

1. Sarnof Mednick, "The Associative Basis of the Creative Process," *Psychological Review* 69, no. 3 (1962): 220–232.

2. Jeffrey Sanchez-Burks, Matthew J. Karlesky, and Fiona Lee, "Psychological Bricolage: Integrating Social Identities to Produce Creative Solutions," in *The Oxford Handbook of Creativity, Innovation and Entrepreneurship*, ed. Christina E. Shalley, Michael A. Hitt, and Jing Zhou, 93–102 (New York: Oxford University Press, 2015).

3. Ap Dijksterhuis and Teun Meurs, "Where Creativity Resides: The Generative Power of Unconscious Thought," *Consciousness and Cognition* 15, no. 1 (2006): 135–146.

4. M. D. Mumford, "Managing Creative People: Strategies and Tactics for Innovation," *Human Resource Management Review* 10, no. 3 (2000): 313–351; James L. Adams, *Conceptual Blockbusting* (New York: Basic Books, 1974).

5. John R. Anderson and Peter L. Pirolli, "Spread of Activation," *Journal of Experimental Psychology: Learning, Memory, and Cognition* 10, no. 4 (1984): 791.

6. Ap Dijksterhuis and Loran F. Nordgren, "A Theory of Unconscious Thought," *Perspectives on Psychological Science* 1, no. 2 (2006): 95–109.

7. Ibid., 95; Lynn Hasher and Rose T. Zacks, "Automatic and Effortful Processes in Memory," *Journal of Experimental Psychology: General* 108, no. 3 (1979): 356.

8. Mark Jung-Beeman, Edward M. Bowden, Jason Haberman, Jennifer L. Frymiare, Stella Arambel-Liu, Richard Greenblatt, Paul J. Reber, and John Kounios, "Neural Activity When People Solve Verbal Problems with Insight," *PLOS Biology* 2, no. 4 (2004): e97.

9. Robert J. Sternberg and Janet E. Davidson, *The Nature of Insight* (Cambridge, MA: MIT Press, 1995).

10. We talk about deliberately attending to and reasoning about particular concepts; others use such terms as *controlled cognitive processing* (see Richard M. Shiffrin and Walter Schneider, "Controlled and Automatic Human Information Processing: II. Perceptual Learning, Automatic Attending and a General Theory," *Psychological Review* 84, no. 2 (1977): 127) or, now common in the decision-making literature, *system 2 processing* (see Daniel Kahneman, *Thinking, Fast and Slow* (New York: Macmillan, 2011).

11. Matthew A. Cronin, "A Strategy for Improving Insight at Work," *Academy of Management Proceedings* 2006, no. 1 (2006), E1–E6.

12. Matthew A. Cronin, Linda Argote, and Kenneth Kotovsky, "Partitioned Cognition in Teams," (working paper, Carnegie Mellon University, n.d.).

13. Marc G. Berman, John Jonides, and Stephen Kaplan, "The Cognitive Benefits of Interacting with Nature," *Psychological Science* 19, no. 12 (2008): 1207–1212.

14. Jarrod Moss, Kenneth Kotovsky, and Jonathan Cagan, "The Influence of Open Goals on the Acquisition of Problem-Relevant Information," *Journal of Experimental Psychology: Learning, Memory, and Cognition* 33, no. 5 (2007): 876.

15. Kimberly D. Elsbach and Andrew B. Hargadon, "Enhancing Creativity Through 'Mindless' Work: A Framework of Workday Design," *Organization Science* 17, no. 4 (2006): 470–483.

16. Carsten K. W. De Dreu, Bernard A. Nijstad, Matthijs Baas, Inge Wolsink, and Marieke Roskes, "Working Memory Benefits Creative Insight, Musical Improvisation, and Original Ideation Through Maintained Task-Focused Attention," *Personality and Social Psychology Bulletin* 38, no. 5 (2012): 656–669; Moss, Kotovsky, and Cagan, "The Influence of Open Goals," 876.

17. Alice M. Isen, Kimberly A. Daubman, and Gary P. Nowicki, "Positive Affect Facilitates Creative Problem Solving," *Journal of Personality and Social Psychology* 52, no. 6 (1987): 1122–1131.

18. Craig A. Kaplan and Herbert A. Simon, "In Search of Insight," *Cognitive Psychology* 22, no. 3 (1990): 374; Richard E. Mayer, "The Search for Insight: Grappling with Gestalt Psychology's Unanswered Questions," in *The Nature of Insight*, ed. R. E. Sternberg and J. E. Davidson, 3–32 (Cambridge, MA: MIT Press, 1995); Steven M. Smith, "Getting Into and Out of Mental Ruts: A Theory of Fixation, Incubation, and Insight," in *The Nature of Insight*, ed. R. E. Sternberg and J. E. Davidson, 229–353 (Cambridge, MA: MIT Press, 1995).

19. Cronin, "Strategy for Improving Insight at Work."

20. Dedre Gentner, "Structure–Mapping: A Theoretical Framework for Analogy," *Cognitive Science* 7, no. 2 (1983): 155–170; Douglas Hofstadter and Emmanuel Sander, *Surfaces and Essences: Analogy as the Fuel and Fire of Thinking* (New York: Basic Books, 2013).

21. Gentner, "Structure-Mapping"; Dedre Gentner and Arthur B. Markman, "Structure Mapping in Analogy and Similarity," *American Psychologist* 52, no. 1 (1997): 45; Dedre Gentner, Keith James Holyoak, and Boicho N. Kokinov, *The Analogical Mind: Perspectives from Cognitive Science* (Cambridge, MA: MIT Press, 2001).

22. We thank Jesse Schell for this example.

23. Dedre Gentner, Mary Jo Rattermann, and Kenneth D. Forbus, "The Roles of Similarity in Transfer: Separating Retrievability from Inferential Soundness," *Cognitive Psychology* 25, no. 4 (1993): 524–575.

24. Jeffrey Loewenstein, "How One's Hook Is Baited Matters for Catching an Analogy," *Psychology of Learning and Motivation* 53 (2010): 149–182.

25. Leonid Rozenblit and Frank Keil, "The Misunderstood Limits of Folk Science: An Illusion of Explanatory Depth," *Cognitive Science* 26, no. 5 (2002): 521–562.

26. Ana Swanson, "The Strange, Hilarious Pictures You Get When You Ask Random People to Draw a Bicycle," *Washington Post*, April 18, 2016, https://www.washingtonpost.com/news/wonk/wp/2016/04/18/the-horrible-hilarious-pictures-you-get-when-you-ask-random-people-to-draw-a-bicycle.

27. Laura Kotovsky and Dedre Gentner, "Comparison and Categorization in the

Development of Relational Similarity," *Child Development* 67, no. 6 (1996): 2797–2822; Jeffrey Loewenstein and Dedre Gentner, "Spatial Mapping in Preschoolers: Close Comparisons Facilitate Far Mappings," *Journal of Cognition and Development* 2, no. 2 (2001): 189–219; Dedre Gentner, Jeffrey Loewenstein, and Leigh Thompson, "Learning and Transfer: A General Role for Analogical Encoding," *Journal of Educational Psychology* 95, no. 2 (2003): 393–408.

28. Brian F. Bowdle and Dedre Gentner, "The Career of Metaphor," *Psychological Review* 112, no. 1 (2005): 193.

29. Arthur B. Markman, Eric Taylor, and Dedre Gentner, "Auditory Presentation Leads to Better Analogical Retrieval Than Written Presentation," *Psychonomic Bulletin & Review* 14, no. 6 (2007): 1101–1106.

30. Kenneth J. Kurtz and Jeffrey Loewenstein, "Converging on a New Role for Analogy in Problem Solving and Retrieval: When Two Problems Are Better Than One," *Memory & Cognition* 35, no. 2 (2007): 334–341.

31. Jeffrey Loewenstein and Dedre Gentner, "Relational Language and the Development of Relational Mapping," *Cognitive Psychology* 50, no. 4 (2005): 315–353; Catherine A. Clement, Ronald Mawby, and Denise E. Giles, "The Effects of Manifest Relational Similarity on Analog Retrieval," *Journal of Memory and Language* 33, no. 3 (1994): 396–420.

32. Keith James Holyoak and Paul Thagard, *Mental Leaps: Analogy in Creative Thought* (Cambridge, MA: MIT Press, 1996).

33. For example, Ikujiro Nonaka and Hirotaka Takeuchi, *The Knowledge-Creating Company: How Japanese Companies Create the Dynamics of innovation* (New York: Oxford University Press, 1995).

34. Denis A. Grégoire, Pamela S. Barr, and Dean A. Shepherd, "Cognitive Processes of Opportunity Recognition: The Role of Structural Alignment," *Organization Science* 21, no. 2 (2010): 413–431.

35. This is often called "conceptual combination" (see Edward J. Wisniewski, "Conceptual Combination: Possibilities and Aesthetics," in *Creative Thought: An Investigation of Conceptual Structures and Processes*, ed. Thomas B. Ward, Steven M. Smith, and Jyotsna Vaid, 51–81(Washington, DC: American Psychological Association, 1997)), or "conceptual blending" (see Mark Turner and Gilles Fauconnier, *The Way We Think: Conceptual Blending and the Mind's Hidden Complexities* (New York: Basic Books 2002).

36. Thomas B. Ward, "Creative Cognition, Conceptual Combination, and the Creative Writing of Stephen R. Donaldson," *American Psychologist* 56, no. 4 (2001): 350.

37. Ziva Kunda, Dale T. Miller, and Theresa Claire, "Combining Social Concepts: The Role of Causal Reasoning," *Cognitive Science* 14, no. 4 (1990): 551–577.

38. See ZipBling Jewelry for some examples, accessed June 23, 2017, http://www.zipblingjewelry.com.

39. Wisniewski, *Conceptual Combination*.

40. There is some discussion of paradoxes and creativity, from "Janusian thinking" (Albert Rothenberg, "The Janusian Process in Scientific Creativity," *Creativity Research Journal* 9, no. 2-3 (1996): 207–231) to paradoxical cognition (Ella Miron-Spektor, Francesca Gino, and Linda Argote, "Paradoxical Frames and Creative Sparks: Enhancing

Individual Creativity Through Conflict and Integration," *Organizational Behavior and Human Decision Processes* 116 (2011): 229–240.

41. Sanchez-Burks, Karlesky, and Lee, "Psychological Bricolage."

42. Susan A. Gelman, *The Essential Child: Origins of Essentialism in Everyday Thought* (New York: Oxford University Press, 2003).

43. Douglas L. Medin and Lance J. Rips, "Concepts and Categories: Memory, Meaning, and Metaphysics," in *The Cambridge Handbook of Thinking and Reasoning*, ed. Robert G. Morrison and Keith James Holyoak, 37–72 (Cambridge, UK: Cambridge University Press, 2005); Gregory Murphy, *The Big Book of Concepts* (Cambridge, MA: MIT Press, 2004); Brian H. Ross and Gregory L. Murphy, "Food for Thought: Cross-Classification and Category Organization in a Complex Real-World Domain," *Cognitive Psychology* 38, no. 4 (1999): 495–553.

44. For example, see Maria A. Brandimonte and Walter Gerbino, "Mental Image Reversal and Verbal Recoding: When Ducks Become Rabbits," *Memory & Cognition* 21, no. 1 (1993): 23–33.

45. Barry Nalebuff and Ian Ayres, *Why Not? How to Use Everyday Ingenuity to Solve Problems Big and Small* (Boston: Harvard Business School Press, 2003); Keith Markman, Matthew J. Lindberg, Laura J. Kray, and Adam D. Galinsky, "Implications of Counterfactual Structure for Creative Generation and Analytical Problem Solving," *Personality and Social Psychology Bulletin* 33, no. 3 (2007): 312–324; Neal Roese, *If Only: How to Turn Regret into Opportunity* (New York: Harmony, 2005).

46. Taking different roles is a part of many discussions, including work on perspective taking, empathy, heterogeneous groups, and more, but among the first noting its importance were Harry C. Triandis, Eleanor R. Hall, and Robert B. Ewen ("Member Heterogeneity and Dyadic Creativity," *Human Relations* 18, no. 1 (1965): 33–55).

47. For example, Adam M. Grant, Ellen J. Langer, Emily Falk, and Christina Capodilupo, "Mindful Creativity: Drawing to Draw Distinctions," *Creativity Research Journal* 16, no. 2-3 (2004): 261–265.

48. Karl Dunker, "On Problem Solving," *Psychological Monographs*, 58 No. 5 (1945): i–113.

49. Joy Paul Guilford, *Intelligence, Creativity, and Their Educational Implications* (San Diego: R.R. Knapp, 1968).

50. Max Wertheimer, *Productive Thinking* (New York: Harper, 1959).

51. For example, see Jack A. Goncalo and Barry M. Staw, "Individualism-Collectivism and Group Creativity," *Organizational Behavior and Human Decision Processes* 100, no. 1 (2006): 96–109; Sarah Harvey and Chia-Yu Kou, "Collective Engagement in Creative Tasks: The Role of Evaluation in the Creative Process in Groups," *Administrative Science Quarterly* 58, no. 3 (2013): 346–386; Jennifer Mueller and Matthew A. Cronin, "How Relational Processes Support Team Creativity," in *Creativity in Groups*, ed. Elizabeth A. Mannix, Margaret Ann Neale, and Jack A. Goncalo, 291–310 (Bingley, UK: Emerald Group, 2009).

52. Kevin Dunbar, "How Scientists Think: On-Line Creativity and Conceptual Change in Science," in *Creative Thought: An Investigation of Conceptual Structures and*

Processes, ed. Thomas B. Ward, Steven M. Smith, and Jyotsna Vaid, 461–493 (Washington, DC: American Psychological Association, 1997).

53. J. Richard Hackman and Greg R. Oldham, "Motivation Through the Design of Work: Test of a Theory," *Organizational Behavior and Human Performance* 16, no. 2 (1976): 250–279; Greg R. Oldham and Anne Cummings, "Employee Creativity: Personal and Contextual Factors at Work," *Academy of Management Journal* 39, no. 3 (1996): 607–634.

54. Matthew A. Cronin and Laurie R. Weingart, "Representational Gaps, Information Processing, and Conflict in Functionally Diverse Teams," *Academy of Management Review* 32, no. 3 (2007): 761–773; K. Williams and C. O'Reilly, "The Complexity of Diversity: A Review of Forty Years of Research," *Research in Organizational Behavior* 21 (1998): 77.

55. Ronald Burt, *Structural Holes: The Social Structure of Competition* (Cambridge, MA: Harvard University Press, 1992); Ronald S. Burt, "Structural Holes and Good Ideas," *American Journal of Sociology* 110, no. 2 (2004): 349–399; Andrew Hargadon and Robert I. Sutton, "Technology Brokering and Innovation in a Product Development Firm," *Administrative Science Quarterly* (1997): 716–749.

56. Jill E. Perry-Smith, "Social Yet Creative: The Role of Social Relationships in Facilitating Individual Creativity," *Academy of Management Journal* 49, no. 1 (2006): 85–101; Jill E. Perry-Smith and Christina E. Shalley, "The Social Side of Creativity: A Static and Dynamic Social Network Perspective," *Academy of Management Review* 28, no. 1 (2003): 89–106.

57. Chi-Ying Cheng, Jeffrey Sanchez-Burks, and Fiona Lee, "Connecting the Dots Within Creative Performance and Identity Integration," *Psychological Science* 19, no. 11 (2008): 1178–1184; Angela Ka-yee Leung, William W. Maddux, Adam D. Galinsky, and Chi-yue Chiu, "Multicultural Experience Enhances Creativity: The When and How," *American Psychologist* 63, no. 3 (2008): 169–181.

58. To learn more about this task (which should help you draw correspondences), you can read this: Rachel Deussom, Wanda Jaskiewicz, Elizabeth Adams, and Kate Tulenko, "Ensuring a Positive Practice Environment: Occupational Safety and Health for Health Worker Productivity," CapacityPlus, August 2012, http://www.capacityplus.org/files/resources/ensuring-positive-practice-environment-occupational-safety-health -worker-productivity.pdf.

CHAPTER 7

1. Teresa M. Amabile, "The Social Psychology of Creativity: A Componential Conceptualization," *Journal of Personality and Social Psychology* 45, no. 2 (1983): 357–376; Beth A. Hennessy and Teresa M. Amabile, "Creativity," *Annual Review of Psychology* 61 (2010): 569–598; Teresa M. Amabile, Sigal G. Barsade, Jennifer S. Mueller, and Barry M. Staw, "Affect and Creativity at Work," *Administrative Science Quarterly* 50, no. 3 (2005): 367–403.

2. Charles A. Holt and Susan K. Laury, "Risk Aversion and Incentive Effects," *American Economic Review* 92, no. 5 (2002): 1644–1655; John W. Pratt, "Risk Aversion in the Small and in the Large," *Econometrica: Journal of the Econometric Society* (1964): 122–136.

3. Geert H. Hofstede, *Culture's Consequences: Comparing Values, Behaviors, Institutions and Organizations Across Nations* (Thousand Oaks, CA: Sage, 2001).

4. C. R. Berger and R. J. Calabrese, "Some Exploration in Initial Interaction and Beyond: Toward a Developmental Theory of Communication," *Human Communication Research* 1 (1975): 99–112.

5. V. H. Vroom, *Work and Motivation* (New York: Wiley, 1964); Albert Bandura, Self-Efficacy: Toward a Unifying Theory of Behavioral Change," *Psychological Review* 84, (1977): 191–215.

6. Janet Metcalfe and David Wiebe, "Intuition in Insight and Noninsight Problem Solving," *Memory & Cognition* 15, no. 3 (1987): 238–246.

7. For example, see "Mosquito Inspired Microneedle," AskNature, September 9, 2015, https://asknature.org/idea/mosquito-inspired-microneedle/#.WIYct5L9F2A.

8. Barry M. Staw, "Why No One Really Wants Creativity," *Creative Action in Organizations* (1995): 161–166.

9. Ed Catmull, *Creativity, Inc.: Overcoming the Unseen Forces That Stand in the Way of True Inspiration* (New York: Random House, 2014), 196.

10. Given the story, we are keeping the company name and person's name confidential.

11. In his book *The Design of Business*, Roger Martin has a very nice model for how inventive notions can be systematized and incorporated into how an organization works. *The Design of Business: Why Design Thinking Is the Next Competitive Advantage* (Boston: Harvard Business Publishing, 2009).

12. This is an enormous topic, and one that we hope the current discussions will help advance. In the meantime, a useful starting point remains; see Teresa M. Amabile, "How to Kill Creativity," *Harvard Business Review*, September/October (1998): 76–87. Then there are more hopeful views about the roles leaders can play to reduce mindless conformity; for example, see Ruth Wageman and Colin Fisher, "Who's in Charge Here? The Team Leadership Implications of Authority," *The Oxford Handbook of Leadership and Organizations* (2014): 455–481.

13. We modified some of the specialized verbiage to mask the characteristic military voice in which it is written so as not to give away our punchline. The exact quote can be found on p. 80 at "Doctrine for the U.S. Coast Guard," U.S. Coast Guard, February 2014, http://www.uscg.mil/doctrine/CGPub/Pub_1.pdf.

14. Greg R. Oldham and Anne Cummings, "Employee Creativity: Personal and Contextual Factors at Work," *Academy of Management Journal* 39, no. 3 (1996): 607–634.

15. Gregory J. Feist, "A Meta-Analysis of Personality in Scientific and Artistic Creativity," *Personality and Social Psychology Review* 2 no. 4 (1998): 290–309; Hsen-Hsing Ma, "The Effect Size of Variables Associated with Creativity: A Meta-Analysis," *Creativity Research Journal* 21, no. 1 (2009): 30–42.

16. See "The Charles Goodyear Story," *Reader's Digest*, January 1958, reprinted at Goodyear Corporate, accessed June 23, 2017,https://corporate.goodyear.com/en-US/about/history/charles-goodyear-story.html.

17. See J. K. Rowling, "The Fringe Benefits of Failure," speech to the Harvard class

of 2008, TED, accessed June 23, 2017, https://www.ted.com/talks/jk_rowling_the_ fringe_benefits_of_failure.

18. Scholars usually call it "intrinsic motivation." Richard M. Ryan and Edward L. Deci, "Self-Determination Theory and the Facilitation of Intrinsic Motivation, Social Development, and Well-Being," *American Psychologist* 55, no. 1 (2000): 68–78; Hennessey and Amabile, "Creativity."

19. Much more work needs to be done here. For a concurring discussion, see Joseph Kasof, Chuansheng Chen, Amy Himsel, and Ellen Greenberger, "Values and Creativity," *Creativity Research Journal* 19, no. 2–3 (2007): 105–122.

20. Dan Pink, "The Puzzle of Motivation," July 2009,https://www.ted.com/talks/ dan_pink_on_motivation.

21. Kimberly D. Elsbach and Andrew B. Hargadon, "Enhancing Creativity Through 'Mindless' Work: A Framework of Workday Design," *Organization Science* 17, no. 4 (2006): 470–483.

22. This has been reiterated in many forms, but it dates back to Graham Wallas, *The Art of Thought* (New York: Franklin Watt, 1926).

23. Arthur B. Markman, *Smart Thinking: Three Essential Keys to Solve Problems, Innovate, and Get Things Done* (New York: Perigee/Penguin Group, 2013).

24. It is not even necessary to identify concepts associated with current concepts. See John Kounios and Mark Beeman, "The Aha! Moment: The Cognitive Neuroscience of Insight," *Current Directions in Psychological Science* 18, no. 4 (2009): 210–216.

25. This characterization comes from Amabile, drawing on Newell, Shaw, and Simon and updated and revisited in 2007 by Amabile and Mueller, the source of the four step characterization here. Teresa M. Amabile and Jennifer S. Mueller, "Studying Creativity, Its Processes, and Its Antecedents: An Exploration of the Componential Theory of Creativity," in *Handbook of Organizational Creativity*, ed. Jing Zhou, 31–62 (Hoboken, NJ: Lawrence Erlbaum Associates). See also Teresa M. Amabile, "A Model of Creativity and Innovation in Organizations," in *Research in Organizational Behavior* 10, no. 1 (1988): 123–167; and Allen Newell, J. Clifford Shaw, and Herbert A. Simon, "The Processes of Creative Thinking," in *Contemporary Approaches to Creative Thinking: A Symposium Held at the University of Colorado*, ed. H. E. Gruber, C. Terrell, and M. Wertheimer, 63–119 (New York: Atherton Press, 2012).

26. This detail is often overlooked, but it is a part of Amabile's formulation.

27. Robert W. Weisberg and Richard Hass, "Commentaries: We Are All Partly Right: Comment on Simonton," *Creativity Research Journal* 19, no. 4 (2007): 345–360; Robert W. Weisberg and Joseph W. Alba, "An Examination of the Alleged Role of 'Fixation' in the Solution of Several 'Insight' Problems," *Journal of Experimental Psychology: General* 110, no. 2 (1981): 169–192.

28. Teresa M. Amabile, *Creativity in Context: Update to "The Social Psychology of Creativity"* (Boulder, CO: Westview Press, 1996).

29. There are extremely detailed models of problem solving, very much including the Alan Newell and Herbert Simon work that was the inspiration for the problem-solving model in wide use in the creativity literature. However, the creativity literature does

not make use of the specificity. We have not made much use of these models because they are nearly entirely focused on what we have called using and adding to the perspective, and do not have much to say about what we have called changing the perspective. This was a weakness Simon himself pointed out in an essay honoring Alan Newell's contributions (Herbert A. Simon, "Bounded Rationality and Organizational Learning," *Organization Science* 2, no. 1 (1991): 125–134).

30. Donald T. Campbell, "Blind Variation and Selective Retentions in Creative Thought as in Other Knowledge Processes," *Psychological Review* 67, no. 6 (1960): 380; Dean Keith Simonton, "Creativity as Blind Variation and Selective Retention: Is the Creative Process Darwinian?" *Psychological Inquiry* (1999): 309–328.

31. Craig A. Kaplan and Herbert A. Simon, "In Search of Insight," *Cognitive Psychology* 22, no. 3 (1990): 374–419.

32. Janet Metcalfe, "Feeling of Knowing in Memory and Problem Solving," *Journal of Experimental Psychology: Learning, Memory, and Cognition* 12, no. 2 (1986): 288. Metcalfe and Wiebe, "Intuition in Insight and Noninsight Problem Solving."

33. Campbell, "Blind Variation," 380.

34. Dean Keith Simonton, "Scientific Creativity as Constrained Stochastic Behavior: The integration of Product, Person, and Process Perspectives," *Psychological Bulletin* 129, no. 4 (2003): 475.

35. We are sort of playing off of Sternberg here. See Robert J. Sternberg, "Cognitive Mechanisms in Human Creativity: Is Variation Blind or Sighted?" *The Journal of Creative Behavior* (1998): 159–176.

36. Metcalfe and Wiebe, "Intuition in Insight and Noninsight Problem Solving."

37. Jeffrey Sanchez-Burks, Matthew J. Karlesky, and Fiona Lee, "Psychological Bricolage: Integrating Social Identities to Produce Creative Solutions," in *The Oxford Handbook of Creativity, Innovation and Entrepreneurship*, ed. Christina E. Shalley, Michael A. Hitt, and Jing Zhou, 93–102 (New York: Oxford University Press, 2015), 93.

38. Merryl J. Wilkenfeld and Thomas B. Ward, "Similarity and Emergence in Conceptual Combination," *Journal of Memory and Language* 45, no. 1 (2001): 21–38.

39. Roni Reiter-Palmon, "Can We Really Have an Integrative Theory of Creativity? The Case of Creative Cognition," *Creativity: Theory—Research—Applications* 2, no. 1 (2014): 256–259; Roni Reiter-Palmon, "Problem Finding," In *Encyclopedia of Creativity 2nd Edition*, vol. 2, ed. M. A. Runce and S. R. Pritzker, 250–253 (San Diego: Academic Press, 2011).

40. Christina L. Gagné and Edward J. Shoben, "Priming Relations in Ambiguous Noun-Noun Combinations," *Memory & Cognition* 30, no. 4 (2002): 637–646.

41. This is the formula provided by Mike Cronin, who invented this example.

42. The suggestion of using a random word generator is not one we made up. We find both practitioners and scholars discussing random cueing as a means of advancing creativity, and websites with random word generators of various kinds to support the endeavor (such as Creativity Games at http://creativitygames.net/random-word-generator/randomwords/8).

43. Examples are taken from Sarah Gold, L. Lee, R. Lipton, and F. MacLaughlin,

New York Public Library Desk Reference (New York: Prentice-Hall General Reference, 1993), 105–126.

CHAPTER 8

1. For example, see National Research Council, *How People Learn: Brain, Mind, Experience, and School; Expanded Edition* (Washington, DC: National Academies Press, 2000).

2. The conception of young children as universal novices is a powerful enlightenment developed by A. L. Brown and J. S. DeLoache, "Skills, Plans, and Self-Regulation, in *Children's Thinking: What Develops?* ed. R. Siegler, 3–35 (Hillsdale, NJ: Erlbaum, 1978).

3. These are all quotes from those we talked to about what they had learned as they went on. The specific participants were producer Bob Dawson (hear better); historian and former provost Peter Stearns (become bolder, though many said that); composer Jesse Guessford (know their own process); and design professor Dan Boyarski (needed, expected, respected).

4. There are communities devoted to developing and sharing these modest creative outcomes, such as found at lifehacker.com.

5. A. G. Lafley, Interview, *Harvard Business Review*, June 23, 2008, https://www.youtube.com/watch?v=xvIUSxXrffc.

6. "CHM Revolutionaries: 'How Google Works' Eric Schmidt and Jonathan Rosenberg," Computer History Museum, October 15, 2014, https://www.youtube.com/watch?v=3tNpYpcU5s4.

7. For an extended treatment of the evaluation of outcomes for creativity, see Jennifer S. Mueller, *Creative Change* (New York: Houghton Mifflin Harcourt, 2017).

8. Beth A. Hennessy and Teresa M. Amabile, "Creativity," *Annual Review of Psychology* 61 (2010): 569–598; Jennifer M. George and Jing Zhou, "Understanding When Bad Moods Foster Creativity and Good Ones Don't: The Role of Context and Clarity of Feelings," *Journal of Applied Psychology* 87, no. 4 (2002): 687–697.

9. Wayne A. Baughman and Michael D. Mumford, "Process-Analytic Models of Creative Capacities: Operations Influencing the Combination-and-Reorganization Process," *Creativity Research Journal* 8, no. 1 (1995): 37–62; Davide Piffer, "Can Creativity Be Measured? An Attempt to Clarify the Notion of Creativity and General Directions for Future Research," *Thinking Skills and Creativity* 7, no. 3 (2012): 258–264; Jeffrey Sanchez-Burks, Matthew J. Karlesky, and Fiona Lee, "Psychological Bricolage: Integrating Social Identities to Produce Creative Solutions," in *The Oxford Handbook of Creativity, Innovation and Entrepreneurship*, ed. Christina E. Shalley, Michael A. Hitt, and Jing Zhou, 93–102 (New York: Oxford University Press, 2015).

10. Again, see Creativity Games at http://creativitygames.net/random-word-generator/randomwords/8.

11. George A. Akerlof, "The Market for 'Lemons': Quality Uncertainty and the Market Mechanism," *The Quarterly Journal of Economics* (1970): 488–500.

12. Mueller, *Creative Change*.

13. Chia-Jung Tsay, "Privileging Naturals Over Strivers: The Costs of the Naturalness Bias, *Personality and Social Psychology Bulletin* (2015), doi:10.1177/0146167215611638.

14. Jasjit Singh and Lee Fleming, "Lone Inventors as Sources of Breakthroughs: Myth or Reality?" *Management Science* 56, no. 1 (January 2010): 41–56; R. Keith Sawyer, *Explaining Creativity: The Science of Human Innovation* (New York: Oxford University Press, 2011).

15. Jeffrey Loewenstein and Jennifer Mueller, "Implicit Theories of Creative Ideas: How Culture Guides Creativity Assessments," *Academy of Management Discoveries* 2, no. 4 (2016): 320–348.

16. J. C. Kaufman, J. Baer, D. H. Cropley, R. Reiter-Palmon, and S. Nienhauser, "Furious Activity vs. Understanding: How Much Expertise Is Needed to Evaluate Creative Work? *Psychology of Aesthetics, Creativity, and the Arts* 7 no. 4 (2013): 332–340.

17. Jennifer Mueller, Shimul Melwani, Jeffrey Loewenstein, and Jennifer Deal, "Reframing the Decision-Maker's Dilemma: Toward a Social Context Model of Creative Idea Recognition," *Academy of Management Journal* (March 2017), doi: 10.5465/amj .2013.0887

18. Dean Keith Simonton, "Creativity as Blind Variation and Selective Retention: Is the Creative Process Darwinian?" *Psychological Inquiry* (1999): 309–328.

19. Matthew J. Salganik, Peter Sheridan Dodds, and Duncan J. Watts, "Experimental Study of Inequality and Unpredictability in an Artificial Cultural Market," *Science* 311, no. 5762 (2006): 854–856.

20. Some fields have higher consensus than others, which is why Simonton often controlled for the domain in which creative merit was being evaluated. See Dean Keith Simonton, "Creative Productivity and Age: A Mathematical Model Based on a Two-Step Cognitive Process," *Developmental Review* 4, no. 1 (1984): 77–111.

21. Matthew A. Cronin and Laurie R. Weingart, "Representational Gaps, Information Processing, and Conflict in Functionally Diverse Teams," *Academy of Management Review* 32, no. 3 (2007): 761–773

22. Ronald A. Beghetto, "Creative Mortification: An Initial Exploration," *Psychology of Aesthetics, Creativity, and the Arts* 8, no. 3 (2014): 266.

23. Colin Camerer, George Loewenstein, and Martin Weber, "The Curse of Knowledge in Economic Settings: An Experimental Analysis," *Journal of Political Economy* 97, no. 5 (1989): 1232–1254.

24. A complementary view and discussion of elements that help in this communication process can be found in Chip Heath and Dan Heath, *Made to Stick: Why Some Ideas Survive and Others Die* (New York: Random House, 2007).

25. Actually, just two are areas of science. The study of quasicrystals won a Nobel Prize; Fraunhofer lines are a phenomenon regarding the light emitted from stars; orb photography is a play on a hobbyist term for reflection artifacts in pictures; and as for chromium reification, we made that one up and so as far as we know that is utter nonsense.

26. Jeffrey Loewenstein and Chip Heath, "The Repetition-Break Plot Structure: A Cognitive Influence on Selection in the Marketplace of Ideas," *Cognitive Science* 33, no. 1 (2009): 1–19.

27. Gordon used the terms *good* to mean well regarded and *right* to mean personally satisfying. Hayes Gordon, *Acting and Performing* (New York: Samuel French Trade,

1992). We found those terms a bit too nebulous, and so we thank Bob Axlerod for suggesting alternatives.

28. Julian Edgerton Orr, *Talking About Machines: An Ethnography of a Modern Job* (Ithaca, NY: Cornell University Press, 1996).

29. Nikolaus Franke and Sonali Shah, "How Communities Support Innovative Activities: An Exploration of Assistance and Sharing Among End-Users," *Research Policy* 32, no. 1 (2003): 157–178; Sonali K. Shah and Mary Tripsas, "The Accidental Entrepreneur: The Emergent and Collective Process of User Entrepreneurship," *Strategic Entrepreneurship Journal* 1, no. 1-2 (2007): 123–140.

30. Teresa M. Amabile, *Creativity in Context: Update to "The Social Psychology of Creativity"* (Boulder, CO: Westview Press, 1996); Teresa M. Amabile, "How to Kill Creativity," *Harvard Business Review*, September/October (1998): 76–87.

31. Ed Catmull, *Creativity, Inc.: Overcoming the Unseen Forces That Stand in the Way of True Inspiration* (New York: Random House, 2014), 196.

32. Maybe creativity does not mean what he thinks it means either.

33. C. Tinsley, J. Schloetzer, M. A. Cronin, and M. Price, "The Science of Confidence," presented at The World Economic Forum Annual Meeting, Davos, Switzerland, 2017.

34. Jack A. Goncalo and Michelle M. Duguid, "Follow the Crowd in a New Direction: When Conformity Pressure Facilitates Group Creativity (and When It Does Not)," *Organizational Behavior and Human Decision Processes* 118, no. 1 (May 2012): 14–23. Note that deep-level diversity, which diversity of perspective would be, creates its own challenges as well. See Sarah Harvey, "A Different Perspective: The Multiple Effects of Deep Level Diversity on Group Creativity," *Journal of Experimental Social Psychology* 49, no. 5 (2013): 822–832. Nonetheless, when harnessed it can produce outstanding results. See Sarah Harvey, "Creative Synthesis: Exploring the Process of Extraordinary Group Creativity," *Academy of Management Review* 39, no. 3 (2014): 324–343.

35. Charlan J. Nemeth, Bernard Personnaz, Marie Personnaz, and Jack A. Goncalo, "The Liberating Role of Conflict in Group Creativity: A Study in Two Countries," *European Journal of Social Psychology* 34, no. 4 (2004): 365–374; Jack A. Goncalo, Evan Polman, and Christina Maslach, "Can Confidence Come Too Soon? Collective Efficacy, Conflict and Group Performance Over Time," *Organizational Behavior and Human Decision Processes* 113, no. 1 (2010): 13–24.

36. Herbert A. Simon, "The Scientist as Problem Solver," in *Complex Information Processing: The Impact of Herbert A. Simon*, ed. David Klahr and Kenneth Kotovsky, 375–398 (Hillsdale, NJ: Lawrence Erlbaum Associates, 1989).

37. See William Ocasio and John Joseph, "Cultural Adaptation and Institutional Change: The Evolution of Vocabularies of Corporate Governance, 1972–2003," *Poetics* 33, no. 3 (2005): 163–178.

APPENDIX

1. Holder of two medical device patents.

2. Recipient of the Outstanding Anthropology Undergraduate Award for her analysis of racial inequalities in alternative food systems.

3. Also a black belt in Tae Kwon Do, certified as a county wild land firefighter, and an accomplished pianist.

4. Also a producer and writer, known for *Last Comic Standing* (2003), *Silver Patriot* (2005), and *Comedy Central Presents* (1998).

5. His noise-canceling walls were featured in Sarah Susanka and Kira Obolensky, *The Not So Big House: A Blueprint for the Way We Really Live* (Newtown, CT: Taunton Press, 1998).

6. She is also an actor known for *Shallow Grave* (1987), *American Risciò* (1990), and *Being Jon Stewart* (2009).

7. Muriel Cooper Prize winner for "outstanding achievement in advancing design, technology, and communications in the digital environment."

8. Also a medical marijuana producer and former herpetologist.

9. Founding editor of ETC Press and its "Well Played" series and journal.

10. While in Tanzania developed a widely regarded blog and then parlayed this into a means for fundraising for the people she was studying.

11. Worked on *The Nameless Mod*; see note 16.

12. Winner of the Best Management Student award, 2013.

13. Three-time Grammy Award nominee and two-time winner.

14. Among other things, worked on the Alto, the prototype desktop computer, and founded Maya Design.

15. Originally an industrial designer. He quit that field to study under Italian master tailor Joseph Centofanti, then was head tailor at world-renowned Martin Greenfield Clothiers in Brooklyn, New York.

16. This story did not make it into the main text, but it is one of the most remarkable we heard (so we tell it here as a kind of Easter egg in plain sight). *The Nameless Mod* was a full-scale revamp of a very significant video game, *Deus Ex*. The designers took the mechanics of one game and made an entirely new one with new characters, levels, stories, and gameplay. Its features include two unique storylines—each with an average of fifteen hours of playtime—over fifty nonlinear levels, more than seventy characters, and over fourteen hours of fully voiced dialogue. Even more remarkable, the team managed to capture the very spirit of the original game (albeit with a bit more humor), right down to the music. It won best single player mod of 2009 and number 8 best overall mod as voted by ModDB (the IMDB of video game mods). This project involved scores of developers and hundreds of actors who contributed from all over the globe (literally). Jonas, Lawrence Laxdal, and Gelo Fleischer were the "executive team" who kept this project on track. Here is the inconceivable part. All the people who worked on this project did so for free over seven years. Jonas, Lawrence, and Gelo were managing a multinational cross-functional team with high turnover over a seven-year period with no formal authority. Also, Jonas and Lawrence were fourteen years old when they started the project. Inconceivable!

17. See note 16.

18. Music writer for *The Nameless Mod*; see note 16.

19. Author of over 130 books.

20. Also an accomplished musician.

21. Turley is a great example of how impactful creativity can be. Turley taught reading to the developmentally disabled adults, and so the shift to landscaping was not an obvious move. But he realized that his students, many of whom could only read at about a third-grade level, and who had a variety of different kinds of challenges (some were deaf or partially blind, or did not have full use of their limbs), would really need a wide variety of tasks. Landscaping could provide such a variety of tasks for all of his people. The man who had a crippled leg and one arm would pick up trash so the lawn could be mowed by the man who was deaf. For ten years, until he had to sell it for family reasons, this company gave all of these people jobs and dignity.

INDEX